The Daily Telegraph
GUIDE TO
BRITAIN'S
MILITARY
HERITAGE

The Daily Telegraph
GUIDE TO
BRITAIN'S MILITARY HERITAGE

Mark Adkin

First published 2006 by
Aurum Press Limited
25 Bedford Avenue
London WC1B 3AT
www.aurumpress.co.uk

ISBN 1 84513 135 5 (paperback)
ISBN 1 84513 183 5 (hardback)

10 9 8 7 6 5 4 3 2 1
2010 2009 2008 2007 2006

Designed by Robert Updegraff
Maps by PerroCarto Ltd
Printed and bound in Singapore

CONTENTS

About this book   1

Introduction: Warfare in Britain   2

ENGLAND   9
South-West   10
The Celts and Their Hill-Forts   24
South-East and London   28
The Roman Occupation   57
West Midlands   62
East Midlands   72
Defence against Invasion   79
Eastern   84
The Battle of Britain   92
North-West   94
North-East   98
The Walls: Hadrian's and the Antonine   116

WALES   121
Norman and Medieval Castles   128

SCOTLAND   133
Borders and Lowlands   134
Military Museums   137
Central Scotland   142
Highlands and Islands   148

Picture credits   162
Index of battles   163
Index of sites   165

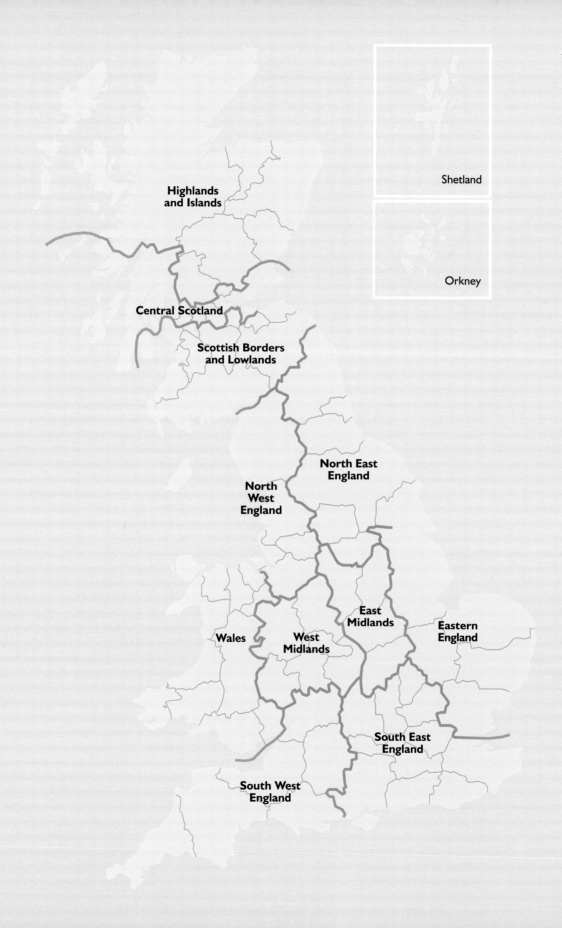

Shetland

Orkney

Highlands
and Islands

Central Scotland

Scottish Borders
and Lowlands

North East
England

North
West
England

Wales

West
Midlands

East
Midlands

Eastern
England

South East
England

South West
England

ABOUT THIS BOOK

Britain has perhaps the most varied and exciting military history of any country in the world. The nations that make up the United Kingdom have been successfully and unsuccessfully invaded, have engaged in several bitter civil wars and have put down rebellions from every part of the islands, while Britain's Armed Services have fought with unrivalled success and courage worldwide. Since Henry VIII the country's independence has been in the hands of, first, the Royal Navy, then the Navy in combination with the Army and finally, after the formation of the RAF following the First World War, of the Combined Services.

This Guide is a first. Strangely, while guides on castles and books on battlefields exist in their hundreds, this is the first guidebook that describes the whole range of military history here in Britain, covering some 350 places worthy of a visit. The Guide covers Iron Age hill-forts, the Roman conquest, Hadrian's Wall and the Antonine Wall, castles, defences against invasion, battlefields and

The central map room of the Cabinet War Rooms

military museums of all three Services. Each of these subjects is introduced by an illustrated overview, enabling readers to discover the answer to such questions as: who were the Celts? How did the Roman Army fight? How was a castle defended or attacked? What weapons or tactics were used at this battle? What will I see in a regimental museum?

A particular debt of gratitude is due to the Battlefields Trust, an organization dedicated to the preservation, interpretation and presentation of battlefield sites as educational and heritage resources. The first phase of the Trust's development of a Resource Centre took place from mid-2002 to mid-2005 and involved their Project Officer, Glenn Foard, visiting forty-eight of the most important English battlefields. Michael Rayner, the Trust's National Coordinator, generously gave me permission to make use of many of the photographs taken by Glenn. They illustrate the bulk of the English battlefield entries in this Guide.

A few words on how to use the Guide:

• England, Scotland and Wales are divided into regions, the boundaries of which are shown on the map opposite. Within each region sites worth visiting are listed in alphabetical order. Every site is marked on the regional map at the beginning of each section, and further details of how to find it are found at the beginning of the entry.

• Each entry starts with details of admission charges (if any), opening hours, facilities available, telephone number and website. 'Usual hours' means daily from 10 a.m. to 4 p.m.; in summer months these are often

extended. For school visits or research prior arrangements are necessary. In many places, but not all, parking is free.

• Admission charges change frequently so it is impossible to keep a guide up to date. However, the approximate level of charge is indicated as follows: £ = less than £3; ££ = £3–4.99; £££ = £5–7.50; ££££ = over £7.50. These are full adult charges, and all sites making a charge offer concessions for children, senior citizens and groups.

Abbreviations and symbols

⚜	National Trust for England and Wales	★ Viewpoint	▲ Memorial
⌗	English Heritage	✘ Battle (date)	■ Other sites
Cadw	Welsh Historic Monuments	⌂ Museum	⚘ Iron Age Fort
NTS	National Trust for Scotland	⛨ Castle or Fort	
HS	Historic Scotland		

WARFARE IN BRITAIN

There are ninety-six battlefields marked on the maps in this guide, including twenty-seven in Scotland but only two in Wales, which saw plenty of bloodshed but mostly on a smaller scale. Of these ninety-six battlefields, twenty of the most historically significant and rewarding to visit are covered in detail with maps and photographs. Some of the remaining battlefields have been built over, some mutilated by motorways, while others, like the two battles at St Albans, involved mostly street fighting. Nevertheless, many have at least one forgotten, half-hidden memorial or plaque to remind the passer-by that history was made and men died nearby.

The Roman Army left Britain in 409, and in the next 1350 years Britain's inhabitants fought against invaders and with each other, with some major civil wars and uprisings. But after Culloden in 1746 their battles were fought overseas. The only exception was the Battle of Britain in 1940 (see pp. 93–3), when the skies over southern England witnessed aerial warfare on a massive scale for weeks on end.

EARLY ENGLAND, 409–1060

This was the period of incursions, raids, invasions and conquest, first by Angles and Saxons, then by the Vikings from what we know today as Norway, Sweden and Denmark. Initially war-bands or raiding parties were usually a few hundred strong, perhaps arriving from across the North Sea in a handful of ships, their occupants bent on pillage and a speedy return to their homeland. Eventually raids became invasions and invasions led to conquest and settlement.

Many Anglo-Saxons were fanatical warriors, joining the war-band of the most successful leader they could find for glory and rewards. The lord of the war-band was expected to be generous to his warriors, providing them with gold rings, arms, armour and horses together with food and wine in his hall. In exchange the warrior gave loyalty unto death. When Earl Byrhtnoth was cut down at the Battle of Maldon in 991, his followers fought on beside his body, determined to die or avenge him. The Saxon warrior was armed with a spear, sometimes a sword or axe, and a round shield. The spear was used both for war and hunting, for throwing and stabbing, and had a long leaf-shaped blade on a 7ft ash shaft. The shield was wooden, slightly convex, covered in leather and strengthened with a metal rim and bands. The lords wore a chain-mail shirt and straight two-edged swords with two shallow grooves running down the centre of the blade, to lighten the weapon without weakening it. These swords were thought to hold some of the courage and skill of the former owner and were often passed down within families; King Offa died in 796, but his sword still existed in the 11th century, when it was bequeathed by Prince Athelston to his brother.

The Danish raiders arrived in strength in the ninth century and fell on an England divided into several warring kingdoms. By the middle of the century fleets of up to 350 ships would descend on the exposed eastern shores and plunder undefended monasteries and churches. The raiders were followed by ever larger bands who wintered in England, riding across the country on stolen horses, plundering, setting fire to villages, even capturing towns like York and London. The Danes were full-time warriors living off the land they conquered. The Saxons, however, had now become farmers as well as fighters. This meant men were needed to tend the crops, so armies could not remain in the field for prolonged periods. King Alfred solved this problem by organizing his manpower in such a way that half were always at home on the farms while the other half were fighting. But it was not until Alfred, after many reverses, defeated the Danes at the Battle of Ethandun in 878 that the invaders were checked.

Well worth a visit
Dyrham, 577 *p. 14*
Ashdown, 871 *p. 30*
Maldon, 991 *p. 88*

THE MIDDLE AGES, 1066–1450

When the Norman William (later 'the Conqueror') landed on the beach at Pevensey in 1066 he was soon to be confronted by a well-organized English army. It was composed of three groups. The first were the 'housecarls', in effect the King's personal guard, full-time soldiers, heavily armed and paid from an 'army tax'. There were both Saxons and Danes among the housecarls at Hastings. Their favourite weapon was the huge Danish battleaxe, wielded with two hands and swung from over the left shoulder so as to strike an enemy's right, unshielded, side. By 1066 many of the lesser lords had their own following of housecarls.

The second group within the army were 'thegns', who owed military service to the King due to their estates. Anyone holding land five 'hides' in size had to provide one man to fight, armed and protected with a helmet and chainmail shirt. Those holding less land would band together to equip one of their number for every five hides, and the greater thegns, with much bigger estates, would supply their quotas of men from their bodyguards or from special tenants subletting land from them. Housecarls, thegns and their followers supplied the bulk of the trained and organized army. In a major battle such as Stamford Bridge or Hastings, however, the 'freemen', those who were neither landowners or serfs, outnumbered them. All freemen could be called on by the king to provide three services – building fortifications, building bridges and giving military service. They were unmounted, lightly armed men fielded only in an emergency. At Hastings they were the men shown by the Bayeux Tapestry using bows, missiles or clubs.

In line of battle the housecarls would form the centre, grouped around the King's Dragon Banner of Saxon England with the thegns on either side and the freemen on either flank. When fighting hand-to-hand the shield was slung across the back.

The Normans relied more on the 5000 mounted knights that William brought with him across the Channel than on any foot soldiers, in contrast to the Saxons who used horses as a means of transport rather than on the battlefield. Like the Saxons, the Norman's armour was the long chain-mail shirt, or 'hauberk'. His helmet was a conical steel skullcap, with a bar acting as nose-guard riveted on, his weapons the sword and spear. William's archers used the bow or crossbow, his tactics being to soften up and disorganize the opposition with arrows and bolts, thus preparing the way for a heavy cavalry attack. Hastings in 1066 was the only large-scale pitched battle fought against the Normans in Britain and the battlefield is well worth a visit.

With the Norman Conquest came the Norman castle, knights and the beginnings of what became known, not entirely justly, as the age of chivalry. After the conquest William distributed large swathes of England to his knights as reward for their services.

A clash between mounted Norman knights and Saxon housecarls at the Battle of Hastings, as depicted in the Bayeux tapestry

These estates, known as knights' 'fees', quickly became hereditary. The Norman knight was first and foremost a soldier, hard, cruel and uncultured, skilled in the use of lance, sword, mace, axe and bow. The next two hundred years were filled with fighting, in the Crusades, the Barons' Wars, against the Scots and, above all, the Hundred Years' War, a struggle between the English and the French interrupted by numerous truces and treaties that lasted from 1338 to 1453. It was the age of plate armour that covered a man from head to toe. Such was his weight that only the strongest horses could carry him, and then only at a walk or trot. Contrary to popular belief, a complete suit of battle armour did not render an unhorsed knight totally immobile, but he was easily taken prisoner (and ransomed) or had his throat slit. The answer to the armoured knight was the English (or Welsh) longbowman. Able to shoot far faster than crossbowmen, these archers destroyed the might of France at such battles as Crécy (1346) and Henry V's famous victory at Agincourt (1415).

The English longbow was made of yew, ash or elm and was the height of the archer. Archery was engrained in English culture, with mandatory practice for men and boys on Sundays and holidays on the village green. Arrows were specially designed for particular targets (e.g. bodkin head for penetrating armour) and had a range of up to 400 yards. The combination of skilled bowmen and powerful weapons was usually deadly. The Scots became particularly apprehensive when faced with massed ranks of English archers, often drawn up in wedges on the flanks. They had a saying that 'Every

Plate armour for man and horse; this set was made in Germany in the 15th century.

English archer carries twenty-four Scots under his belt.' At Bannockburn in 1314 tight formations of Scottish spearmen defeated repeated assaults by English knights and men-at-arms. At Halidon Hill seventeen years later the tables were turned. The attacking Scots were shot to pieces by an arrow storm before they could close with the English.

In the second quarter of the 14th century appeared the weapon that would ultimately make both armour and the medieval castle obsolete – the cannon. By the early 15th century siege trains of guns and ammunition wagons had become commonplace, with iron or brass guns pulled ponderously along on carriages drawn by teams of horses or oxen. They were still primitive pieces of ordnance, but breached the walls of Harfleur for Henry V in 1415 – later enabling Shakespeare to give Henry a rallying cry of 'Once more unto the breach, dear friends, once more!' By 1450 some guns were exceedingly powerful. 'Mons Meg' at Edinburgh, cast in around 1460, is 13ft and 2in long with a bore of nearly 20in. It fired a stone ball weighing 549lb. It was also during this period that the first rudimentary handguns were introduced – actually small cannons lashed to a wooden stock.

Well worth a visit

Lewes, 1264 *p. 42*
Shrewsbury, 1403 *p. 68*
Northallerton (The Standard), 1138 *p. 110*
Bannockburn, 1314 *p. 150*

THE WARS OF THE ROSES AND AFTERWARDS, 1450–1550

This period saw the final touches put to the knight's plate armour. To get dressed for a battle or tournament required considerable time and the assistance of a squire to put on the suit piece by piece. The armour of foot soldiers varied considerably with the wealth of their town, village or captain; some had quilted jackets with long sleeves and skirts while others, more wealthy, could afford jackets with small steel or horn plates fastened on, known as brigandines. A simple helmet and thick quilted doublet protected archers. Neither bowmen or billmen (who were armed with long-shafted axes) could handle a shield while using their primary weapons so they often carried a small round shield called a 'buckler' that hung over the sword hilt or from the belt, for use if they were forced to resort to sword fighting.

In addition to swords and daggers, a variety of polearms were in common use for fighting on foot. These included 4–6ft shafted axes with a heavy beak or hammerhead behind the axe head, with narrow strips of steel fixed on the shaft below the head to prevent it being chopped off in combat. The poleaxe had a sharp spike at each end with a steel guard fixed to the shaft to protect the hand; it could smash through

Cannon and equipment, late 15th century

helmet and skull down to a man's teeth if wielded properly. A glaive was a strong one-edged blade on a long shaft suitable for thrusting and cutting, and the halberd a cleaver-like axe with a heavy spike behind the head and another on the top. The Swiss pike with an exceptionally long shaft became common in Europe but did not reach England until the reign of Henry VIII.

The Wars of the Roses – the red rose of the House of Lancaster against the white rose of York – were largely fought with armies composed of dismounted men-at-arms supported or flanked by archers. It was common for both sides to close in quickly for the kill to avoid the deadly hail of arrows. Only at Northampton did the Yorkists build a fortified camp defended by a number of guns (made useless by heavy rain).

These civil wars took place within a space of thirty years and saw some fifteen set-piece battles, all of which are marked on the Guide maps.

The Wars of the Roses virtually extinguished the old feudal aristocracy. Henry VIII assumed the throne of England in 1509 but, blinded by his territorial and military ambitions, failed to recognize the value of Scottish neutrality. In 1512 James of Scotland, concerned that Henry's acquisitive eye might one day alight on his kingdom, signed a mutual defence pact with Louis XII of France. Henry invaded France in early 1513 so Louis immediately activated the agreement, encouraging James to march into England at the head of a huge army of 35,000 men, including 5000 Frenchmen. The result was the particularly bloody battle of Flodden, at which the English archers and billmen under the Earl of Surrey defeated the Scottish pikemen. James was killed, it is said, by no fewer than five halberd blows and one arrow.

Well worth a visit

Mortimer's Cross, 1461 *p. 67*
Bosworth, 1485 *p. 74*
Flodden, 1513 *p. 102*
Towton, 1461 *p. 112*

1550–1660 AND THE ENGLISH CIVIL WAR

The second half of the 16th century saw the development of cannons, muskets and pistols. English armies were composed of 'shot' (musketeers with matchlocks), archers, halberdiers and pikemen, plus both heavy and light cavalry. Armour was still worn; indeed suits of expensive and decorative plate armour were often purchased from Italy, Germany or France. Although archers were still an element of every army it was becoming increasingly difficult to find men well trained in the art; it was far easier and quicker to train a musketeer than a longbowman. Heavy horsemen wore a leather cuirass and were armed with sword and heavy lance, while their light comrades had a mail shirt, sword and light lance. Artillery was now a well-established arm with heavy siege guns and lighter field guns called 'culverins', also in use by the Navy. A siege gun could throw a 50lb iron ball 2000 paces and a culverin a 9lb ball 2500 paces.

The 17th century finally saw firearms defeat armour. A musket ball would penetrate all but the thickest of plate. Even when wearing just a breastplate soldiers complained of its weight. At times carts had to be hired to carry the armour on the march; at others men demanded extra money to wear it! At the start of the century an infantry regiment consisted half of pikemen to hold off cavalry and half of musketeers. By the time the Civil War between Royalists under King Charles I and Parliamentarians began in 1642 the proportion of pikemen had fallen to a third. Infantry regiments usually had about 500 musketeers who were formed up in two blocks on either side of the pikemen. The musketeers took at least a minute to reload their piece, and in high wind or rain the whole process became almost impossible – thus the vital role of the pikemen was to protect the musketeers from cavalry attacks during these vulnerable moments. If all went well, repeated volleys of musketry delivered by successive ranks of men firing and falling back to reload would damage the enemy's close-packed ranks enough to allow a charge with levelled pikes to sweep them away.

Most Civil War battles were simple head-on clashes between long lines of infantry regiments grouped together into brigades. The cavalry were drawn up on the flanks and usually fought their opposing cavalry. Their half-armour, swords and pistols were no match for the massed pikes or heavy volleys of a steady infantry brigade of perhaps 2000 men, but they could prevail by catching the infantry in flank or rear (rather than dashing off in wild pursuit of fleeing enemy horsemen as the Royalist horsemen were apt to). Against enemy horsemen the drill books stated that

cavalry should be drawn up in six ranks just out of range of the enemy. Each rank would take it in turn to trot forward, fire its pistols and trot to the rear to reload (it being impossible to reload on the move). When the opposition became disorganized that was the time to charge. At the Battle of Edgehill in 1642 the Royalist cavalry commander, Prince Rupert, declined to fight by the book. He lined his men up in three ranks and trotted forward as if to fire pistols, but instead of doing so charged immediately. The demoralized Parliamentarians turned and fled, hotly pursued off the field by the jubilant cavaliers.

In the end it was money that turned the tide in Parliament's favour rather than tactics. Parliament controlled London, with its commercial wealth, and the Navy, meaning they could deny supplies to the King while purchasing their own abroad and, crucially, pay their troops. Charles never had the funds to keep his volunteers in pocket for long. His troops lived off the country (never popular with the locals) and tended to slip away to tend their land at harvesting or seed time. When Parliament raised Britain's first standing army the end was in sight. The 'New Model Army' was properly paid, disciplined and trained. It consisted of 12 regiments (each 1200 strong) of infantry, 11 of horse with 600 troopers, 1000 dragoons (mounted infantry) plus an artillery train. The victory of this Army over the King at Naseby in 1645 effectively brought the first of the three periods of the Civil War to an end, although it spluttered on until the following year when Charles's last field force was scattered at Stow-on-the-Wold. The Royalist garrison of Harlech Castle held out until March 1647 and fired the final shots for the King.

The other two civil wars were really much shorter continuations of the first. Charles escaped imprisonment and fled to Carisbrooke Castle on the Isle of Wight, where he thought he had a loyal friend in the governor. He was mistaken, and found himself imprisoned in the castle, from which he made three unsuccessful attempts to escape. From there he tried to persuade the Scots to support him by promising that he would restore Presbyterianism – the more rigorous Scottish version of Protestantism – in England for a three-year trial period if they would take up arms on his behalf. He was further encouraged to make a comeback by Royalist revolts in South Wales, Kent and Essex as well as the New Model Army's discontent over arrears of pay. This second civil war speedily ended in tears for the King when Oliver Cromwell defeated the Royalist Scots at Preston in August 1648. Five months later the axeman removed Charles's head. The monarchy was, temporarily, abolished.

The third phase of the civil wars began with the arrival of Charles's eldest son in Scotland. The Scots were prepared to accept him as King Charles II provided he accepted the 'Solemn League and Covenant' reflecting their Presbyterian beliefs. He did, and was proclaimed king in July 1650. But neither the Scots at Dunbar in September 1650 nor the Scots and English at Worcester a year later could withstand Cromwell's better disciplined and experienced troops.

Until the restoration of the monarchy in 1660 England was ruled by the military under Cromwell. The country was divided into regions, each with a military governor and troops to ensure compliance with government edicts. It was an unpopular regime, and following Cromwell's death in 1659 Charles II regained the crown, not by force of arms, but at the invitation of Parliament.

Well worth a visit

Lansdown Hill, 1643 *p. 18*
Cheriton, 1644 *p. 37*
Edgehill, 1642 *p. 64*
Naseby, 1645 *p. 76*
Marston Moor, 1644 *p. 108*

THE STUART UPRISINGS, 1660–1746

When Charles II died in 1685 without legitimate heirs he was succeeded by his Catholic brother James II. However, Charles's illegitimate son the Duke of Monmouth claimed he was the true Stuart heir, and set sail for England in June 1685 to incite a Protestant uprising. On landing in the West Country he received a warm welcome, and declared himself king before local magistrates, who acclaimed him with swords held at their throats. But his followers were more a rabble than an army and quickly dwindled in numbers when James's force appeared. Monmouth felt his only chance was a surprise night attack on the English camp at Sedgemoor.

Like so many night attacks before and since it went disastrously wrong, and Monmouth was crushed and captured. For treason there was only one penalty – beheading. Monmouth was a brave man. On the scaffold he tested the blade of the axe with his thumb before encouraging the executioner to strike well; unsuccessfully, as it took five strokes to remove Monmouth's head.

James II finally lost his throne in 1688, to his daughter Mary II and her husband William III of Orange. But James and his heirs did not give up easily. The first of the so-called Jacobite rebellions occurred in 1689 but was quickly put down at the Battle of Killicrankie in July of that year. In 1715 James's son, another James, invaded Scotland to pursue his claim to the throne, but his rebel army was defeated by King George I's Government Army at Sheriffmuir. Another thirty years were to pass before the Jacobite banner was raised again. This time the contender for the throne of England was the twenty-five-year-old 'Bonnie Prince Charlie', son of the would-be James III, who sailed from France to make his bid, again enlisting Scottish help. It started well. The Highlanders' fearsome charge at Prestonpans in September 1745 swept the Hanoverians from the field in a matter of minutes. Again the next year the English were savagely mauled at Falkirk, the Highlanders countering a charge of dragoons by lying on the ground and thrusting their dirks into the horses' bellies, dragging the rider to the ground and finishing him off. But despite these earlier triumphs Bonnie Prince Charlie's Highlanders finally met their match in the sustained fire and bayonets of the Hanoverian muskets of the Duke of Cumberland at Culloden in 1746. It was the last battle on British soil.

Well worth a visit

Culloden, 1746 *p. 154*
Killiecrankie, 1689 *p. 158*
Sheriffmuir, 1715 *p. 160*

ENGLAND

SOUTH-WEST

Ackling Dyke Roman Road (Dorset)

Farmland. Free. Open access. On either side of the B3081 east of the roundabout on the A354, about midway between Blandford Forum and Salisbury.

This is a substantial stretch of Roman road not covered in tarmac that you can walk along. Nearly 2000 years ago Roman surveyors would have laid out the direction of the road by taking sightings between hill features. Next, centurions would have organized the legionaries into working parties. Any woodland would be cleared to a width of 90ft with ditches ploughed to mark the edges. Ploughs would be used to cut two more parallel ditches down the centre of the area about 30ft apart. This marked the road proper. An embankment was built up between the central ditches creating the *agger* or causeway. Layers of large stones, then smaller ones and finally gravel were compacted to form the surface – now buried under topsoil.

Badbury Rings (Dorset) 🌿

Free. Easy access, open countryside. Parking possible. Three miles north-west of Wimborne Minster on the B3082.

This Celtic hill-fort has not yet been excavated but was probably built two or three hundred years before the Romans arrived. It is close to the junction of four Roman roads, including Ackling Dyke (above), next to an avenue of magnificent trees that line this stretch of the B3082. Strangely, no Roman town developed here, although there was a market at the road junction. The hill-fort is not large but well worth a walk up the not too steep slope to the tree-covered summit. The ramparts are some 40 feet high (recently restored) and there is an atmosphere of history inside the fort. Legend has it that King Arthur fought his battle of Mount Baden against the Saxons here (in fact, it was probably close to the Badbury near Swindon) and that he lives on as a raven in the woods on the summit.

Bovington Tank Museum (Dorset)

££££. Usual hours. Shop. Bookstall. Refreshments. Special events in summer. Library. Parking. Tel: 01929 405096. www.tankmuseum.org/home.html About two miles north of Wool. From Poole take the A35 and then the A351 to Wareham then turn onto the A352 towards Dorchester. Follow museum signs.

An impressive museum containing the most comprehensive collection of tanks and armoured vehicles in the world, from the First World War to the Gulf – it can take up to three hours to see it all. The collection is brought to life with live demonstrations and vehicle rides. Special events, including mock tank battles, feature throughout the year except in winter (telephone for details), and there is a special 'trench exhibition' that highlights the stark reality of warfare during the First World War, ending with a visit to a German trench to witness a tank attack from the receiving end. A new 'For Valour' medal display illustrates the courage of tank men through the ages. There are activities for younger visitors and families including Home Front tours, dressing up, quizzes, code breaking and model making. A splendid day out.

Bradock Down, Battle of, 1643 (Cornwall)

Free. Some farmland. Mostly open access. Follow lane off A390 to Bradock Church. Across the road in the field opposite, Ruthin's force was drawn up facing south-west. Hopton's army attacked from the direction of Bocannoc House. There is no monument and the dead are supposedly buried in one of the nearby tumuli.

English Civil War battle fought 19 January 1643, at which Royalist Cornishmen under Sir Ralph Hopton routed the heavily outnumbered Parliamentarians under Colonel Ruthin. Both armies were drawn up on high ground on either side of a shallow valley. Hopton positioned two guns atop a Bronze Age barrow. Their firing signalled a general advance and charge uphill, infantry in the centre with long pikes and muskets, cavalry on the flanks. Ruthin's force fled after feeble resistance, abandoning several guns.

Cobbaton Combat Vehicle Collection (Devon)

££. Usual hours (closed Saturdays), limited hours November–March. Shop. Refreshments. Play area. Parking. Tel. 01769 540740. www.cobbatoncombat.co.uk In the village of Chittlehampton between the A361 Tiverton–Barnstaple road and the A377 Exeter–Barnstaple road. Follow brown tourism signs.

A private collection of over fifty Second World War artillery pieces and vehicles, together with several hundred weapons and items of equipment. A separate building is devoted to the civilian aspects of the war.

Corfe Castle (Dorset) 🌿

£££. Usual hours. Shop. Tea-room. Parking. Tel. 01929 481294. www.nationaltrust.org.uk/hbcache/property 295.htm In centre of Corfe Castle village on the A351 halfway between Wareham and Swanage.

Once one of the greatest strongholds in England, Corfe Castle started out as a Norman motte and bailey castle guarding a gap in the Purbeck hills,

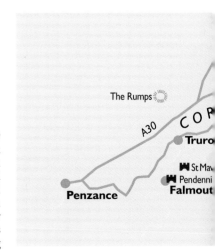

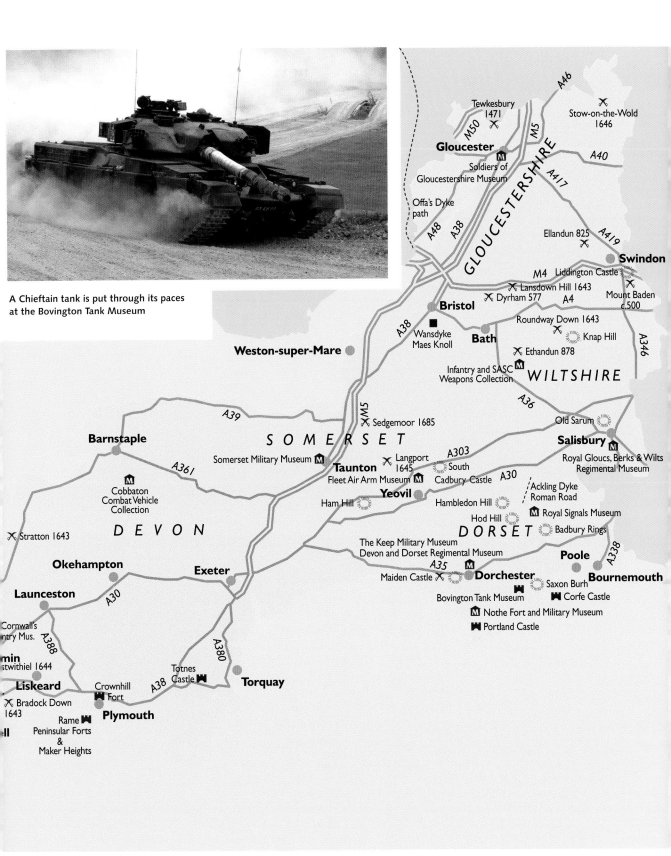

A Chieftain tank is put through its paces at the Bovington Tank Museum

Corfe Castle, ruined but still impressive

developed in the Middle Ages, and was finally destroyed on the orders of Parliament in 1646. The Royalist Lady Bankes defended it during the Civil War but it fell to treachery from within. Although in ruins it is probably the finest castle in the south-west, and a tour is a rewarding experience. At the top of the bailey is the south-west gatehouse, split dramatically in two by an explosion during the course of demolition. The views from the castle are spectacular. Steam trains run close to Corfe on a railway line to Swanage.

Crownhill Fort (Devon) (Landmark Trust)

££. Usual hours April–October, groups by arrangement November–March. Guided tours. Special events. Parking. Tel. 01752 793754. www.landmarktrust. org.uk/otherOptions/crownhill.htm Crownhill Fort Road, Plymouth. Signposted off the A386 and B3373.

One of 'Palmerston's Follies', this is a huge Victorian fort now restored to its original state. It's a wonderful place to explore, with a maze of tunnels, four fighting floors with thirty-two gun positions, many with guns in place.

The fort contains the world's only working Moncrieff Disappearing Gun – it rises up above the parapet to fire, then sinks down out of sight. It was continually occupied by the military for 114 years and visitors can experience life in recreated Victorian and Second World War barrack rooms. There is also a display of artefacts discovered during restoration.

The Devon and Dorset Regimental Museum (The Keep Military Museum) (Dorset)

££. Usual hours. Shop. Tel. 01305 264066. Dorchester town centre.

The Keep was formerly the entrance to the Dorset Regimental Depot but has been converted into a state-of-the-art military museum covering the history of Devon and Dorset soldiers over the last 300 years. There are three floors with medals, uniforms, badges, model soldiers, maps and a command bunker with introductory video. Visitors will enjoy the 'hands-on' interactive battle system which lets you try out automatic weapons against electronically activated soldiers, artillery and tanks. The highlight of the exhibits is one of

Hitler's desks, removed from his office in Berlin by the Russians and then given to the British. It contained personal stationery as well as Christmas cards to and from Hitler. Lieutenant-Colonel 'H' Jones, who won a posthumous VC in the Falklands commanding the 2nd Battalion of the Parachute Regiment, served most of his time in the Devon and Dorset Regiment.

Duke of Cornwall's Light Infantry Museum (Cornwall)

£. Usual hours, plus Sundays in July and August. Parking opposite. Tel. 01208 72810. The Keep, Castle Canyke Road, Bodmin.

Tells the story of the DCLI (amalgamated with the Somerset Light Infantry in 1959) by means of numerous splendid pictures, uniforms, weapons and artefacts . The Regiment's forebears captured Gibraltar in 1704. Highlights on display include George Washington's bible, captured in a raid in Massachusetts in 1778, and a FOR VALOUR case containing all the eight VCs awarded to the Regiment along with photographs and citations. The most recent winner (posthumously) was Lieutenant Phillip Curtis in Korea.

Ethandun, Battle of, 878 (Wiltshire)

Downland. Free. Open access. Uncertain, but likely to be near the cross tracks on the ridge some three miles south of Bratton village on the B3098 east of Westbury. It can be approached by car along the minor road leading south from Bratton.

A decisive victory for the Saxon King Alfred over the Danes under Guthrum. Alfred marched his army to Iley Oak, near Warminster, en route to the Danish base around Chippenham. The opposing shield walls clashed just south of Edington village. The Vikings were overwhelmed, pursued to Chippenham and their camp surrounded.

Fleet Air Arm Museum (Somerset)

££££. Usual hours. Shop. Restaurant. Picnic area. Adventure playground. Video games arcade. Airfield viewing gallery. Parking. Tel. 01935 840565. www.fleetairarm.com/index2.htm North of Yeovil on the B3151 just off the A303 near Ilchester.

Covering six and a half acres, this is one of the largest aviation museums in Britain, situated alongside an operational airfield. The history of British naval aviation is told through service aircraft, audio-visual presentations and working models, with exhibits designed to appeal to visitors of all ages. Of particular significance are the Super X Flight simulator, the Aircraft Carrier Experience and the Merlin Experience, introducing the RN's latest helicopter.

Half Moon Battery (in Pendennis Castle grounds) (Cornwall) ⌗

££. Usual hours. Picnic spot. Parking. Tel. 01326 316594. One mile south-east of Falmouth city centre – signposted as Pendennis Castle.

In use throughout the Second World War to protect the Fal estuary, the Half Moon battery is just below the Elizabethan ramparts with its observation post built into them. It is well worth seeing during a visit to Pendennis Castle (p. 20); visitors can descend through secret underground tunnels for a look at this more modern coastal defence installation.

Hambledon Hill (Dorset) ⌗

Free. Open access. Limited parking at entrance to Hod Hill. Five miles north-west of Blandford Forum off the A350 Shaftesbury road. A footpath leads to the top from the side of the cricket ground in Shroton village.

Hambledon Hill is one of the most attractive and spectacular of British hill-forts and it is well worth the walk to the top, if only to admire the superb views. There were three stages of construction, starting in the north in around 3000 BC. The second took in the centre portion of the hill with a set of cross-banks, with the final phase being constructed between 50 BC and the Roman conquest of the south-west in AD 43. At the highest point inside the fort is a massive Neolithic long barrow. The causewayed camp, surrounded by a ditch and inner bank, was of great ritual importance; the ditch contained many human bones including crouched infant burials and skulls placed at intervals, and it is possible the camp may have been an open-air cemetery where corpses were left exposed. Another structure lies 75 yards to the south-east, with a large ditch containing much charcoal, perhaps indicating a palisade destroyed by fire. More skulls severed from their bodies have been placed around its

circuit. It seems the fort was attacked and taken as an intact skeleton was found near the entrance with an arrowhead embedded in his chest.

In 1645 a band of 2000 'Clubmen' (local peasants opposed to the English Civil War) were dispersed from their camp on Hambledon Hill by 50 of Cromwell's dragoons.

Ham Hill (Somerset)

Free. Privately owned but run by local District Council. Open access. Picnic spot. Pub (Prince of Wales). Countryside ranger service available. Parking at various places on the hill. Tel. 01935 823617. Five miles north-west of Yeovil at the village of Stoke sub Hamdon just south of the A303.

Ham Hill is the centre of a country park managed by the South Somerset District Council with stunning views to the Mendips, Exmoor and even, on a clear day, to the Brecon Beacons. It was once an Iron Age hill-fort but has been quarried since Roman times for its famous honey-coloured stone, which has given a distinctive character to many of the surrounding villages. An excellent place for gentle walks along the network of ramparts, ridges and terraces, Ham Hill is also the start of at least one exploratory trail that is a delight for those interested in flora and wildlife.

An enormous range of aircraft are on show at the Fleet Air Arm Museum

Dyrham (Deorham), Battle of, 577 (Somerset)

Fields. Free. Open access. Parking off-road. Picnic area nearby. On A46, half a mile south of Junction 18 on M4.

There is still disagreement as to the exact location of this engagement, one of the most important battles fought in England. After a century during which the Saxons gradually pushed the Britons westward this major clash was decisive. The siting of the battlefield in this Guide follows the careful, logical reasoning of an experienced soldier, the late Lieutenant-Colonel A.H. Burne, who based his analysis on the only real authority, the *Anglo-Saxon Chronicle*. It is worth quoting a passage: 'A.D. 577. Cuthwin and Ceawlin fought with the Britons and slew three kings … on a place that is called Deorham and took from them three cities Gloucester, Cirencester and Bath.'

The three native British 'kings' had assembled their army to stop the Saxons, who had been advancing cautiously through the Cotswolds, headed for the Bristol Channel. The Saxon approach was probably along the ancient track-way that is now the minor road immediately south of, and parallel to, the M4 between the tiny villages of Nettlefold and Hinton. We can imagine the Britons moving east along the track, with the fortified camp on Hinton Hill at their backs, looking for suitable ground to deploy their large force in a blocking position across the Saxons' line of advance. Hinton Hill was a promontory camp; that is, it was built on a steep escarpment that jutted west pointing to the Bristol Channel, which is plainly visible from the camp. It may have been used as a sanctuary for families or it may have been intended as a last stand position to which the Britons could retreat if need be. However, it was never the intention to base the British defence on the camp as it was too small for the three armies and the approach from the east was too easy.

For the British, defeat with the sea virtually at their backs would be a catastrophe – they must fight to the end. The first possible position was a few hundred yards east of the camp, a low ridge that crossed the road at right angles and now carries the Cotswold Way path. Perhaps there was a pause while the leaders considered it. Almost certainly it was rejected as some 600 yards further ahead was another slightly higher ridge, which the British would have moved forward to occupy. The Tolldown Farm crossroads sits towards the southern end of this low ridge, which provided a splendid view of the approaching Saxons from the east.

We know little of the Saxon attack itself other than that the outcome was decisive, the Britons were destroyed and their three 'kings' killed. This implies that the fighting was bitter and bloody, that the British were pushed back, perhaps some retreating into the camp, and that they were, in the end, surrounded – this is implied by the death of all British 'kings'. There may have been a last-ditch stand in Hinton Hill camp by some but if so it did no more than briefly postpone the end. Following their defeat the Britons became divided, with those to the north retreating to Wales, the southern tribes to Cornwall.

Visitors are recommended to approach the battlefield via the A46 leading to or from Junction 18 on the M4 and stop at the Tolldown Farm crossroads. Face east towards Nettlefold and you can see a long way down a gentle slope – from here the British watched the Saxons march up and deploy. Turn left (north) and on the ridge on which you are standing stood a solid line of British warriors with shields, swords, javelins and spears together with some bowmen, stretching about 800 yards. Turn south, and where the ridge falls away after 300 yards was the British right flank. The Saxons attacked all along the line, slowly pushed their enemy back, possibly as far as the first position (see map), and there began to outflank the British. The 'kings' may have sought respite in the camp, but more likely they went down fighting in the open defended by their guards.

If you have time, drive up to Hinton Hill, look back at the field of battle and then look west to the sea – the view is splendid.

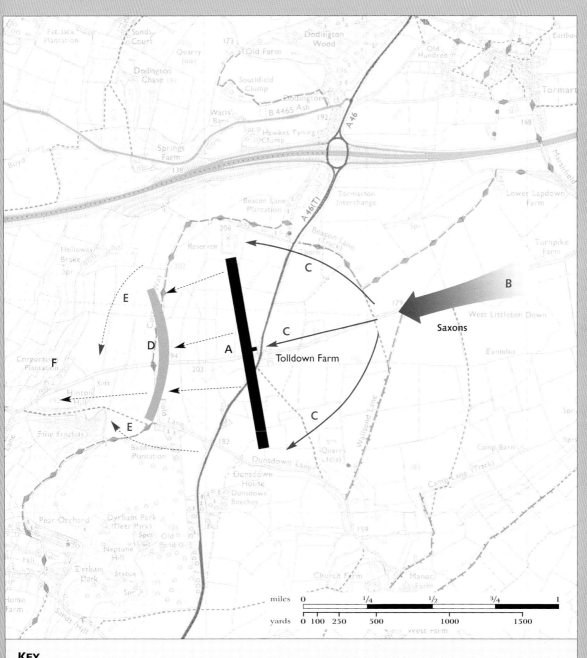

KEY

■ British
■ Saxons

A Three British kings assemble their armies to block the approaching Saxons.

B Large Saxon army advances from the east.

C The Saxons attack and eventually push the British back.

D The British retreat, possibly making a final stand on this ridge.

E The Saxons manage to outflank and surround the British, whose kings are killed.

F Some British may have sought a final refuge in Hinton Hill fort.

Hod Hill (Dorset) 🌿

Free. Easy access, open countryside. Small car park nearby. Four miles north-west of Blandford Forum. A steep footpath leads to the fort from the car park on the minor road leading to Child Okeford from the A350.

An immensely imposing hill-fort built on an isolated hill rising almost sheer from the banks of the River Stour. It is protected on all sides by steep slopes and huge ramparts that have a deep ditch on the outside and quarry pits behind them. The area, 55 acres, is the largest surrounded by ramparts of any hill-fort in Dorset (including Maiden Castle). Excavations have revealed that Hod Hill was in the process of being renovated when attacked by Vespasian's 2nd Augusta Legion in AD 43. The British defenders made extensive use of slingshots, as several piles of reserve ammunition prove. The Romans bombarded the fort with arrow-firing ballistae and many iron bolt heads have been found scattered around the interior. There is no direct evidence that the fort was stormed and then burnt, rather that the British may have capitulated after prolonged bombardment. Unusually, the Romans took over the fort for themselves and constructed a smaller fort for a cohort in the north-west corner. Its earth ramparts are still well defined.

Infantry and Small Arms School Corps Weapons Collection (Wiltshire)

Free (donations encouraged). Limited access by appointment, Tuesday–Thursday. Not suitable for children. Parking. Tel. 01985 222487. HQ Small Arms School Corps, Warminster Training Centre, Warminster.

There are almost 3000 exhibits on display here, illustrating the development of military small arms from the 16th century to modern times. These include pistols, rifles, sub-machine guns, light and medium machine guns and mortars, grenades and anti-armour weapons. The Collection also contains an extensive reference library including manuscript trial records dating back to 1853.

Knap Hill (Wiltshire)

Free. Open countryside. Open access. Parking nearby. 12 miles south of Swindon. Take the minor road to Alton Priors off the A345. Turn right in the village and the car park is a mile down this road. Knap Hill looms above you on your right.

A fine example of a Neolithic 'causeway camp'; that is, a stronghold with several causeways across concentric rings of ditches rather than defensive gateways through ramparts. This indicates that the Knap Hill site may have initially been built for ceremonial purposes, a proposition strengthened by the nearby Bronze Age round barrows and Iron Age enclosure to the north. It has a single ditch up to 12ft wide and 8ft deep, with an inner bank crossed by five causeways. Its location, superbly situated on a steep scarp overlooking the Vale of Pewsey, makes one wonder if it was intended to have defensive as well as ceremonial functions, although there is no archaeological evidence of fighting.

Hod Hill, a scene of fierce fighting by the Romans in AD 43

Langport, Battle of, 1645 (Somerset)

Farmland. Free access. Parking in Huish Episcopi village. Battlefield is about 1000 yards east of Langport on the B3153 to Somerton. If you can get permission to climb the Huish Episcopi church tower there is a rewarding view of the battlefield to the north and east.

A Parliamentary victory for Sir Thomas Fairfax with 10,000 men over the Royalists' 7000 under Lord Goring, fought on 10 July 1645. Goring was falling back on Bridgewater and had sent most of his guns and baggage to the rear. He deployed on rising ground overlooking a marshy area over which there was only one road bridge. This carried the road from Long Sutton along which Fairfax approached. The Parliamentary guns overwhelmed Goring's two remaining cannons and their musketeers got the better of a lengthy exchange among the hedges in the low ground. At this point Fairfax's cavalry charged across the bridge four abreast. The Royalist cavalry were pushed back and Fairfax's horsemen were reinforced. Infantry followed and a hand-to-hand fight ensued. Eventually Goring's men fell back in flight. This defeat broke the morale of the Royalists in the south-west and contributed to the end of the First Civil War.

Liddington Castle (Hill-fort) (Wiltshire)

Free. Easy access, open hillside, downland. Two miles south of Swindon. At Junction 15 on the M4 take the A346 south. Turn left onto the minor road just after the B4005 at Chiseldon – this is the old Ridgeway track. The hill-fort dominates the road on your right. After about 1000 yards a path leads to the top.

A fine, well-preserved hill-fort, worth the walk up the pathway to the top from the minor road south of Badbury village. It was occupied from the sixth century BC, later abandoned, then reoccupied and refortified in the early Dark Ages. Oval-shaped with a single rampart and ditch enclosing over seven acres, it dominates the ancient Ridgeway

track (the road from which you climbed the hill) and the downland to the south. It is also the most likely site for the great Battle of Mount Baden, in which King Arthur defeated the Anglo-Saxon army in about 500 (see below).

Lostwithiel, Battle of, 1644 (Cornwall)

Free. Farmland. Limited access. Parking possible. Lostwithiel lies on the A390 between St Austell and Liskeard. Restormel Castle (EH site. £. Picnic area. Parking.) lies a mile north of the town with Beacon Hill a mile to the east of it; both the scenes of fighting can be visited without difficulty.

In the summer of 1644 the Parliamentary army under the Earl of Essex with about 10,000 men had been forced to take up a defensive position north of Lostwithiel guarding the small port of Fowey. Essex was isolated in a hostile Cornwall and relied entirely on supplies shipped in through Fowey. He was short of food and morale was low. A Royalist cordon of 14,000 troops under King Charles closed in. Scattered fighting took place around the town, and some of Essex's cavalry broke out on 31 August but his main body was slowly forced back within a shrinking perimeter. Disjointed fighting took place in the fields and houses. The Royalists took Lanhydrock House and then Restormel Castle. By nightfall the Parliamentarians still held the earthworks of Castle Dore. However, Essex abandoned his men and slipped away by boat to Plymouth. A council of war by the remaining senior officers agreed a surrender, and some 6000 men became prisoners.

Maiden Castle (Dorset) ⌗

Free. Open access. Parking. One mile west of Dorchester. Take the A354 Dorchester–Weymouth road, turn right just before reaching the junction with the Dorchester bypass and follow signs.

The most famous hill-fort in Britain and the largest Iron Age fort in Europe. The climb up is challenging but rewarding. Its huge banks enclose an area the size of 50 football pitches

and would have been the home for at least 200 families. The site was developed in two stages; its final form was surrounded by three sets of ramparts with complex outworks at either end to protect the entrances against attack. Thousands of pebbles have been found inside, in ammunition dumps for the slingers. However, they were no defence against the disciplined assault of the future Roman Emperor Vespasian with the II Augusta Legion in AD 43. The main attack was a bloody one at the eastern entrance. Near here were buried thirty-eight bodies of Britons, many with sword cuts in their bones, along with food and drink for the afterlife. One skeleton was found with a ballista bolt embedded in his spine, which can be seen in the Dorchester Museum.

Mount Badon, Battle of, *c.*500 (Wiltshire)

Free. Open access, downland. Parking possible on minor roads. Two miles south of Swindon and immediately east of Badbury.

A resounding victory by King Arthur over the Saxons that drove them back and secured peace for Christian Britain for fifty years. Historians dispute the location of the battlefield but Lieutenant-Colonel A.H. Burne has argued compellingly in favour of placing it north of, and on, Liddington Hill south of Swindon. The Saxons were initially drawn up on the hill immediately east of Badbury village.

During the first day the Britons attacked continuously but without great success. At dusk as the armies drew apart, the Saxons pulled back 2000 yards to the summit of Liddington Hill, on top of which was the Iron Age hill-fort, although this was too small to be of use to the defenders. The Saxon line extended all along the hill. The next day Arthur attacked again. Once more the battle raged most of the day with the Britons struggling up the slope, the Saxons charging down. Finally, Arthur himself led a cavalry charge up the gentler slope on the Saxon right. It swept his enemy off the hill with great slaughter.

Lansdown Hill, Battle of, 1643 (Somerset)

Free. Farmland. Open access. Parking. Lansdown Hill is four miles north of Bath and can be reached from the A420 Chippenham to Bristol road. When approaching from Chippenham, turn left onto the minor road 1000 yards past the A420 and A46 junction. As you reach the top of the hill Sir Bevil Grenville's monument is on your left.

An inconclusive battle fought on 5 July 1643 between Royalists under Sir Ralph Hopton and Parliamentarians under Sir William Waller. The Royalists approached Lansdown Hill from the north, following the line of the road. Drawn up along the crest of a sharp slope was Waller's army, which had positioned guns in the centre across the road and reinforced the front with breastworks. It was an exceedingly strong position to attack frontally. After some hesitation and consultation Hopton decided to accept the challenge of assaulting straight up the hill. It was late afternoon and he chose an unusual formation. In the centre he put his cavalry, spread up to the right of the road. On the road itself were his Cornish pikemen under the redoubtable Sir Bevil Grenville. Extended on either flank, with orders to advance up through the trees, were the musketeers. Hopton had completely reversed the normal battle formation whereby the infantry was in the centre with cavalry on the flanks. The object of the musketeers was 'to gain the flank of the enemy on the top of the hill'. They advanced into the trees without much difficulty and slowly began to fight their way up the slope.

In the centre it was much more difficult. The pikes and horse received the full weight of the plunging fire from the cannons on the crest. Both Royalist pikemen and horse suffered serious losses as they struggled with the slope and the hail of fire from above. The whole slope was blanketed with smoke and noise. The first to give way were the Royalist cavalry who melted back to the rear, some galloping all the way to Oxford spreading tales of disaster. At the end of the day Hopton had only 600 demoralized cavalry left out of 2000. The Cornishmen were made of sterner stuff and forced their way to the crest. A furious 'push of pike' took place across and through the barricades. Waller's cavalry counter-attacked but Grenville's Cornishmen formed a hedgehog of steel-tipped

Lansdown Hill looking north-east from Hanging Hill (Battlefields Trust)

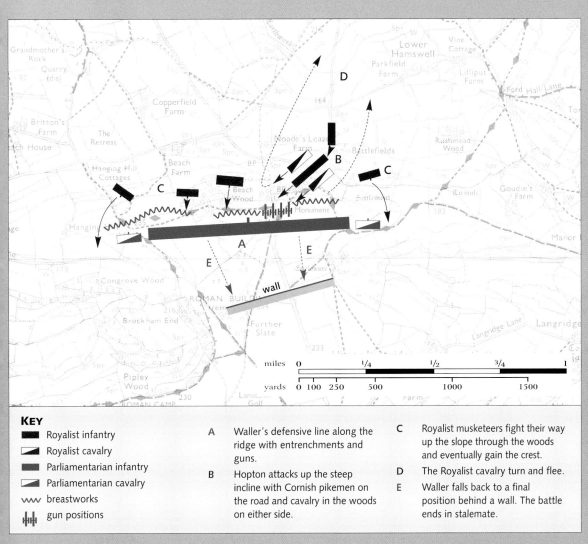

KEY

■■	Royalist infantry
◪	Royalist cavalry
■■	Parliamentarian infantry
◪	Parliamentarian cavalry
⌇⌇⌇	breastworks
⊞⊞	gun positions

A   Waller's defensive line along the ridge with entrenchments and guns.

B   Hopton attacks up the steep incline with Cornish pikemen on the road and cavalry in the woods on either side.

C   Royalist musketeers fight their way up the slope through the woods and eventually gain the crest.

D   The Royalist cavalry turn and flee.

E   Waller falls back to a final position behind a wall. The battle ends in stalemate.

pikes that succeeded in keeping the horsemen at a distance, although they were at this stage almost surrounded and outnumbered.

Meanwhile the Royalist musketeers had made progress through the woods on the flanks and eventually gained the crest all along the line – but at a huge cost. Waller's line fell back in some disorder, but with their guns intact, to the shelter of a stone wall some 400 yards to the rear. Here they reformed and turned to face their attackers again. Both sides were exhausted and the Royalists had suffered heavily, leaving the slope and crest of the hill littered with dead and wounded. Just at the time Hopton needed his cavalry to outflank the new position they had disappeared. Casualties, extreme fatigue and a shortage of ammunition forced Hopton to halt on

the ground he had won. A counter-attack by Waller at this moment would surely have sent his enemy tumbling back down the hill to ruin. It never came. During the night Waller's army slipped away behind the welcoming walls of Bath.

Park your car off the road opposite Grenville's monument and you are standing about in the centre of Waller's defences. Walk along the side of the road to the crest of the hill. Lined up across the road at this point were the Parliamentary guns, with their infantry positions extending through the woods and trees on either side of the road. Along the line of the road and on either side the Cornish pikemen struggled uphill, with bitter hand-to-hand fighting all around. Turn and walk back about 400 yards and you will find the stone wall behind which Waller rallied his men.

Nothe Fort and Military Museum (Dorset)

££. Usual hours. Shop. Refreshments. Guided tours. Council parking nearby. Tel. 01305 766626. Barrack Road, Weymouth. Well signed from outskirts of town. A ferry runs across the harbour in summer from the Pavilion end of the Esplanade.

The Fort, which comprises over seventy rooms on three levels (ramparts, courtyard and magazines), was built between 1860 and 1872 as part of the defences of the naval base. It contains numerous displays, dummy figures, dioramas and tank, ship, gun and aircraft models illustrating how soldiers lived and worked from Victorian times to the Second World War. There is a Victorian gun-deck with massive 30-ton guns, and at magazine level the displays provide snapshots of local history as it might have been seen from the Nothe headland.

Offa's Dyke (Gloucestershire) ⚏

Free. Open access. Forestry car park a mile from dyke. Take the B4228 north of Chepstow and follow the Forestry sign to the car park. Follow the left fork of forest track and turn right when it reaches a rough road, then turn left at the footpath sign.

Offa's Dyke is the longest earthwork in Britain, running for 120 miles from a point north-west of Wrexham to the low cliffs above the River Severn at Sedbury, near Chepstow. It was built in the late 780s by King Offa as a check on the Welsh tribes, and as such was half boundary and half defensive barrier. There was a deep ditch on the Welsh side and a wooden palisade topped the bank. The actual earthworks are only 80 miles long, but much of it is accessible following the opening up of the Offa's Dyke Long Distance Path in 1971. The section north of Chepstow is the only part in the care of English Heritage and makes for a very enjoyable half-hour walk through woods and fields culminating in a superb view of Tintern Abbey and the Wye valley. However, it is not the best place to view the Dyke; for that you should go to Shropshire or into Wales (see pp. 66 and 125).

Old Sarum and Castle (Wiltshire) ⚏

££ for castle. Usual hours. Shop. Picnic spot. Parking. Tel. 01722 335398. Signposted on the A345 two miles north of Salisbury.

The massive Iron Age hill-fort of Old Sarum (Old Salisbury) was reused by the Romans, Saxons and Normans. It was here that William the Conqueror built a great palace and the original Salisbury cathedral. Part of the Doomsday Book was written here, and it was to Sarum that William summoned all the landowners of England to swear allegiance. However the cathedral became redundant when the new town of Salisbury grew up in the 13th century. Worth a visit but probably not paying to see the castle, of which only the foundations remain; you can look at the rest for free.

Pendennis Castle (Cornwall) ⚏

££. Usual hours. Shop. Refreshments (summer only). Picnic spot. Special events. Parking. Tel. 01323 316594. On Pendennis Head, one mile south of Falmouth. Signposted.

The castle is part of a chain built by Henry VIII as protection against attack from Europe; it was later the penultimate Royalist stronghold to surrender during the English Civil War, and adapted over the next 300 years to meet new enemies. It is a splendid place to visit. Features include a hands-on Discovery Centre, the sights and sounds of battle on a Tudor gun-deck, garrison life before the First World War, underground wartime defences, the Half Moon Battery of Second World War guns (p. 13) and an attack alert in a Second World War observation post.

Portland Castle (Dorset) ⚏

££. Usual hours. Shop. Tearoom. Tel. 01305 820539. Overlooking Portland Harbour in Castleton, Isle of Portland. Signposted at roundabout on A354 at southern end of causeway.

Portland Castle guards the south of Weymouth harbour. Its squat, fan appearance is typical of Henry VIII's forts, of which it is one of the best-preserved examples. It saw fighting during the English Civil War; there is a story that a Royalist captain captured the castle by dividing his men into two groups, one dressed as Parliamentarians who were chased down the beach by the Royalist group. The Parliamentary garrison, thinking to save their comrades, opened the gates and thus lost the castle. In the First World War it was a seaplane station and in the Second World War it played a key role in the planning of D-Day.

Rame Peninsular Forts (Devon)

Free. Public footpaths follow the coast around the peninsula. Open access to area. Parking. Directly opposite Plymouth, approached by the A387.

These forts were built between 1790 and 1890 to defend the naval base of Plymouth, and form the western part of the most extensive and complete historic coastal defences in the UK. There are sixteen redoubts and batteries spread along the coastline overlooking Whitsand Bay to Cawsand Bay to Cremyll village, including the Maker Heights Anti-Aircraft site. Unfortunately, many are overgrown or privately owned. The Cawsand Battery was in use until 1926 but has been converted to residential use. Tregantle Battery, dramatically sited atop the cliffs of Whitsand Bay, can be seen for several miles along the coast. It is still in regular use for military live firing practice. With its coastal and woodland paths the Rame Forts area offers superb walking and a unique insight into our military heritage.

Roundway Down, Battle of, 1643 (Wiltshire)

Free. Easy access, open downland. Parking possible on minor road. Two miles north of Devizes. Take the A361 from Devizes, turn left onto minor road in Bishops Cannings signed Calne. Stop at the next track junction on the left – you are now in the area from which Wilmot charged westwards. Take the next left and continue for another mile to the prehistoric camp of Oliver's Castle close to the 'Bloody Ditch'.

After the inconclusive battle at Lansdown (pp. 18–19), Hopton's dispirited Royalists withdrew into Devizes pursued by Sir William Waller. On 13 July 1643, 1800 Royalist horsemen under Wilmot, sent by King Charles from Oxford to relieve Hopton, met the Parliamentary force of 2000 cavalry and 3000 infantry that Waller had drawn up on the slopes of Roundway Down, blocking their route to Devizes. Waller had infantry in the centre and cavalry on each flank. Wilmot ignored the enemy centre and charged the opposing horsemen. After thirty minutes of hacking and slashing the Royalist cavalry gained the upper hand. Meanwhile, in the centre Waller's musketeers could merely gape at the mêlées on either side of them.

Waller's horsemen fled westwards with their opponents snapping at their heels. After about 2500 yards they saw, opening up in front of them, a precipitous drop of 300ft! Over the edge they went like lemmings, stumbling and crashing to the bottom of what is now known as the 'Bloody Ditch'. Waller's cavalry was destroyed. His infantry surrendered when Hopton's force sallied out from Devizes.

The Royal Gloucestershire, Berkshire and Wiltshire Regiment Museum, 'Redcoats in the Wardrobe' (Wiltshire)

£. Usual hours (closed December and January). Shop. Bookstall. Tel. 01722 419419. Housed in 'The Wardrobe', 58 The Close, Salisbury.

Situated in the beautiful Cathedral Close within easy walking distance of the city centre and car parks, this is an award-winning military museum that tells the story of the Duke of Edinburgh's Royal Regiment and its predecessors, with a series of fine displays covering several hundred years of military history to the present day.

Royal Signals Museum (Dorset)

£££. Usual times. Shop. Café. Picnic area. Parking. Tel. 01258 482248. www.army.mod.uk/royalsignalsmuseum/ Blandford Camp two miles north-east of Blandford Forum off the A354.

This museum depicts the history of military communications, science and technology from the Crimea to the present. There are permanent displays, featuring amongst others animals at war, the Special Operations Executive, Cryptography, ENIGMA codes, the Long Range Desert Group, women at war and airborne forces. The displays are supplemented by hands-on activities, fun trails and competitions.

The Rumps, Hill-forts (Cornwall) ❧

Free. Easy access. Limited parking at Pentire Farm. On the tip of Pentire Point west of Newquay. NT footpaths explore the cliffs along Pentire Point starting at New Polzeath. The views are spectacular.

The site of three Iron Age promontory forts is reached by a narrow isthmus. The local population exploited existing gullies caused by geological faults to build a series of ditches and ramparts to protect the landward side. Originally they had facing walls and breastworks leading to a substantial defensive gateway. Visitors still use this prehistoric entrance, which leads into a flattish area which was large enough to hold flocks of sheep and several circular wooden huts built on levelled platforms.

St Mawes Castle (Cornwall) ⌗

££. Usual hours. Shop. Picnic area. Parking. Tel. 01326 270526. Next to A3078 west of St Mawes village.

The most perfectly preserved of Henry VIII's coastal forts, St Mawes was built to counter the invasion threat from Europe, working in partnership with its twin castle, Pendennis, across the Fal Estuary. It fell to Parliamentary forces without firing a shot in 1646 and was not properly refortified until the late 19th and early 20th centuries. It is clover-

leaf-shaped with two stories and a basement. Guns were mounted on the roof and in embrasures throughout the castle.

Saxon Burh (Dorset)

Free. Open access. Parking. Wareham car park.

Saxon burhs were fortified towns surrounded by steep banks up to 10ft high with a timber palisade and wall-walk, and a ditch beyond. They first appeared in Mercia c.800, probably to counter Viking attacks at strategic places such as population centres or river crossings. Some were quite large, such as that at Hereford which enclosed thirty-three acres. Large numbers were built from the reign of Alfred the Great (871–99). They appear to have been successful defensive works until increasing population rendered them ineffective. One of the few burh ramparts remaining today and easily accessible is this one, whose banks run along the main car park in Wareham.

Sedgemoor, Battle of, 1685 (Somerset)

Free. Farmland. Limited access. Parking possible. Three miles south-east of Bridgewater on A372. A signposted track leads from the outskirts of Westonzoyland to the Royal camp area. There is a monument at Bussex Farm but the terrain has changed considerably since the battle.

In June 1685 the Protestant Duke of Monmouth (King Charles II's eldest illegitimate son) landed at Lyme Regis to raise the standard of rebellion against his unpopular Catholic uncle James II. Those who joined him were untrained, ill-armed country yeomen. James sent his regular troops under Earl Feversham to crush him. Although Monmouth had nearly 3000 foot, 800 horse and 17 guns against 1800, 700 and 4 respectively, Feversham's regiments were the pick of the Army.

On the night of 5–6 July Monmouth, realizing the poor quality of his forces, launched a surprise night attack against his enemy, who was encamped just north of

Colonel A.J. Palmer of the Royal Gloucestershire Hussars, on show at the Soldiers of Gloucestershire Museum

Westonzoyland on Sedgemoor, and protected by a deep drainage ditch called the Bussex Rhyne. As with many night attacks things quickly went wrong. A sentry was alerted and Faversham's force stood to arms. Monmouth sent his cavalry under Lord Grey ahead to find the Upper Plungeon crossing (bridge) but they spurred away into the darkness leaving their guide to chase after them on foot! It was a fiasco. Grey never found the crossing and was scattered by hostile musketry volleys from across the Rhyne. At dawn Faversham unleashed his horsemen on either flank and Monmouth's men quickly disintegrated.

Monmouth was later captured and beheaded – the executioner taking five swings of his axe to complete the job.

Soldiers of Gloucestershire Museum (Gloucestershire)

££. Usual hours, April–October. Shop. Tel. 01452 522682. Custom House, Gloucester Docks, Gloucester.

Good interactive displays including life-size dioramas, sound effects and archive film.

Somerset Military Museum (Somerset)

Free. Usual hours. Shop. Parking. Tel. 01823 320201. Taunton town centre.

Housed within the County Museum in the old Norman castle, the site of Judge Jeffreys's 'Bloody Assize' following Monmouth's Rebellion in 1685, this museum displays the regimental collections of all the former Somerset regiments, including the Somerset Light Infantry, portraying their history from 1685 to the present. Of special interest is the coverage of the two World Wars and the exhibition of some 600 sets of medals.

South Cadbury Castle (Hill-fort) (Somerset)

Free. Private land. Open access, but keep to paths. Parking in South Cadbury village. Leave A303 west of Wincanton at the South and North Cadbury turning. Castle Lane in South Cadbury leads to the hill-fort.

Perhaps the most fabled hill-fort site in Britain, as it is a contender for the title of 'Camelot', the palace of King Arthur. Alas, there is no certain evidence of this, although the hill-fort was heavily refortified around AD 500 and excavations have revealed a large hall and much pottery – Arthur's banqueting hall? It is a magnificent hill-fort to visit with ramparts rising up to 500ft. It was first occupied *c.* 3300 BC and there followed thousands of years of abandonment and occupation evidenced by strengthening and improvement of its defences. It was a thriving population centre when the II Augusta legion arrived. A little later thirty people, including women and children, were massacred by the south-west gate and left to rot. The Romans made a camp within the fort, which was used as late as the reign of Ethelred the Unready, when it became a Saxon burh. Cadbury was destroyed around 1020, possibly on orders from King Canute.

Stow-on-the-Wold, Battle of, 1646 (Gloucestershire)

Free. Farmland, open fields. Reasonable access. Parking possible in Donnington. Take the A429 north out of Stow-on-the-Wold. Turn left to Donnington and park. Follow the path out of the village to the north, continue until a belt of trees is reached. These trees mark the centre of the battlefield.

An English Civil War battle fought on 21 March 1646 between the Royalists under Sir Jacob Astley and the Parliamentarians commanded by Sir William Brereton. With the king's cause virtually lost Astley had managed to scrape together 3000 men and was marching to join King Charles at Oxford when he was intercepted at Stow-on-the-Wold. Astley occupied the high ground but Brereton nevertheless ordered an attack up the slope. The Royalists managed to force the Parliamentarian left to retreat but their own left was dispersed by Brereton's cavalry. The flight of the Royalist left was soon followed by their infantry and Astley's force disintegrated. Many Royalists were trapped and killed in the market square of Stow-on-the-Wold.

Stratton, Battle of, 1643 (Cornwall)

Free. Fields. Open access. Off-road parking. Three miles east of Bude. A good starting (or finishing) point for the visitor is the Tree Inn in Maiden Street, Stratton, which boasts a picture of Anthony Payne (a 7ft giant who fought for the Royalists) and several scythes said to have been bloodied in the fight. From there walk up Poundfield Lane and continue across the A39 to a wicket gate which leads to the top of Stamford Hill. On the summit is a monument to the battle. It is easy to imagine the attacks coming in from all sides.

This remarkable little Royalist victory on 16 May 1643 was part of the struggle for the West Country during the English Civil War. The Parliamentarians under the Earl of Stamford had deployed over 5000 men atop the 200ft Stamford Hill on the northern outskirts of Stratton village. Sir Ralph Hopton, commanding around 3000 Royalists whose musketeers were short of ammunition, decided on a bold plan of attack. Splitting his force into four units he ordered simultaneous attacks up the hill from three sides with pike and sword. The issue was in doubt for a while but the flight of Stamford and the turning of captured guns on the Parliamentarians decided the day. The Royalist booty included 1700 prisoners and £5000.

Tewkesbury, Battle of, 1471 (Gloucestershire)

Free. Some open ground, parkland, housing estates. Reasonable access. Parking available. On southern outskirts of Tewkesbury west of the A38.

The turning to Tewkesbury Park (now a golf club) is signposted to Bloody Meadow. A battlefield plan has been erected here and is the starting point of a walk signed by metal flags. The Park south of the Abbey (The Vineyards) has a monument to the battle.

One of the most decisive battles of the Wars of the Roses. On 14 May the Lancastrian Army of 6000 was drawn up across 'The Vineyards' immediately south of the Abbey. The right division was commanded by the Duke of Somerset, the centre by Lord Wenlock and Prince Edward, the left by the Earl of Devonshire. Opposite, the 5000 Yorkists under King Edward IV were also in three divisions. On their left (opposite Somerset) was the Duke of Gloucester, in the centre the King and on the right Lord Hastings. However, Edward had concealed 200 mounted spearmen in the wooded hill on his extreme left near the present golf course. Both armies deployed guns and archers.

After an exchange of arrows and artillery fire Somerset advanced against the Yorkist left. However, Wenlock (a lukewarm Lancastrian who had fought for the Yorkists at Towton) in the centre failed to support him. Thus Somerset's left was exposed to an attack from the King commanding the Yorkist centre. Engaged in front and on the left, Somerset was extremely hard pressed. At this moment the 200 spearmen dashed down and hit him on the right. His men fled, many being cut down in what became known as 'Bloody Meadow'. The remainder of the Lancastrian forces were put to flight, during which the Prince of Wales was killed and Margaret of Anjou captured. Somerset was executed two days later.

West Wansdyke (Somerset)

Free. Footpath. Open access. Parking off-road. Immediately south of Bristol. Take the A37 and turn right onto the first minor road after Whitchurch. After a mile Maes Knoll is on the right and a footpath is signposted.

The western section of this ditch and bank that runs from the Avon Valley to Savernake Forest near Marlborough is best seen from the viewpoint on Maes Knoll hill-fort. The bank was built by the Saxons, probably in the sixth century, and faces north.

South Cadbury hill-fort; according to legend this was Arthur's Camelot

THE CELTS AND THEIR HILL-FORTS

THE WARRIOR CELTS

The Stone, Bronze and Iron Ages are the familiar names given to the main phases of Britain's prehistory. They are crude descriptions as the phases overlapped, often by many hundreds of years. In Britain change and development came late. Only the most daring or desperate would risk the journey into the unknown from an island protected by wind, water and currents. Over the centuries, however, progressive waves of migrants and invaders, themselves often fleeing more powerful tribes from central Europe, brought the new technologies to our shores – invariably the southern or eastern ones first.

The hunter-gatherers of 8000 BC, with their flint and stone implements, gradually gave way to men who could make bronze weapons and tools. From about 500 BC to 100 BC the people now known as 'Celts' gradually infiltrated the British Isles, crossing the Channel from France. They brought with them the magic of iron. Accessible, plentiful and durable, it revolutionized life for our forebears. Heavy soils could be ploughed and heavy swords could be forged, swords that kept their edge. Farming and warfare thrived.

Physically the Celts' build and features varied considerably; according to Caesar 'they wear their hair long, and shave the whole of their bodies except the head and the upper lip'. Some Celts were small and dark, with Mediterranean blood, while others were tall and big-boned with reddish or fair hair. Many Scotsmen are descended from this stock. In the Scottish clans we can recognize the type of tribal organization that both bound and divided them; a map of twenty-one Celtic tribes can be seen here.

Druids – high priests – officiated at religious ceremonies that not infrequently involved human sacrifice. Caesar wrote:

> Some tribes have colossal images made of wickerwork the limbs of which they fill with living men. They are then set on fire, and the victims burnt to death. They think that the gods prefer the execution of men taken in the act of theft or brigandage ... but when they run short of criminals, they do not hesitate to make up with innocent men.

Druids also acted as judges, arbitrators in disputes, teachers and healers. They had enormous influence, including the right to speak ahead of the king in council.

Celts regarded the human head as the source of all spiritual power. Thus a severed enemy head was a way of securing his spirit, and several such trophies often adorned the entrances to their arched timber, wicker-walled, thatch-roofed huts. These dwellings were primitive, clustered together within a banked enclosure with the tribal leaders only slightly better housed. The Celtic chiefs commanded in war – a favourite activity. They, and their women, were fond of magnificent personal ornaments: gold and enamelled brooches for their cloaks, beautifully fashioned swords,

Celtic tribes in 54 BC

PICTII

OTADINI

Tweed

SELGOVAE

NOVANTAE

BRIGANTES

Ouse

Trent

DEGEANGLI

CORNOVII

ORDOVICES

CORITANI

Welland

ICENI

Severn

DEMETAE

SILURES

DOBUNI

CANUVELLAUNI

Thames

TRINOVANTES

ATREBATES

CANTII

BELGAE

REGNI

DUMNONII

DUROTRIGES

shields, horned helmets, necklaces and bracelets of pale Irish gold.

By the time the Romans invaded Britain in strength the chariot had gone out of use in warfare in mainland Europe but not in Britain, where the tribes of northern Scotland used them well into the third century AD. When mounted in his light, two-wheeled, two-horsed chariot in full regalia the chief was a splendid sight. The chariot was controlled by a driver, while the chief or other warrior either skirmished from it, hurling javelins at speed, or jumped down to fight on foot, remounting when hard pressed – an ancient form of mounted infantry. Caesar was impressed by their skill:

They began by driving all over the field, hurling javelins; and the terror inspired by the horses and the noise of the wheels is usually enough to throw the enemy ranks into disorder. Then they work their way between their own cavalry units, where the warriors jump down and fight on foot. Meanwhile, the drivers retire a short distance ... and station the cars in such a way that their masters, if outnumbered, have an easy means of retreat to their own lines. In action, therefore, they combine the mobility of cavalry with the staying power of foot-soldiers.

The ordinary Celtic warrior often, though not always, fought bare-chested. 'All Britons dye their bodies with woad, which produces a blue colour, and this gives them a more terrifying appearance in battle,' Caesar noted. When fighting on foot the Celt bore a sword and wooden shield, with an asymmetric central decoration of bronze, embellished in places with enamel. For more open warfare away from their settlements some British tribes mobilized light cavalry as well as chariots. These men were armed with spear and sword, or javelins and sword, and commonly protected themselves with large oval wickerwork shields faced with leather. British coins often depict these horsemen wearing helmets like modern jockey caps. Ordinary infantry wore woollen trousers; some had long-sleeved shirts and fought with a mixture of long, straight swords for slashing, javelins and spears. Some shields were oval, covering much of the body, while those used by the javelin men were smaller and circular. The missile men were the slingers, with their ammunition stashed in a leather bag slung on the belt. The British slingers who faced the Romans were, like the charioteers, skilled specialists. Although they used rounded seashore pebbles about the size of a golf or snooker ball, rather than the lead shot used by more advanced nations, a continuous hail of hundreds of such missiles proved extremely effective in defence of their hilltop settlements. An advantage for the slinger over the archer was that he could also handle a shield to deflect enemy missiles.

HILL-FORTS

There are some two thousand Iron Age hill-forts in England. This guide looks at twelve that are worth visiting for a good walk and some impressive views, if you relish a stiff climb. The great majority are in the south-west of the country, with Dorset and Wiltshire being particularly well endowed. The heyday for building hill-forts was from about 700 to 500 BC. These forts predominated in cereal crop areas, thus signifying a fairly stable population. They vary in size from under 1 to 200 acres although most enclose areas from 3 to 30. The very small ones were used as fortified residences for perhaps a single family; larger forts were often the seat of a tribal leader sheltering substantial communities with their cattle.

There are several types of fort, varying according to the topographical setting. They include promontory forts, contour forts (a prime example being Maiden Castle in Dorset), plateau forts and, something of a misnomer, lowland forts. Caesar described one of the latter (probably Wheathampstead, which is double the size of Maiden Castle) as being defended by woods and marshes – 'they have fortified thickly wooded spots with rampart and ditch'. Basic hill-forts consisted of a bank, or rampart, and one ditch; these are called 'univallate' forts. Others, called 'multivallate' forts, have a series of banks and ditches that usually represent several stages of construction and improvement over many centuries. From earliest times wooden palisades topped the bank behind the ditch. A later development was the box rampart, while some forts, in Wales for example, had stone walls.

Walking along the ramparts of the larger forts, it is impossible not to wonder at the massive amount of labour required. Many ramparts are not just piled-up earth but were strengthened with rocks and stones or were laced with a criss-cross of timber, a major feat of primitive engineering. Inside, occupation and the construction of the circular huts, granaries and storage pits was often random and disordered. Occasionally, as at Hod Hill, there is evidence of some attempt at rudimentary street planning and the allocation of space for cattle.

From a defensive point of view the hilltop fort had two major problems. The first was lack of water. A year-round supply of water within the fort was not possible, so withstanding a prolonged siege was not an option – indeed there is evidence the smaller forts were often used seasonally or in an emergency. The second problem was the vulnerability of the entrances to attack. There were never more than two entrances, usually defended by elaborate outerworks – even guardhouses were built into some ramparts. The most complex works of this kind are the colossal entrance

Maiden Castle, one of the greatest Iron Age hill-forts

approaches to Maiden Castle, from the top of which hundreds of slingers would hurl showers of stones down at the attackers as they tried to reach the main gates. Thousands of sling stones have been found on and around the entrance at Danebury, together with a pit containing 6000 more just inside the entrance – a Celtic ammunition dump.

These forts were designed to resist attack from rival tribes, not the sophisticated tactics or siege engines of the Romans. Caesar gives an account of how the Celts themselves organized an assault:

> *The Gauls and Belgae use the same method of attack. They surround the whole circuit of the walls with a large number of men and shower it with stones from all sides, so that the defences are denuded of men. Then they form a testudo ['tortoise'; a wedge of men with shields interlocked over their heads], set fire to the gates and undermine the walls.*

Well worth a visit

Badbury Rings, Dorset *p. 10*
Ham Hill, Somerset *p. 13*
Hambledon Hill, Dorset *p. 13*
Hod Hill, Dorset *p. 16*
Knap Hill, Wiltshire *p. 16*
Maiden Castle, Dorset *p. 17*
The Rumps, Cornwall *p. 21*
South Cadbury Castle, Somerset *p. 22*
Stanwick, North Yorkshire *p. 114*
Castell Henllys, Wales *p. 124*

BROCHS AND DUNS

These are small, fortified Iron Age sites scattered across Scotland. There are 120 on Orkney alone and at least 500 in Scotland. Their heyday was the three hundred years from the second century BC through to the first century AD.

Brochs were mostly high, circular stone towers probably built by local clan chiefs both as a defended residence and as an expression of their wealth and influence. They suggest a period when defences against raiders were necessary and the people looked to the chief for protection. Their circular walls rose up to 30ft or more, much wider at the base than the top. From outside they resembled a giant, tapering chimney. There were two walls, an inner and an outer, joined at intervals by courses of wide, flat, stone slabs. This space between the walls allowed for the construction of a stairway inside with the slabs forming corridors inside the walls. From them doorways could lead into wooden-floored rooms at different levels. The broch was also roofed over. Many had small guardrooms built into the wider wall at ground level.

Well worth a visit

Dun Telve, Western Highlands *p. 153*
Mousa Broch, Shetland *p. 157*

The word 'Dun' is the Gaelic for 'castle'. It is also used, confusingly, in the names of some brochs such as Dun Telve. They also date from the Iron Age and are found on the west coast of Scotland, mostly located near the sea on a rocky hill or promontory, often with an outer wall cutting off access on the landward side. Duns are similar to brochs (which they predate) but smaller, with solid walls seldom over 10 feet high. They were, basically, round, stone, fortified houses.

Well worth a visit
Dun Beag, Skye *p. 152*

Mousa Broch in its spectacular Shetland setting

SOUTH-EAST AND LONDON

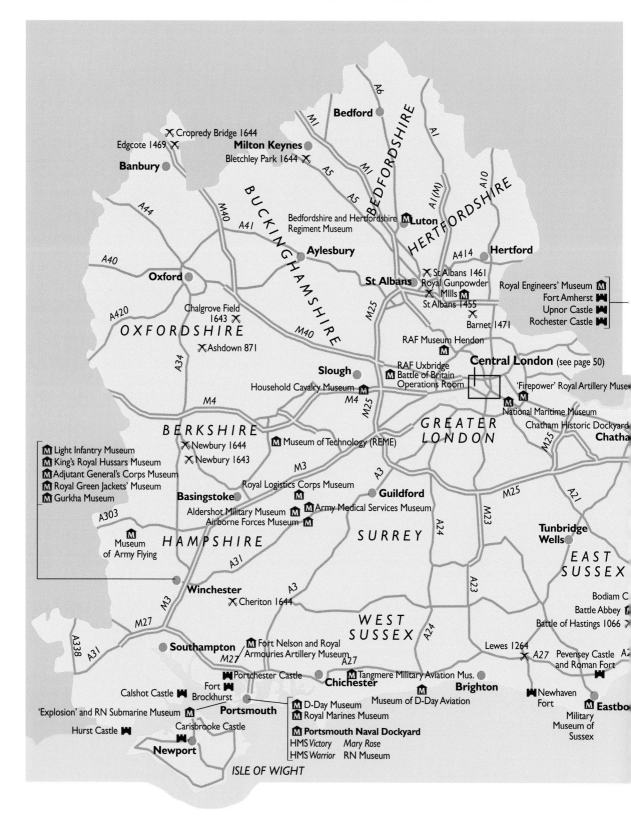

Bedford

Cropredy Bridge 1644

Edgcote 1469

Milton Keynes

Banbury

Bletchley Park 1644

BEDFORDSHIRE

BUCKINGHAMSHIRE

HERTFORDSHIRE

Bedfordshire and Hertfordshire
Regiment Museum

Luton

Aylesbury

Hertford

St Albans 1461
Royal Gunpowder
Mills
St Albans 1455

St Albans

Oxford

Royal Engineers' Museum
Fort Amherst
Upnor Castle
Rochester Castle

Chalgrove Field
1643

OXFORDSHIRE

Barnet 1471

Ashdown 871

RAF Museum Hendon

Central London (see page 50)

Slough

RAF Uxbridge
Battle of Britain
Operations Room

Household Cavalry Museum

'Firepower' Royal Artillery Museum

GREATER
LONDON

National Maritime Museum

BERKSHIRE

Museum of Technology (REME)

Chatham Historic Dockyard

Chatham

Light Infantry Museum
King's Royal Hussars Museum
Adjutant General's Corps Museum
Royal Green Jackets' Museum
Gurkha Museum

Newbury 1644

Newbury 1643

Royal Logistics Corps Museum

Guildford

Basingstoke

Aldershot Military Museum
Airborne Forces Museum

Army Medical Services Museum

Tunbridge
Wells

Museum
of Army Flying

HAMPSHIRE

SURREY

EAST
SUSSEX

Winchester

Cheriton 1644

Bodiam C
Battle Abbey
Battle of Hastings 1066

WEST
SUSSEX

Lewes 1264

Pevensey Castle
and Roman Fort

Southampton

Fort Nelson and Royal
Armouries Artillery Museum

Portchester Castle

Tangmere Military Aviation Mus.

Newhaven
Fort

Calshot Castle

Fort
Brockhurst

Chichester

Museum of D-Day Aviation

Brighton

Eastb

'Explosion' and RN Submarine Museum

Portsmouth

D-Day Museum
Royal Marines Museum

Military
Museum of
Sussex

Hurst Castle

Carisbrooke Castle

Portsmouth Naval Dockyard

Newport

HMS Victory   Mary Rose
HMS Warrior   RN Museum

ISLE OF WIGHT

The Adjutant General's Corps Museum (Hampshire)

Free. Usual hours. Visitors' centre. Refreshments. Tel. 01962 828598. www.winchestermilitarymuseums.co.uk/agc.html *Peninsula Barracks, Romsey Road, Winchester city centre.*

The Adjutant General's Corps (AGC) was only formed in 1992, but it is made up of six older and very interesting corps – the former Women's Royal Army Corps, The Royal Military Police, The Royal Army Pays Corps, The Army Legal Corps and The Military Provost Staff Corps – whose varied and exciting stories are told here.

There are another four splendid museums in the same barracks: the Gurkha Museum (p. 38), The King's Royal Hussars (p. 39), The Light Infantry (p. 39) and The Royal Green Jackets (p. 47).

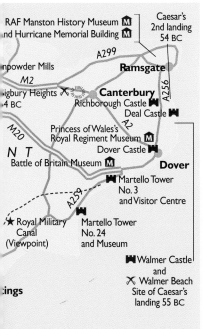

Airborne Forces Museum (Hampshire)

££. Usual hours. Shop. Parking. Tel. 01252 349619. Browning Barracks, Aldershot. M3 motorway to Farnborough then A325 to Aldershot Military Town and follow museum signs.

This splendid museum, covering the history of airborne forces from 1940 to the present, has displays and exhibits for the Parachute Regiment and all Corps and Arms of service connected with Airborne Forces. They include Second World War models, glider cockpits, equipment, weapons and uniforms as well as a special section on the Falklands conflict.

Aldershot Military Museum (Hampshire)

£. Usual hours. Refreshments. Special events. Parking. Tel. 01252 314598. www.hants.gov.uk/museum/aldershot *Queen's Avenue, Aldershot.*

This museum tells the story of the 'Home of the British Army', with photographs, models, displays and an original Victorian barrack room illustrating the soldier's life over 145 years. Vehicles include a Chieftain main battle tank, anti-tank guns, trucks and armoured cars. In addition to badges, medals and weapons there are several 'hands-on' activities suitable for younger visitors. These include trying a training tunnel, solving puzzles, experiencing a 'ride' in an armoured reconnaissance vehicle and listening to the roar of a drill sergeant.

Army Medical Services Museum (Hampshire)

Free. Usual hours (not public holidays). Shop. Research facilities. Parking. Tel. 01252 868612. Keogh Barracks, Ash Vale, Aldershot. M3 exit 4 then A331 for 1½ miles until exit signed Mytchett, then follow brown tourist signs for RAMC Museum. www.army.mod.uk/medical/ams_museum

A fascinating museum that illustrates the story of the Royal Army Medical

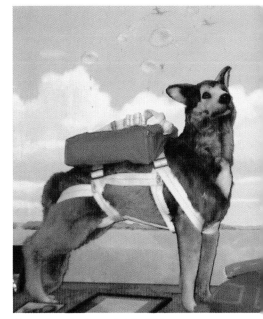

Bing, a 'paradog' awarded the Dickens Medal (the animal equivalent of the Victoria Cross), is one of the most striking exhibits at the Airborne Forces Museum

Corps, Royal Army Dental Corps, Royal Army Veterinary Corps and the Queen Alexandra's Royal Army Nursing Corps. There are exhibits of medical and veterinary care in the Army from 1660 together with displays of uniforms, surgical equipment and ambulances. Recent redevelopment will make the museum a major resource for the study of military medicine, nursing, dentistry and veterinary science.

Battle Abbey
(East Sussex; see also Hastings, p. 40) ⊞

£££. Usual hours. Shop. Children's play area. Parking. Tel. 01424 773792. www.english-heritage.org/battleabbey *Battle village, six miles NW of Hastings on the A2100.*

In 1070 William the Conqueror established Battle Abbey on the site of his famous victory. A few portions of the Abbey remain today, though little from William's time. The best-preserved feature is the Great Gatehouse, the finest of all surviving

Ashdown, Battle of, 871 (Berkshire)

Free. Open downland/farmland. Easy access. Parking off-road. Twelve miles NW of Reading. Follow the A329 northwards from Reading, and turn left onto the B4009 signed to Aldworth at Streatly. From Aldworth follow the lane signposted The Downs for 2¹/₂ miles until it meets the Ridgeway. This is the centre of the fiercest fighting, close to the stunted thorn-tree. The battlefield is easy to explore on foot from here.

From the middle of the ninth century the Vikings began to establish permanent settlements in England rather than just making seasonal raids. By late 870 the Danes were encamped outside Reading under the Kings Bagsecg and Halfdan and began launching concerted attacks on Wessex, opposed by the Saxons under King Aethelred and his brother Alfred. In bitter January weather the Saxons had advanced towards Reading along the Ridgeway. They drove back the Danish outposts but on following up were surprised by a sudden rush from behind the earthworks. The Saxon army retreated north-west up the Ridgeway, calling for reinforcements and setting a rendezvous at the track junction at Lowbury Hill, the highest point on the eastern Berkshire Downs. The Danes returned to their camp and 'sat down for a steady drink'. The Danes eventually moved out on 7 January and by dusk had sighted the Saxon camp

at the track junction under Lowbury Hill 1000 yards away.

No doubt both armies spent a sleepless night huddled close to campfires. At dawn the Danes formed up in two divisions, one on either side of the Ridgeway. The right, under the Viking nobles, was about 400 yards west of the present Warren farm. The left under the two kings was a similar distance west of Starveall farm. Just 1000 yards away were the Saxons, again in two divisions, Aethelred on the left facing the Viking nobles, Alfred on the right. The Danes had a slight height advantage. At this point there was a pause, the Danes no doubt hoping to hold their stronger position and act defensively. Over in the Saxon camp King Aethelred thought this an appropriate moment to hold mass in his tent. However, the Vikings soon got tired of waiting and resolved to attack. Both divisions moved down the slope with loud war cries and clashing of shields, with their enemy commander still in the middle of divine service. Aethelred was no doubt told that the enemy was advancing but refused to cut short the service.

The young Alfred watched the enemy getting nearer with mounting concern. When they were about 600 yards off he made his decision. Although the Saxons had intended to remain on the defensive

The crossing place which saw the fiercest fighting of the Battle of Ashdown, very little changed today. A thorn tree can still be seen to the left of the photograph. (Battlefields Trust)

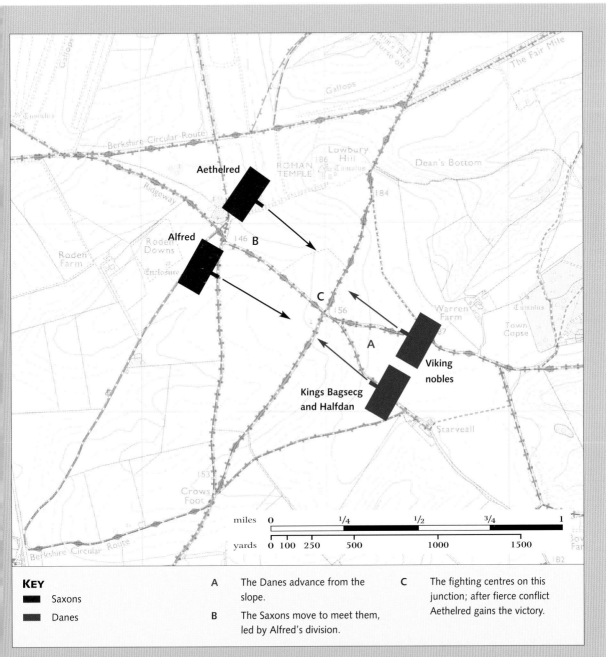

KEY

Saxons

Danes

A The Danes advance from the slope.

B The Saxons move to meet them, led by Alfred's division.

C The fighting centres on this junction; after fierce conflict Aethelred gains the victory.

and the king was still on his knees, Alfred gave the order for his division to advance. His column rolled forward with, probably, most of the king's division following moments later, although still without their sovereign. The clash, when it came, was brutal and prolonged. The fighting took place in the valley, which was afterwards known traditionally as 'Awful Bottom'. The Danes were pushed back up the hill to a junction of five tracks, beside which was a single, stunted thorn-tree. Bishop Asser in his *Life of King Alfred* (written about twenty years later) tells us that the fighting round here was particularly savage. At some stage Aethelred rose from his knees and led his household troops into the fray, finally clinching victory. The Danes fled. The pursuit continued until nightfall. Among the bodies strewn over the plain of Ashdown was that of King Bagsecg.

medieval abbey entrances, built in 1338. Other features of the site include a Discovery Centre with an activity-based exhibition, an analysis of the battle, and an interactive audio tour of the battlefield.

Battle of Britain Museum (Kent)

££. Usual hours but closed October–Easter and Mondays. Shop. Refreshments. Parking. Tel. 01303 893140. www.kbobm.org Aerodrome Road, Hawkinge, near Folkestone. Hawkinge is on the A260 between Folkestone and Canterbury.

The museum is housed in Hawkinge RAF station, which was at the fore-front of the Battle of Britain. Its hangars, some of which date back to the 1920s, house the most important collection of Battle of Britain artefacts in the country, alongside full-size repli-cas of German Me109Es, Spitfires and Hurricanes together with every vehi-cle in use on a Fighter Command Station. Also on view are a German V-1 flying bomb plus ground-based and airborne weaponry and German and British uniforms and insignia of 1940. The old Operations Block con-tains items gleaned from over 600 Battle of Britain aircraft as well as descriptions of the exploits of many of the pilots who fought and lost their lives.

Three Hurricanes guarding the Battle of Britain Museum

Bedfordshire and Hertfordshire Regiment Museum (Bedfordshire)

Free. Usual hours (Sundays 1–5 p.m.). Shop. Refreshments. School visits. Picnic area. Parking. Tel. 01582 546722. Luton Museum, Wardown Park, Old Bedford Road, Luton. Turn east off the A6 onto the A505 and take the first right; the entrance to the Park is half a mile down on the right.

This regimental museum is a part of the Luton Museum and Gallery, to which entry is free. It tells the story of the former 16th Regiment of Foot, formed in 1688, which eventu-ally became The Bedfordshire & Hertfordshire Regiment until it was amalgamated with the Essex Regiment in 1958. The 16th Foot fought with Marlborough and car-ried the battle honour 'Blenheim' on its Colours.

The museum is primarily devoted to the Regiment's more recent service in the two World Wars. There are dis-plays, photographs, pictures, uni-forms and medals relating to its role in the withdrawal from Dunkirk, the Chindit operations in Burma, the 5th Battalion's experiences as prisoners of war of the Japanese working on the 'railway of death', the North Africa Campaign (Tobruk) and the Battle of Monte Cassino in Italy.

The astonishing medieval gatehouse of Battle Abbey

Bigbury Heights, Caesar's second invasion, 54 BC (Kent)

Free. Open access. Parking off-road. Three miles east of Canterbury. Take the A2050 from Canterbury and turn right onto the minor road signed Rough Common. Bigbury Heights are on the left after half a mile.

Caesar's invasion in 54 BC was much more serious than his previous year's reconnaissance in force. This time he came in 800 ships with 5 legions and 2000 cavalry. After an unopposed landing near Sandwich in July the Romans marched inland. They encountered the British in strength behind the River Stour and had to fight their way across. The British retreated some three miles to an encampment (a Celtic hill-fort) on Bigbury Heights. In his *Commentaries*, Caesar states the British 'enjoyed a position with extremely good natural and manmade defences ... many trees had been cut down and used to block all the entrances ... The Britons came out of the woods in small groups to fight, and tried to stop our men penetrating their fortifications. But the soldiers of the Seventh Legion, holding up their shields to form a protective shell, piled up earth against the fortifications and captured the place.'

Bletchley Park (Bucks)

£££. Usual hours. Café. Picnic area. Guided tours. Special events. Parking. Tel. 01908 640404. www.bletchleypark.org.uk Bletchley, on southern outskirts of Milton Keynes. Signposted off the A5 Dunstable Road and the A421 from Buckingham.

Bletchley Park, also known as 'Station X', was home to the famous code-breakers of the Second World War and the birthplace of modern computing and communications. The Government Code and Cypher School acquired the mansion in 1938 and built wooden huts to house the 12,000 people who worked within the 28-acre site.

Guided tours take about two and a half hours, with the highlight being the Cryptology Trail and Enigma Exhibition. The Enigma machine was the main coding device of the German Forces, railways and police. Some of the finest brains in Britain

An Enigma cipher machine: this typewriter-like device was used by the Germans to encode their messages, until the Bletchley Park cryptanalysts discovered its secret.

Bletchley Park: the country house at the centre of the wartime decoding effort

were assembled at the Park for the purpose of breaking the Enigma codes – which they succeeded in doing. Visitors can follow the trail of a coded message from its interception to decipherment and interpretation. Other exhibits include a Churchill memorabilia collection, Second World War uniforms and vehicles, US, German and British re-enactment groups, a toy museum and post office, a wartime amateur radio station and a computer museum.

Bodiam Castle (East Sussex)

££. Usual hours. Refreshments. Parking. Tel. 01580 830436. Twelve miles north of Hastings. Take A21 and turn right onto B2244 and follow signs.

Bodiam is one of the most widely visited castles in Britain. Extensively restored in the 1920s, it now resembles a typical toy castle with high walls and towers at each of the four corners, surrounded by a water-filled moat. It is a courtyard castle in that it has no inner keep, the courtyard space being used for the garrison's accommodation, stores, bakeries and brewhouses. Bodiam was completed in 1388. It saw action twice, in 1483 when it fell to the Earl of Surrey for Richard III, and in 1643 when it surrendered to Parliamentary forces; on both occasions it capitulated without much of a fight.

It is an excellent castle to visit, particularly for children, with lots of stairs to climb and battlements to explore.

Calshot Castle (Hampshire)

£. Usual hours, 29 March–31 October. Parking. Tel. 02380 892023. Off B3053 on spit two miles SE of Fowley.

One of Henry VIII's artillery forts completed in 1540, Calshot's purpose was to guard the sea passage to Southampton. The hangars behind were used during the Second World War and flying boats were also stationed here. The barrack room has been restored to its pre-First World War artillery garrison appearance. Splendid view of the Solent from the roof.

Bodiam Castle: just how a castle should look

Carisbrooke Castle: a charming mix of periods

Carisbrooke Castle (Isle of Wight, Hampshire) ⌗

£££. Usual hours. Tearoom (April–October). Parking. Tel. 01983 522107. Ferry from Portsmouth, Southampton or Lymington. Castle is on the western outskirts of Newport.

A small but interesting castle set in the centre of the island. Originally a Roman fort, then a Saxon burh, then a Norman motte and bailey, its outer walls date from the 1130s and the outer set of 'star' fortifications that surround the castle were added in around 1600. They are well worth walking round. Donkeys are used to demonstrate the working of the well – the task of prisoners until the 16th century. King Charles I was imprisoned here and twice attempted to escape and a story is told of a single bowman who fought off French raiders in 1377. An interactive museum in the Old Coach House shows the history of the castle.

Chatham Historic Dockyard (Kent)

££££. Usual hours 12 February–30 October; weekends only in November; closed December and January. Bookstall. Shop. Library. Refreshments. Guided tours. Lecture hall. School visits. Picnic area. Parking. Tel. 01634 823800. www.chdt.org.uk Chatham. Follow signs to Chatham along the A229 from M20 Junction 6 or the A289 from M2 Junction 1.

An excellent working museum within the world's most complete dockyard from the age of sail. The Chatham docks supported the RN for over 300 years, repairing hundreds of ships and building over 400, including HMS *Victory*. The 80-acre site contains many attractions, including three historic warships (one a submarine), a demonstration of the trades involved in constructing wooden ships, the Ropery, focusing on rope making and testing, and a museum. A whole day is needed for a full visit and there is plenty of fun for children.

Chalgrove Field, Battle of, 1643 (Oxfordshire)

Free. Open fields. Limited access. Off-road parking. Chalgrove lies on the B480 between the villages of Cuxham and Stadhampton. The battlefield is to the west of the minor road from Chalgrove to Warpsgrove. Hampden's monument is by the crossroads.

A large cavalry skirmish, important because the Parliamentarian leader John Hampden was mortally wounded when his pistol accidentally exploded in his hand. A 1000-strong Royalist horse under Prince Rupert was covering the withdrawal of the infantry to Oxford when Parliamentary dragoons unexpectedly caught up with them. Rupert turned to confront his pursuers with only a hedge between them. In typical Rupert fashion he spurred his horse through or over the hedge with his men following as best they could. A brief but furious mêlée saw the Parliamentarians in full flight.

Cropredy Bridge, Battle of, 1644 (Oxfordshire)

Free. Farmland. Easy access. Parking in Cropredy or off-road. Four miles NE of Banbury off the A36. There is a plaque on Cropredy Bridge, a modern replacement in the same location.

On 29 June 1644 Sir William Waller with 9000 men caught up with the rearguard of King Charles's similarly sized army withdrawing towards Daventry on the far side of the River Cherwell. The Royalists seemed well strung out so Waller determined on a two-pronged attack to cut off the rearguard. He sent nine companies of foot and two regiments of horse under Lieutenant-General Middleton across the bridge into Cropredy and himself took 1000 men across at the Slat Mill Ford a mile south. Middleton brushed aside some enemy dragoons but then dashed ahead of his infantry and disappeared in pursuit. Seizing the opportunity, a large force of Royalist cavalry commanded by the Earl of Cleveland charged forward and drove Middleton's remaining men back towards the bridge.

Meanwhile Waller's advance had met with stiff resistance and was pushed back by a spirited counter-attack by the Royalist rearguard under the young Earl of Northampton. The King then arrived with the main body. These reinforcements resulted in Middleton being driven back over Cropredy Bridge and the overrunning of Parliamentary guns deployed east of the bridge. Charles was unwilling to follow across the river so the battle ended in stalemate.

D-Day Museum (Hampshire)

£££. Usual hours. Shop. Refreshments. Parking. Tel. 023 9282 7261. Clarence Esplanade, Southsea.

The centrepiece of this museum is the magnificent Overlord Tapestry, commissioned as a tribute to the sacrifice and heroism of all those who took part in Operation Overlord (the code name for the D-Day landings) in 1944. There is a commentary on the Tapestry together with considerable film footage of the actual landings. Displays show the sights and sounds of Britain at war, a munitions factory, troops preparing for D-Day and a crashed glider.

Deal Castle (Kent) ⌗

££. Usual hours. Shop. Parking nearby. Tel. 01304 372762. On seafront at Deal next to A258.

One of Britain's great strongholds, now restored to virtually its original condition. It was built by Henry VIII as an artillery fort to counter the threat of invasion by Catholic France and Spain in the mid-16th century. Its huge, rounded bastions once carried sixty-six guns with heavy ones mounted on the keep's roof. It is a fascinating castle to explore, especially for children, with long dark passages, battlements and a massive basement housing an exhibition showing all of Henry's forts built along the south coast. Splendid coastal views.

Dover Castle (Kent) ⌗

££££ (but worth it). Usual hours. Shop. Refreshments. Picnic area. Parking. Tel. 01304 201628. Dover. Clearly signposted from the town centre.

Probably Britain's greatest stronghold, Dover Castle has been in constant use, and constantly improved or modified, from Norman times until the Second World War. It's expensive to visit but excellent value for money as you can easily spend a whole day exploring. The four main attractions are the Roman lighthouse and Saxon church, the medieval tunnels, the 'secret' Second World War tunnels in the cliffs, and the Norman keep. Among the fascinating things to see are a reconstruction of Henry VIII's visit in 1539; a siege experience of 1216; the Princess of Wales's Royal Regiment Museum (p. 46); the complex tunnel system and the Second World War command centre where 700 personnel were employed. It became the Combined Headquarters for the most exposed sector of coastal defence throughout the Second World War – appropriately nick-named 'Hellfire Corner'.

Explosion – The Museum of Naval Firepower (Hampshire)

£££. Usual hours. Shop. Refreshments. Picnic area. Play area. Parking. Tel. 023 9250 5600. www.explosion.org.uk Priddy's Hard, Gosport. M27 to Junction 11 then follow A32 to Gosport and signs at the end of Heritage Way.

Explosion is an award winning new museum of naval armaments and the people who worked with them over the centuries. It contains a unique collection of small arms, cannons, mines, torpedoes and modern missiles. Walk around the Grand Magazine, a magnificent gunpowder vault which hosts the multimedia film *The Priddy's Hard Story*. Suitable for children, who can interact with Guy Fawkes stacking racks of barrels of gunpowder, dodge mines or load shells on a rolling gun-deck.

The Priddy's Hard Story: **an impressive multimedia experience**

Cheriton, Battle of, 1644 (Hampshire)

Free. Open fields/farmland. Easy access. Parking in Cheriton. Eight miles east of Winchester off the A272. Take the minor road from Cheriton to Ropely Dean. This crosses the battlefield and there is a monument at the T-junction. Several paths cross the battlefield for exploration on foot.

At dawn on 29 March 1644, 6000 Royalists under Sir Ralph Hopton were drawn up along the two-mile ridge north-east of Cheriton village. They faced 10,000 Parliamentarians under Sir William Waller deployed across the fields from Cheriton village to Cheriton Wood. Waller had placed musketeers in the wood to threaten Hopton's left flank. As the mist cleared Hopton realized the importance of the wood and sent four regiments of pikes and musketeers to occupy it. A confused fight among the trees ensued, with much difficulty experienced by both sides in manhandling pikes and firing their muskets. Eventually the Royalists had the better of it

Hopton's intention to remain on the defensive was ruined by the unauthorised advance of one of his regiments under Sir Henry Bard, which was destroyed by Waller's horse in the area of Middle farm. The battle became general but Bard's loss and the Parliamentarians' superior numbers soon forced a Royalist retreat through Alresford.

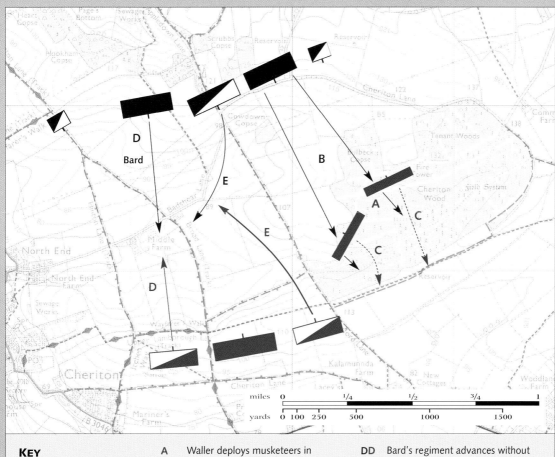

KEY		A	Waller deploys musketeers in Cheriton Wood to threaten Hopton's left flank.	DD	Bard's regiment advances without authorisation and is attacked by the Parliamentary cavalry.
▰	Royalist infantry				
◣	Royalist cavalry	B	Hopton sends 4 regiments of pikes and musketeers to take the wood.	EE	Royalist cavalry attempts to come to Bard's assistance but gets caught in a narrow lane by more enemy horse and scatters. Hopton is soon forced to retreat.
▰	Parliamentarian infantry				
◳	Parliamentarian cavalry	C	The Parliamentary musketeers are driven out of the wood after a prolonged hand-to-hand fight.		

Fort Brockhurst; one of Palmerston's Follies, it never fired a shot in anger

Fort Amherst (Kent)

££. Usual hours. Shop. Refreshments
Tel. 01634 847747.
www.fortamherst.com Dock Road,
Chatham. Signposted from Chatham town.

Built on a hillside overlooking Chatham in the 1750s, this massive fort was intended mainly to protect the RN's largest docks from overland attack by an invading force. At its peak it housed 125 guns, mostly 24-pounders. Perhaps the most unusual feature is the huge tunnel system cut into the chalk cliffs under the fort. Restored areas include the tunnels, Gatehouse, Great Barrier Ditch, Haxo Casement, main magazine and many original gun batteries. There is also a Civil Defence museum with artifacts from the Second World War when the Fort was a Civil Defence HQ and accommodated an anti-invasion planning unit. Numerous static displays give a vivid insight into the lives of the garrison.

Fort Brockhurst (Hampshire)

££. Usual hours. Tel. 02392 581059.
Gunner's Way, Gosport. Follow A32
towards Gosport for three miles and the fort
is on the left in Elson.

One of the five forts strung across the Gosport peninsula, Fort Brockhurst is probably the best 19th-century stronghold open to the public. Its main features are its enormous brick and earth ramparts and moated central keep. The outward-facing sides housed the gun casemates or barracks when under siege. The keep could house over 300 officers and men but it was never fully garrisoned or armed.

Fort Nelson (Hampshire)

Free. Usual hours. Café. Shop. Guided
tours. Special events. Parking. Tel. 01392
233734. www.royalarmouries.org
Down End Road, Fareham. Exit the M27
at Junction 11 and follow brown tourist
signs for Royal Armouries.

Another of 'Palmerston's Follies' that never faced attack, this is one of six forts along Portsdown Hill overlooking Portsmouth harbour, but facing inland to repel overland assault.
Fort Nelson houses the Royal Armouries collection of historic artillery, including the famous Iraqi Supergun. From the smallest cannon to the giants from the days of the battleship they are all there, and twice a day guns are fired. Moreover, it has a top-quality special events calendar with exciting shows including Artillery in the First World War, Heroes of Waterloo, a Military Tattoo, Medieval Siege Warfare and Life in the Trenches. If you only visit one Victorian fort make it Fort Nelson.

Gunpowder Mills (Kent)

Faversham Society. Free. Limited opening:
Easter–October, Saturdays, Sundays and
bank holidays only. Shop. Parking off-road
opposite. Tel. 01795 534542. Off
Stonebridge Way, Faversham.

These mills are the oldest of their kind in the world – they made gunpowder for Nelson at Trafalgar and Wellington at Waterloo. The Faversham Society rescued them from the bulldozer in 1966 and then restored them. There is an interesting display which includes a video on the explosives industry and others on the Boer War and the First and Second World Wars.

Gurkha Museum (Hampshire)

£. Usual hours. Shop. Parking. Tel. 01962
842832. www.thegurkhamuseum.co.uk
Peninsula Barracks, Romsey Road,
Winchester.

The museum is a fine tribute to the service given by Gurkha soldiers to the Crown since 1815. There are two floors of displays and tableaux covering, among many other subjects, the North-West Frontier of India, the Indian Mutiny, the World Wars, the Partition of India in 1947, Malaya, Borneo, the Falklands and the Brigade of Gurkhas today. There is also a Gurkha Memorial Garden nearby.

Household Cavalry Museum (Berkshire)

Donations encouraged. Usual hours (closed weekends and bank holidays). Shop. Parking. Tel. 01753 755112. www.householdcavalry.gvon.com/museum.htm Note: closed for refurbishment until early 2007, when it will reopen along with a second museum in London. Combermere Barracks, St Leonard's Road, Windsor. From A332 between Windsor and Ascot turn into Windsor Great Park. Take first exit at large roundabout and follow road past hospital.

This collection relates to the Life Guards, the Horse Grenadier Guards, The Royal Horse Guards (Blues), 1st Royal Dragoons and The Blues and Royals. It is one of the richest and best presented military collections with a first-class display including Household Cavalry head-dress, uniforms, swords, firearms, standards, guidons, drum banners, medals, silver and kettledrums, illustrating 350 years of history. Some of the many battle honours are displayed as dioramas. The Regiment's more recent operational duties in the Falklands, the Gulf War, Bosnia, Kosovo and the Iraq War are well illustrated.

Hurst Castle (Hampshire) ⚏

££. Usual hours, 29 March–31 October. Refreshments. Tel. 01590 642344. www.hurst-castle.co.uk On pebble spit south of Keyhaven. Best approached by ferry from Keyhaven (01590 642500) but you can walk along the spit if the weather is kind and you feel energetic.

Another of Henry VIII's forts, built at the end of a narrow shingle spit over a mile long that reaches out across the Solent until it almost touches the Isle of Wight. It was completed in 1544 with a two-storey, twelve-sided keep, basement and roof-mounted guns, surrounded by a curtain wall and moat. The Victorians updated it with massive gun batteries housing sixty-one heavy guns on either side of the keep, and early in the 20th century quick-firing guns and searchlights were added. It was garrisoned throughout both World Wars with anti-aircraft guns and not vacated until 1956. Opposite on the Isle of Wight are Forts Victoria and Albert. It can be a wild and windswept but invigorating place to visit.

King's Royal Hussars Museum (Hampshire)

Free. Usual hours (closed Mondays except bank holidays and half-term and for two weeks over Christmas and New Year). Some parking. Tel. 01962 828541. Peninsula Barracks, Romsey Road, Winchester.

The museum tells the story of the 10th, 11th, The Royal and The King's Royal Hussars from 1715 to the present, with a series of displays showing how the cavalry lived and fought throughout this period. Of particular interest are the battered bugle carried by Lord Cardigan's trumpeter during the Charge of the Light Brigade, RSM Roy Smith's diary of 'The Charge' and the actual French cupboard where Private Fowler hid for three years behind enemy lines during the First World War. Visitors can explore the Regiment's latest tanks using the interactive Challenger 2 CD-ROM simulator.

Light Infantry Museum (Hampshire)

Free. Usual hours. Shop. Guided tours. Parking. Tel. 01962 828550. Peninsula Barracks, Romsey Road, Winchester.

This museum has a totally new theme in that it tells the story not so much of a particular regiment but of the modern light infantry since its inception in 1968. This puts the emphasis on Berlin, the Berlin Wall, the Gulf War and the Iraq War as well as peacekeeping operations, all enhanced by the use of video CDs.

Martello Towers (East Sussex and Kent) ⚏

Free. Number 3 usual hours; Number 24 limited (summer holidays only). Parking. www.martello-towers.co.uk No. 3 on the coast on eastern outskirts of Folkestone, off the B2011. No. 24 on the coast on the A259 at Dymchurch.

Yet another line of defensive works against invasion from Europe constructed after the Roman Saxon Shore Forts and Henry VIII's artillery forts. They are named after a similar fort on Mortella Point in Corsica, which had successfully resisted the hugely superior fire of two British warships in 1794. Seventy-four were built between 1805 and 1808 along the south coast, sited so their fire was mutually supporting. They are oval-shaped, tapered and about 35ft high. Some had a rear-facing drawbridge over a moat, others a ladder to the entrance at first floor level. They housed a garrison of an officer and 24 men, with a 24-pounder gun on the roof that could rotate through 360 degrees.

Most have long gone but twenty-five remain, of which several are private residences. No. 3, used as a look-out tower in the Second World War, houses a visitors' centre/local history museum. No. 24 has been restored to its original state and for that reason is worth a visit.

Military Museum of Sussex (East Sussex)

££. Usual hours, April–November. Shop. Refreshments. Special events. School visits. Parking nearby. Tel. 01323 410300. www.eastbournemuseums.co.uk Eastbourne promenade. Five minutes' walk east of the pier along the seafront.

The museum is housed in the Redoubt Fortress, which was built between 1804 and 1810 and remained part of Britain's front-line defences until 1945. It contains the collections of The Royal Sussex Regiment, The Queen's Royal Irish Hussars and the Sussex Combined Services Museum, altogether over 5000 exhibits covering the history of the three Services over the last 300 years. Displays include a German general's staff car, items from the Charge of the Light Brigade, women's uniforms of the 20th century and a splendid collection of model soldiers. A highlight is the collection of the seventeen medals awarded to Major O'Shaugnessy including his MBE, MC, GM, and Croix de Guerre. Telephone for details of special events.

Looking north to the Abbey from the valley bottom, showing the gentle lower slope of Senlac Hill up which the Normans attacked. (Battlefields Trust)

Hastings, Battle of, 1066 (East Sussex)

Free. Easy access. Open fields. Parking and toilets at Battle Abbey. Six miles north of Hastings at the village of Battle. Information boards and models marking walks across the battlefield are useful in tracing events. A good Norman view of Senlac Ridge can be obtained from Telham Hill a mile to the SE.

On 28 September 1066 William, Duke of Normandy, set sail for England with about 9000 men to enforce his claim to the English throne. His army, although numerically small for a campaign of conquest, consisted of picked men with a high proportion of horsemen and archers, arms in which King Harold was deficient. On landing at Pevensey it is said he stumbled and fell, which at the time was considered a bad omen.

Harold heard the news of the landing at York while celebrating his victory at Stamford Bridge (p. 114) over King Harald Hardrada of Norway. He immediately started his army marching for London 190 miles south while he rode on ahead. He arrived in London six days later and his troops trickled in over the next five days – an amazing achievement. A few days were spent resting and gathering more men before Harold set off south again on 12 October to meet his destiny and death at Hastings – a battle that changed the course of English history for ever.

The battle began early on 18 October. Harold had drawn up his 7500 men in a dense line 800 yards long and twelve men deep on top of Senlac Ridge with his centre immediately south of where the ruins of Battle Abbey now stand. The housecarls formed the front of the shield wall with the less well-equipped fyrd (band of peasant warriors) behind. William determined to attack. The first phase was the advance of his crossbowmen to within about 150 yards of the English. From there they began a continuous barrage of bolts against their opponents, whose only response was to shelter behind their shields – a successful tactic as eventually the Normans ran out of ammunition with the wall still unbroken above them.

Next, the dismounted Norman knights and foot soldiers advanced up the hill. Now the advantage was with the defenders on the higher ground. The Normans proved no match for the housecarls in the front rank, backed by the fyrd. The first to give were the Bretons on the Norman left, who turned and fled downhill, hotly, and foolishly, pursued by the English right wing. Within the Norman ranks there was now confusion, the beginnings of panic and, critically, shouted rumours that William was down. Just in time, William removed his helmet so he could be recognized and spurred forward amongst the fugitives. He brought forward a group of mounted knights and flailed into the over-eager and disorganized English who had rushed down the slope. They were scattered like so much chaff in the wind.

William then launched the bulk of his cavalry force at the shield wall. However, there was no question of a charge up that slope. At a laboured trot at best, mostly at a walk, the horsemen struggled to face the hurled javelins, arrows and swinging axes. The fighting was brutal and bloody all along the line but the wall held firm with the Normans losing heavily and falling back. Despite their earlier error groups of ill-disciplined English dashed down the hill, only to be charged and destroyed by fresh horsemen.

In the final phase in the afternoon William showed he had learnt the lessons of the morning. His bowmen, restocked with ammunition, were ordered to fire at high angle (indirect fire) rather than straight at the enemy shields (direct fire). Now a rain of bolts fell on the rear ranks of less well-protected men. As the bowmen fired overhead the mass of Norman infantry could advance again – this tactic was a forerunner of the infantry advances behind the rolling artillery barrages of the First World War. On both flanks this assault was successful, pushing the English back and threatening to envelop them. At around this time an arrow struck Harold in the right eye. Despite the shock and pain the King pulled it out and remained on his feet. As with William in the morning, the word went round that Harold was hit and something like panic gripped the shire levies, many of which turned to flee. The housecarls closed in around their King and the battle in the centre still raged. The Normans hacked and slashed their way to where the Royal Banner of Wessex was still flying. A group of mounted knights smashed their way through to where the dying Harold was leaning on his shield. A heavy blow to the thigh brought him to the ground, where he was finished off under a flurry of swords. Even with their King dead little groups fought on until darkness allowed a few to slip away into the woods.

William's pursuit was relentless. Many fleeing English died when they fell into a ravine afterwards known as the Malfosse. The Duke of Normandy had earned the title 'William the Conqueror' and gained the Crown of England.

KEY

- English – housecarls (shield wall)
- English – fyrd (less well equipped)
- Normans
- ▲▲▲▲ crossbowmen
- men-at-arms

A   The Norman crossbowmen advance and begin firing, ineffectually.

B   The Norman men-at-arms advance but fail to break shield wall; the Bretons give way on Norman left.

C   The English right wing dash down slope in pursuit of Bretons.

D   A body of mounted knights counter-attacks and disperses the English.

E   The rest of the Norman cavalry attack but still fail to dislodge the main English line.

F   The Normans use high-angle archery and an infantry assault to push back both English flanks. Harold is killed and the English flee.

Lewes, Battle of, 1264 (East Sussex)

Free. Reasonable access, open fields. Some off-road parking. Immediately NW of Lewes, approached by a path off the A275 opposite Offham Church. On the top of the ridge you are in the centre of de Montfort's position with a good view of the battlefield.

A battle fought on 14 May 1264 at the start of what became known as the Barons' War, between Henry III and a group of barons under Simon de Montfort, whose aim was to force the king to share some of his power.

De Montfort drew up his army of 5000 men along the top of Offham Hill facing south-east towards Lewes where the King and his son Prince Edward had bivouacked with their force of 10,000. De Montfort's line extended for about 1000 yards from the chalk pits on his left to near where the racecourse grandstand is now. Early on the 14th, Prince Edward, without waiting for the rest of the army to assemble, launched an impulsive mounted attack against de Montfort's left, which he scattered and pursued off the field. The King was forced to follow up belatedly with an infantry assault. It was a stiff climb, with an even stiffer fight at the top. The King had lost Edward's men and the scales were turned decisively against him when de Montfort launched his reserve. The King was forced back downhill and into Lewes where considerable street fighting took place for several hours. The King sought refuge in the Priory and, with his army dispersed, signed a truce, which gave England its first Parliament.

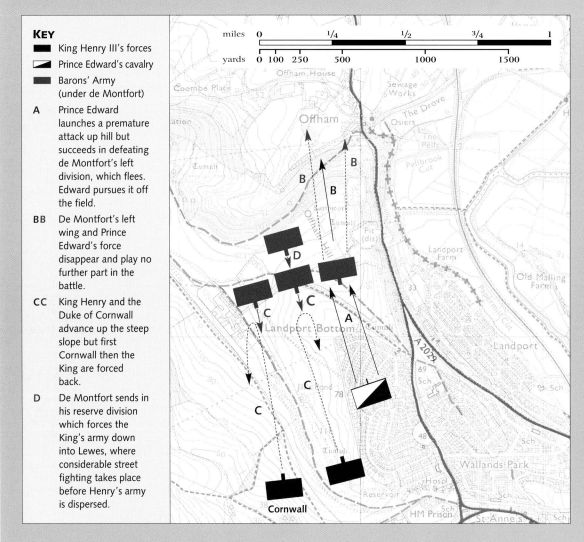

KEY

■ King Henry III's forces

◩ Prince Edward's cavalry

▬ Barons' Army
(under de Montfort)

A Prince Edward launches a premature attack up hill but succeeds in defeating de Montfort's left division, which flees. Edward pursues it off the field.

BB De Montfort's left wing and Prince Edward's force disappear and play no further part in the battle.

CC King Henry and the Duke of Cornwall advance up the steep slope but first Cornwall then the King are forced back.

D De Montfort sends in his reserve division which forces the King's army down into Lewes, where considerable street fighting takes place before Henry's army is dispersed.

Museum of Army Flying (Hampshire)

£££. Usual hours. Shop. Café. School visits. Parking. www.flying-museum.org.uk *Middle Wallop, Stockbridge. Five miles SW of Andover on A343.*

Celebrating over 100 years of Army aviation, this award-winning museum is home to one of Britain's finest collections of kites, gliders, aeroplanes and helicopters. Dioramas trace the development of Army flying from pre-First World War to today's Army Air Corps. Models, weapons, equipment, photographs and a free film show support these displays. Also included is an interactive and science centre that will appeal to children featuring a Sensory Trail, light effects, an IT suite, flying simulator and optical illusions.

Museum of D-Day Aviation (West Sussex)

££. Usual hours, March–October inclusive. Shop. Picnic area. Guided tours. Special events most weekends. School visits. Tel. 01273 971971. Shoreham Airport. At the junction of the A27 and A283 follow signs to Shoreham Airport.

This museum occupies the site of a Second World War bunker at Shoreham Airport. It has an extensive collection of medals, uniforms and photographs. On display are Second World War aircraft engines, a Typhoon cockpit and the inside of a Horsa glider. There is also an Air Sea Rescue section that depicts how the Marine Branch saved the lives of thousands of Allied and Axis airmen.

Museum of Technology (Berkshire)

££. Usual hours. Shops. School visits. Parking. Tel. 0118 9763375. www.rememuseum.org.uk *Isaac Newton Road, Arborfield. From A327 from Reading to Arborfield village, follow signs to Arborfield Garrison along B3349 Wokingham road.*

This is the museum of the Royal Electrical and Mechanical Engineers (REME), whose task it is to recover and repair all types of military vehicles, tanks, guns, small arms and equipment used by the Army. The museum shows the history of the Corps from its formation in 1942 to the present day. Exhibits include several life-size displays showing the REME at work, photographs, uniforms, medals, dioramas, models and engineering technology.

Newbury, Battle of, 1643 (Berkshire)

Free. Open access to Round Hill area. Off-road parking. Immediately SW of Newbury. From Newbury the A343 leads to the crossroads marked by the Lord Falkland monument, which marks the centre of the original Royalist line. Continue down Essex Road and a path on the right leads to Round Hill, the focal point of the battle.

King Charles I had withdrawn his army from besieging Gloucester on the approach of the Earl of Essex with his Parliamentary force. On 19 September the King set up a defensive position just west of Newbury to block Essex's route to London. His error was in not occupying the dominating ground of Round Hill half a mile to the west. During the night the Parliamentary Army occupied this hill. Both armies had around 10,000 men but the Royalists had more and better cavalry.

On the following morning the King attacked up the hill after being awakened by Essex's guns firing from the summit. Numerous hedges (most have now gone) restricted both infantry and cavalry movement. The Royalists slowly forced Essex's men back to the north of Round Hill as far as Skinner's Green Lane – almost to where the railway line is now. They could not, however, force the London Trained Bands off the hill itself. The fighting went on all day with a resultant stalemate at dusk. The King withdrew to Oxford during the night and Essex resumed his march to London. The total killed was around 3500.

Newbury, Battle of, 1644 (Berkshire)

Free. Limited access due to field being mostly obscured by the buildings of Speen and Newbury. Donnington Castle can be reached via the A34 Oxford Road and provides a good viewpoint.

Some dauntingly complex field artillery computer equipment, in the Museum of Technology

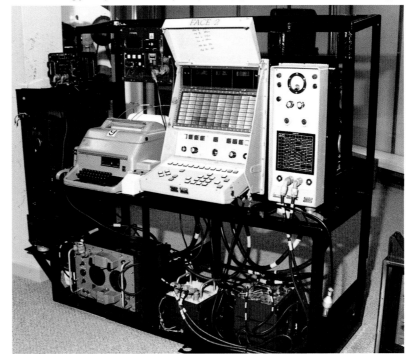

The second Battle of Newbury saw King Charles with some 10,000 men in Newbury facing around 19,000 Parliamentarians under Sir William Waller and the Earl of Manchester in the east. The Parliamentary plan was for Waller to undertake a 13-mile outflanking march to the north of the town with 12,000 men and advance on the King's position from the west. Meanwhile, Manchester would make feint attacks from Clay Hill in the east. Waller's guns firing would be the signal for a combined attack.

On the evening of 26 October Waller's flank march was spotted by the Donnington Castle garrison but the news was not relayed to the King, who was occupied with Manchester's attack, which developed into something more than a feint. Waller attacked at 3 p.m. but, although surprised, the Royalists held their own in Speen village. Manchester's main attack from Clay Hill down onto the Shaw House area did not start until 4 p.m. and was repulsed in hard fighting. At nightfall both sides drew off in a stalemate, with Charles withdrawing to Oxford during darkness.

Newhaven Fort (East Sussex)

£££. Usual times March–end October, weekends in November. Shop. Refreshments. Picnic area. Parking. Tel. 01273 517622. www.newhavenfort.org.uk Fort Road, Newhaven. Clearly signed in the centre of the town.

This fort, another of Palmerston's follies, was built in the early 1860s to guard the approaches to Newhaven. It is sited on top of, and under, the white cliffs and overlooks the docks. Inside, the fort has been well restored and houses an interesting museum illustrating life in the fort and recent military history, especially the Second World War, with a focus on coastal defence, the Dieppe raid, D-Day, the Royal Observer Corps and the Home Front. Good use is made of sound effects, and the visitor can descend seventy steps through a tunnel to emerge in a forward gun position at the foot of the cliffs. A place well worth exploring.

Pevensey Castle and Roman Saxon Shore Fort (East Sussex) ⌗

££ (Roman walls free). Usual hours. Shop. Refreshments. Council parking. Tel. 01323 762694. Westham village NE of Eastbourne. Clearly signed off the A27.

The Roman fort was built late, around 340. William the Conqueror landed at Pevensey in 1066 and immediately made the Roman fort his base. Later the site was expanded into a Norman castle set within the Roman walls. The impressive curtain walls and squat round towers were built in the 1250s. After hundreds of years of neglect the castle was given a new lease of life in the Second World War when it became an observation and command post. An interesting diversion for the visitor is to try to discover the Second World War pillboxes that are still hidden among the fallen masonry.

Portchester Castle and Roman Saxon Shore Fort (Hampshire) ⌗

Grounds free, castle ££. Usual hours. Shop. Picnic area. Parking. Tel. 02392 378291. On the south side of Portchester off the A27, Junction 11 on M27.

An excellent place to visit. The Roman walls are said to be the best preserved in northern Europe, while the Norman keep has also lasted well. Henry V set sail from here on his Agincourt campaign, and the castle was used during the English Civil War and Napoleonic Wars to incarcerate prisoners; there is graffiti on the walls from some of the latter. The most impressive place to explore is the keep and it is possible to climb up to the roof for a splendid view. There is an inclusive interactive tour and castle exhibition.

The striking keep of Portchester Castle; visitors can climb right to the top

HMS *Victory*: perhaps the world's most famous ship, on show in Portsmouth Harbour

Portsmouth Historic Dockyard (Hampshire)

££££ (fully inclusive price to visit all ships and museum). Usual hours. Five shops. Restaurant. Group visits (special rates). Special functions. Educational functions. Parking. Tel. 02392 861512/861533. www.flagship.org.uk/welcome.html Historic Ships and Naval Dockyard, HM Naval Base, Portsmouth. From Junction 12 on M27 follow brown Historic Waterfront signs and Historic Dockyards signs in Portsmouth.

The world's leading naval heritage centre – you will need a whole day to see everything. There are five major attractions:
• HMS *Victory*. Nelson's flagship at Trafalgar, on whose quarterdeck he was mortally wounded. It's now magnificently restored and maintained. Visitors are taken on pre-timed guided tours of the ship, except in summer holidays and peak times when a free-flow, non-guided system is used.
• the *Mary Rose*, Henry VIII's favourite warship, sunk in a storm in 1545. She was raised in 1982 and the long process of conservation begun. Over 1200 objects from the ship are also on display, including cannons, longbows, gold coins, silk clothing, wooden bowls and tankards, all preserved by the silt in the Solent.
• HMS *Warrior*. Launched in 1860, she was the world's first steam-powered, iron-hulled battleship. A fascinating tour.
• the Royal Naval Museum. It contains four award-winning exhibitions. First, 'Trafalgar!' – a true-to-life recreation of the great sea battle of 1805 including a sights and sounds tour of a gun-deck as *Victory* went into action. Second, the 'Story of HMS *Victory*' from 1759 to the present. Third, 'Horatio Nelson', with audio-visual presentations, interactive exhibits and many of Nelson's personal belongings. Fourth, 'The Sailing Navy', an interactive exhibition enabling visitors to discover life aboard an 18th-century warship, let out sails, handle a musket and fight their own battles at the helm of a 74-gun ship.
• 'Action Stations!' A new interactive exhibition that gives an exciting insight into life aboard a modern Type 23 Frigate, including a film of HMS *Monarch*'s bid to rescue hostages from modern-day pirates.

The Princess of Wales's Royal Regiment (Dover Castle, Kent)

£££ (museum entrance included in castle charge). Usual hours. Comprehensive facilities as for Dover Castle.
Tel. 01227 818053. Dover Castle.

The museum traces the story of the Princess of Wales's Royal Regiment and its twelve forebear regiments. There are walk-through life-size displays including the Peninsular War (1808–14), the 19th-century wars in India, the Boer War, trench life in the First World War and service in Northern Ireland. There is an excellent medal collection and the actual football kicked across no man's land by the East Surreys as they advanced to attack in the First World War. Videos of the Second World War record experiences of former members of the Regiment.

RAF Manston History Museum (Kent)

£. Usual hours. Shop. Café. Parking.
Tel. 01843 825224. www.rafmanston.co.uk
The Airfield, Manston Road, Ramsgate. It is housed alongside the Memorial Building car park.

A privately run museum devoted to the history of Manston Airfield since 1916. Good use is made of dioramas, displays of ejector seats, cockpits and artefacts. There is also a section devoted to the Home Front in the Second World War and another on Search and Rescue as well as a comprehensive collection of aircraft.

Richborough Castle and Saxon Shore Fort (Kent) ⌗

££. Usual hours. Shop. Parking.
Tel. 01304 612013. Three miles north of Sandwich. Take the old A357 from Sandwich towards the bypass. Turn right before the railway crossing and the castle is signposted.

The Roman gateway to Britain: it was near here that the Romans landed in AD 43 at the start of their conquest. The fortified walls and massive foundations of flint in mortar of a triumphal arch that stood 80ft high still survive. In the early third century the arch provided a signal station; it was later reconstructed as a Saxon shore fort of which the 25ft-high stone walls

The atmospheric interior of Rochester Castle: visitors can climb right to the top.

the visitor sees today were a part. Richborough became a thriving port and community; more than 50,000 Roman coins were found during excavations, some of which are displayed here in a museum with other Roman artefacts.

Rochester Castle (Kent) ⌗

££. Usual hours. Shop.
Tel. 01634 402276.
Rochester town centre.

Sited at a strategic spot between the Channel ports and London, Rochester's Norman keep is the most impressive in the country, with walls 130ft high and four towers adding another 12ft. Visitors can climb to the top and from the battlements look down into the massive, but empty interior. In 1215 King John besieged the castle for two months. It surrendered when mining under the south-east tower brought it down – pig fat being used to burn the timber props that supported the roof of the mine. A round

tower was built as a replacement, which explains why Richborough has three square and one round.

Royal Engineers' Museum (Kent)

££. Usual hours (closed Mondays). Shop. Refreshments. Picnic area. Family activities. Special events. Parking.
Tel. 01634 822261. Brompton Barracks, Chatham. Clearly signposted from Chatham and Gillingham town centres.

Twenty-six galleries chart the history of military engineering with some 6000 exhibits. Highlights include Wellington's map of Waterloo, Victorian guided torpedoes, and exhibits on early flying and fortifications. The medal collection is of national importance and contains twenty-five VCs. There is something for all the family – the embroidered robes presented to General Gordon, a First World War dugout, working models of engineering equipment and a Harrier jump jet.

The Royal Green Jackets' Museum (Hampshire)

£. Usual hours. Shop. Regimental archives. Parking. Tel. 01962 828549. www.royalgreenjackets.co.uk/museumframe set.htm Peninsula Barracks, Romsey Road, Winchester.

A superb museum, surely one of the best. It records vividly and entertainingly the history of the RGJs and their antecedent regiments from 1741 to the present. Highlights are the Waterloo Diorama with 22,000 model soldiers; the Medal Room with nearly 8000 decorations and medals; the VC display with its touch-screen access to data on the Regiment's fifty-nine VC-holders; and the Recent History section telling the story of the RGJs since 1966. There is also an electronic range where visitors can fire a Baker rifle at an advancing enemy in a realistic setting.

The Waterloo diorama at The Royal Green Jackets' Museum with its 22,000 model soldiers

Royal Logistics Corps Museum (Surrey)

£. Usual hours (closed Saturdays October–Easter and all Mondays, Sundays and bank holidays). Shop. Research archives. Parking. Tel. 01252 833371. www.army.mod.uk/rlc/museum/ Deepcut, Camberley. Follow the B3015 from M3 Junction 3.

Recently built to house a large display area, lecture room and seating. The museum tells the story of the Royal Corps of Transport, Royal Army Ordnance Corps, Royal Pioneer Corps, Army Catering Corps and the Postal and Courier Service. The visitor explores how soldiers have been transported, fed and supplied with arms and equipment over the last 500 years. Many realistic tableaux depict scenes from the Crimean War Commissary's Office up to bomb disposal in Northern Ireland. Numerous artefacts explain technical developments in clothing, ammunition, rations, transport and communications over the centuries.

Royal Marines Museum (Hampshire)

££. Usual hours. Shop. Tea rooms. Special events. Tel. 023 9281 8420. www.royalmarinesmuseum.co.uk The Esplanade, Southsea, Portsmouth. From the M27 or A3(M), turn off the A27 onto the A2030 to Southsea seafront, from which the museum is signposted.

An award-winning museum illustrating the history of the Royal Marines, which is brought to life through a series of dramatic and interactive displays. It is housed in one of the most splendid former officers' messes in the country complete with beautiful gold-leaf ceilings, paintings and grand staircase. Among the highlights are the collection of awards and medals, one of the most comprehensive in the world, which includes all ten VCs won by Royal Marines. Visitors can watch and listen to the Beating Retreat ceremony in the Band Room as well as examine the instrument display. There is a jungle

warfare room and if you like hands-on experience you can fire a flintlock pistol, carry a Marine's rucksack or learn to tie life-saving knots.

Royal Military Canal (Kent)

Free. Open access along footpath. Parking nearby in most parts. Runs from Hythe to Winchelsea with a good viewpoint at the village of Appledore.

Completed in 1806 after two years' work, the Royal Military Canal stretches for twenty-eight miles along the old cliff line that borders Romney Marsh from Hythe in the north-east to Cliff End in the south-west. It was built as the third line of defence, the others being the Channel (and Royal Navy) and then the line of Martello Towers, against invasion by Napoleon. At every 500 yards a short kink was made in the line to enable cannons to cover each stretch. There was a parapet on the landward side and a towpath on the seaward side with station houses (guardhouses) at every bridge.

Today the canal has a public footpath along its full length and makes an excellent waymarked, long-distance trail with numerous information panels. The canal is a haven for wildlife such as kingfishers, dragonflies and noisy marsh frogs.

Royal Navy Submarine Museum (Hampshire)

££. Usual hours. Shop. Refreshments. Picnic area. Guided tours. Parking. Tel. 02392 529217. www.rnsubmus.co.uk Haslar Jetty Road, Gosport; well signposted from the A32 Gosport road.

A splendid museum with lots to see and do. The RN's first submarine, *Holland 1*, is on display in a new gallery after being recovered from seventy years on the sea bed in 1982. The museum presents 100 years of submarines and submariners' life. A highlight is a walkthrough of HMS *Alliance*, built in 1945 and now restored to service condition. Visitors can search the harbour through a working periscope, and examine midget submarines, torpedoes, guns and missiles. There is a fun trail for the family including science workshops. Learn about the pirates' 'Jolly Roger' flag and try out the controls of a modern submarine's hydroplane.

Spitfire and Hurricane Memorial Building (Kent)

Free (donations welcome). Usual hours. Shop. Café. Picnic area. Parking. Tel. 01843 821940. The Airfield, Manston Road, Ramsgate.

The Memorial Building is situated on the site of one of the few remaining airfields that participated in the Battle of Britain. RAF Manston was only ten minutes' flying time from the enemy coast, and thus bore the brunt of the early Luftwaffe attacks in 1940. The Spitfire Memorial Building houses Spitfire TB 432, one of the few surviving Spitfires with a wartime record, now beautifully restored to pristine condition. The Hurricane Memorial Building contains Hurricane LF 752. Other exhibits associated with the Second World War aircraft are displayed, including the Battle of Britain Tapestry, based on the stained-glass memorial window in Westminster Abbey.

St Albans, Battle of, 1455 (Hertfordshire)

Free. Easy access. Car parks available. Centre of St Albans.

King Henry VI temporarily lost his sanity in 1453 and his cousin Richard, Duke of York, was declared Chief Councillor. York had his rival and the king's favourite, the Duke of Somerset, locked in the Tower. Inconveniently for York the King recovered his senses in 1455 and Somerset was released, while York and his followers fled north to raise an army. The Wars of the Roses were about to begin.

York (with the Earls of Warwick and Salisbury) led his army south on London and Henry (with Buckingham, Clifford and Somerset) led his north from London. They met in St Albans, which Henry had barricaded to block York's march down Watling Street, on 21 May 1455. The King's force of some 3000 men lined the town ditch and wall. York advanced along Victoria Street, while Salisbury attacked up Sopwell Lane. Then Warwick, advancing in the centre via the London Road, found an undefended part of the ditch and scrambled across. He got behind the defenders and emerged by what is now the

Queen's Hotel. The Lancastrian line was broken and outflanked and the final phase of the fight took place in St Peter's Street (today's marketplace). A brief but bloody mêlée ensued in which the King and Buckingham were wounded. Somerset was among the dead and a plaque opposite the Leeds Building Society marks the spot where he fell. The Yorkists had triumphed.

St Albans, Battle of, 1461 (Hertfordshire)

Free. Open access, although much of the area is urban. Parking possible. Central St Albans and on either side of the B651 between the northern outskirts of St Albans and Sandridge village.

Once again the streets of St Albans became the scene of considerable bloodshed, although this time the Yorkists under Warwick were defending the town and the Lancastrians under Queen Margaret were on the offensive. The second battle of St Albans took place in winter (17 February) and was in three phases, each on different ground. Initially Margaret's men, attacking the town ditch up George Street, were checked by a storm of arrows but an outflanking movement up Folly and Catharine Lanes eventually forced them back. The Yorkists then formed up across Barnard's Heath (now built up) with their centre astride the B651 road to Sandridge and their right resting on Beech Bottom. Warwick protected his front with caltrops and other obstacles. The Lancastrian attack in a snowstorm could at first make little headway, although several of the enemy cannons blew up and the hand-gunners could not light their firelocks in the wind. However, as the pressure grew as more and more of Margaret's men arrived and Warwick failed to support the line with his reserve, the Yorkists' line cracked. Warwick's reserve came up in time to see most of his army in flight. He formed a final position on Sandridge, just north-west of the modern village, where he fought on until dusk, thereafter making a reasonably orderly retreat.

Tangmere Military Aviation Museum (West Sussex)

££. Usual hours. Shop. Café. Picnic area. Parking. Tel. 01243 775223. www.tangmere-museum.org.uk Tangmere Airfield, nr Chichester. Take the turning to Tangmere village off the A27 from Chichester.

The museum tells the story of military flying from the earliest days to the present, in four halls. Tangmere Hall illustrates in pictures, words and models the history of Tangmere from 1917 to 1970. One part is devoted to the Lysander pilots who flew secret agents into and out of German-occupied Europe. Merston Hall is built like a hangar to house two aircraft that beat world speed records, together with full-size replicas of a Spitfire and Hurricane. The Battle of Britain Hall has a large collection of memorabilia such as aircraft remains, personal effects, photographs and paintings, both British and German, to remind the visitor of the intense air battles that took place in the late summer of 1940. The Middle Hall contains models, including one of the Mohne Dams, uniforms and armaments. There are simulators for 'flying' a Spitfire, a Lancaster bomb aimer and the 'Lorenz' guidance system of a German Heinkel He 111.

Upnor Castle (Kent) ⌗

££. Usual hours (closed November–December). Parking. Tel. 01634 718742. At Upnor, on unclassified road off the A228 – follow signs to village car park.

A well-preserved 16th-century gun fort, small but neat, built to protect Queen Elizabeth I's warships moored in the Medway. It saw action against raiding Dutch ships, but was later downgraded to become a supply fort providing powder and shot to ships on the river. It is well worth a visit to explore the various buildings and to enjoy the tranquility of the location.

Walmer Beach, Caesar's Landing, 55 BC (Kent)

Free. Open access. Off-road parking. Walmer beach immediately south of Deal.

This pebble beach is the site of Caesar's first reconnaissance in force in 55 BC. The beach was crowded with thousands of Celtic warriors and chariots and the Romans hesitated to jump down into the water. As Caesar recorded, 'the troops … weighed with a mass of heavy armour, they had to jump from their ships, stand firm in the surf, and fight at the same time. But the enemy knew their ground, could hurl their weapons boldly from dry land or shallow water, and gallop their horses, which were trained for this kind of work. Our men were terrified.' The eagle-bearer of the 10th Legion bravely led the way, and the rest of the legionaries then followed him. The Roman discipline eventually triumphed, but it was touch and go for a while. With a little imagination the visitor will find this historic spot rewarding.

Walmer Castle (Kent) ⌗

£££. Usual hours. Shop. Restaurant. Gardens. Parking. Tel. 01304 364288. Two miles south of Walmer, signposted from the A258.

Another of Henry VIII's forts built to resist the Spanish or French, although its defences were never put to the test. It serves as the official residence of the Warden of the Cinque Ports, so called because he controlled the five most important medieval ports on the south coast. Previous wardens include William Pitt, the 1st Duke of Wellington (who died there), and Winston Churchill. Because it is still occupied, Walmer Castle is more like a stately home than a castle and thus makes an interesting contrast to nearby Deal Castle. Walmer has some very attractive gardens that can be explored by visitors.

Walmer Castle: now more of a stately home than a fort

Apsley House – Wellington Museum

££ (free on Waterloo Day, 18 June). Usual hours. Guided tours. School visits. Shop. Parking (Park Lane). Tel. 020 7499 5676. www.english-heritage.org.uk/apsleyhouse 149 Hyde Park Corner. Nearest tube Hyde Park.

Here the Duke of Wellington made his London home after his victories in India, Portugal and Spain, culminating in his triumph over Napoleon at Waterloo. The relics displayed include famous paintings, orders, decorations, magnificent porcelain dinner services, the silver-gilt Waterloo Shield and personal items of the Duke.

Barnet, Battle of, 1471

Free. Field extensively built over. Restricted access. Parking possible. Ten miles north of London on the A1000. The Hadley High Stone (monument) in Hadley Green is about 400 yards north of the Lancastrian line. The battlefield is best viewed from the third tee of the Hadley Golf Course.

A Wars of the Roses battle in which King Edward IV's 10,000 Yorkists crushed 15,000 rebel Lancastrians under the Earl of Warwick. The armies formed up astride today's A1000 after dark on 14 April with Edward in three divisions on the northern outskirts of Barnet and Warwick opposite in a similar formation centred on Hadley Green. At dawn, in poor visibility due to fog, the armies advanced. The Earl of Oxford on the Lancastrian right outflanked Lord Hastings, commanding the Yorkist left. Oxford's charge drove his enemy back down the present A1081 from St Albans, many fugitives not stopping until they reached London. On the other flank the reverse happened. The Duke of Gloucester initially missed the Lancastrian left due to the fog but then turned to make a flanking attack. In the resultant mêlée the Yorkists gradually gained the upper hand. Meanwhile Oxford had regrouped with difficulty and returned to the fray from the south.

But his men were fired on by some of Warwick's men, who mistook them for Yorkists. There were cries of 'Treason' and a general collapse of Lancastrian morale amid the confusion, which saw Warwick's army retreat in disarray. Warwick was killed by a sword thrust through his visor while trying to escape through dense bushes, having foolishly left his horse in the rear.

Britain at War Experience

£££. Usual hours. Shop. School visits. Parking behind museum. Tel. 020 7403 3171. www.britainatwar.co.uk 64–66 Tooley Street, London Bridge. Nearest rail/tube London Bridge.

This exhibition pays tribute to Britain's Home Front during the Second World War, exploring the everyday life and hardships of Londoners including evacuation, air raids, rationing and the blackout.

Cabinet War Rooms

£££. Usual hours. Shop. Café. School visits. Audio guide (free). Tel. 020 7930 6961. cwr.iwm.org.uk Clive Steps, King Charles Street, Whitehall. Nearest tube Westminster.

In August 1939, one week before war began, the Cabinet War Rooms became operational in a former government storage basement. Visitors can view all the twenty-one cramped rooms where Winston Churchill, his War Cabinet and the Chiefs of Staff of Britain's Armed Services worked and slept throughout the air raids on London. It became the nerve centre of Britain's entire war effort. Of particular interest are the Cabinet Room, Map Room, Churchill's kitchen and Mrs Churchill's bedroom. They have been kept exactly as they were before the lights were finally turned off after six years of war. In 2005 a permanent exhibition about Churchill's life was opened.

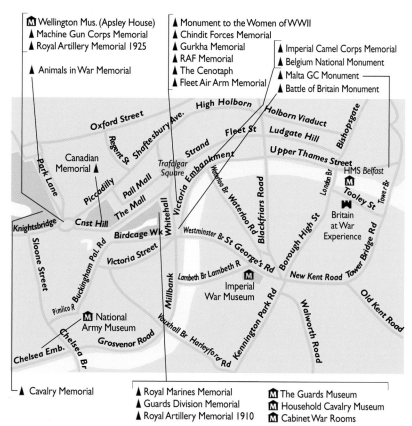

HMS *Belfast*, moored in a splendid position in central London

Firepower – The Royal Artillery Museum

£££. Usual hours. Shop. Café. Parking. Tel. 020 8855 7755.
www.firepower.org.uk
The Royal Arsenal, Woolwich. Nearest rail station Woolwich Arsenal.

A really impressive museum set in the Royal Arsenal on the Thames at Woolwich, Firepower tells the dramatic story of artillery through the ages with numerous interactive experiences. The centerpiece is the 'Field of Fire', an audio and visual extravaganza that gives the visitor an idea of what it is like to be in the centre of an artillery barrage. A History Gallery illustrates the development of artillery from Roman times. In the Real Weapon Gallery you can try firing a tank gun or have a go on the rifle simulator. There is also a Gunnery Hall with a vast array of 20th-century equipment and a Medal Gallery with a splendid display of Victoria Crosses and the stories of gallantry that go with them.

HMS *Belfast*

£££. Usual hours. Shop. Special events. Café. Parking in Tooley Street car park. Tel. 020 7940 6320.
hmsbelfast.iwm.org.uk Morgan's Lane, Tooley Street, London Bridge. Nearest rail and tube station London Bridge.

Launched in 1938, the cruiser HMS *Belfast* served throughout the Second World War, playing a leading role in the destruction of the German battle-cruiser *Scharnhorst*, the Arctic convoys and the D-Day landings. A tour will take up to two hours, taking you from the quarterdeck to the top of her bridge and down through nine decks to her massive boiler and engine rooms. Visitors are able to see inside her triple 6in gun turrets; operate her light anti-aircraft guns; explore the heavily armoured shell rooms and magazine and see the cramped mess-decks, officers' cabins, galley and sick bay. Explanatory videos illustrate the operation of the ship and there is an exhibition, 'HMS *Belfast* in War and Peace'.

H.M. Tower of London (World Heritage Site)

££££. Usual hours. Shop. Restaurant. Special events. Tel. 0870 7567070.
www.hrp.org.uk/webcode/tower_home.asp
Nearest tube Tower Hill, nearest rail Fenchurch Street. Riverboat from Charing Cross, Westminster or Greenwich to Tower Pier.

Probably London's most famous site, the Tower is a unique example of a Norman keep within a concentric castle, begun around 1078 by William the Conqueror. Visitors should expect to spend a whole day exploring. Highlights include the White Tower, which houses Henry VIII's original armour and historic instruments of torture as well as the executioner's block and axe. The Crown Jewels, including the huge Cullinan 1 diamond, are introduced by colour footage of Queen Elizabeth II's coronation. A recreation of Sir Walter Raleigh's thirteen-year imprisonment can be seen in the Bloody Tower. Other places of

The Tower of London seen from the river

great historical interest include Traitor's Gate, the site of the scaffolding where two of Henry VIII's wives were executed, and the Beauchamp Tower with the inscriptions carved by prisoners on the walls. Yeoman Warders conduct 'Beefeater Tours' throughout the day.

HQ No. 11 (Fighter) Group Battle of Britain Operations Room

Free but donations requested. By prior arrangement. School visits. Parking. Tel. 01895 815400 (curator). RAF Uxbridge, Middlesex. One mile from A40 (B467 signposted Uxbridge), three miles from M25 Junction 16. Nearest tube Uxbridge (ten minutes' walk).

The Fighter Group HQ was responsible for the defence of London and the south-east of England during the Second World War. The Operations Room at RAF Uxbridge is maintained exactly as it was on 15 September 1940 at the height of the Battle of Britain when Churchill visited it. Visitors can see the plotting room with its large table map displaying friendly and hostile aircraft and aircraft readiness states. The glass-fronted control rooms house displays of models, weapons, uniforms, insignia, documents and photographs. Presentations are given, tailored to the age of the group and illustrated by archive film footage.

Imperial War Museum

Free. Usual hours. Shop. Café. Special events/exhibitions. School visits. Tel. 020 7416 5320. www.iwm.org.uk Lambeth Road. Nearest rail Waterloo or Elephant and Castle, tube Lambeth North or Elephant and Castle.

This massive, award-winning museum illustrates all aspects of both World Wars and other operations involving Britain and the Commonwealth since 1914. The numerous galleries contain Britain's most outstanding collection of weapons, military equipment, medals, uniforms, photographs, documents, posters, personal mementos and paintings. There is a wide range of permanent and temporary exhibitions, the former including the Western Front, the Blitz, the life and career of Field Marshal Montgomery and the Holocaust. A new permanent exhibition is devoted to Crimes against Humanity, examining ethnic conflict and genocide in Armenia, Nazi-occupied Europe, Cambodia, East Timor, Bosnia, Rwanda and elsewhere. Allow a day to explore the whole museum.

National Army Museum

Free. Usual hours. Shop. Café. Special events/ talks. School visits. Tel. 020 7730 0717. www.national-army-museum.ac.uk Hospital Road, Chelsea. Nearest rail Victoria Station, tube Sloane Square. The museum is adjacent to the Royal Hospital.

Portrays the history of the British Army from 1485 to the present, as well as the story of the Indian Army to independence in 1947 and other Colonial Land Forces. Displays and exhibitions illustrate 500 years of how soldiers lived and fought. There are life-sized reconstructions and audio-visual displays and one of the largest collections of uniforms in the world. Visitors are able to handle a Tudor cannonball, try on helmets, explore a recreated First World War trench, test their military skills on computer challenges and view an enormous model of the Battle of Waterloo.

National Maritime Museum (World Heritage Site)

Free (excluding special exhibitions). Usual hours. Shop. Café. Special events/ exhibitions. School visits. Library. Research facilities. Lecture room. Tel. 0870 7804263. www.nmm.ac.uk Greenwich. Nearest rail Greenwich.

Under an impressive glass roof, this modern museum looks at Britain's association with the sea and seafarers

from the Viking explorers to visions of the future, using art, sounds, models and modern technology. Galleries include 'Ships of Discovery', 'Charting the Globe', 'Costume', 'Art and the Sea', 'Ships of War' and 'Nelson'. As its name implies this is a 'maritime' museum, rather than one devoted to the military aspects of Britain's naval history – for that a visit to Portsmouth is essential.

RAF Museum Hendon

Free. Usual hours. Shop. Café. Restaurant. Guided tours. Special events. School visits. Research facilities. Parking. Tel. 020 8358 4964. www.rafmuseum.org.uk Grahame Park Way, Hendon. Thirty minutes from central London; follow brown tourist signs from M1, M25, A41 or A45. Nearest rail Mill Hill Broadway, tube Colindale.

Sited on ten acres of the former RAF station, this is probably the finest RAF museum in the country and requires a day to do it justice. The displays cover the history of the RAF and its predecessors in three aircraft halls – the Main, Bomber Command and Battle of Britain Halls. Some

eighty aircraft are on display, from wood and canvas machines to helicopters and jet fighters. The Battle of Britain Hall includes a recreation of the sights and sounds of London during the Blitz, while in a 'fun 'n' flight' gallery visitors can experiment with cockpit controls, engine lifting, speed, drop zone and flying aptitude tests.

The Royal Regiment of Fusiliers' Museum

£. Usual hours. Shop. Research facilities. Tel. 020 7488 5610. H.M. Tower of London. Nearest tube Tower Hill, nearest rail Fenchurch Street. Riverboat from Charing Cross, Westminster or Greenwich to Tower Pier.

This first-class museum is located inside the Tower of London with only a small extra charge for admission. A series of impressive displays illustrate the history of the Royal Fusiliers from 1685 to 1968 and that of the Royal Regiment of Fusiliers to date. The exhibits include uniforms, weapons, medals, equipment, colours and dioramas of the battles of Alma (Crimean War), Mons and Cassino.

A Hawker Hart on display at the RAF Museum Hendon

There are a substantial number of war memorials in the City of London, including those erected in schools and by companies, societies and guilds to their employees. They all commemorate men who died in war and whose comradeship is exemplified by the inscription on the First World War Artillery Memorial, 'Here was a Royal Fellowship of Death'. But perhaps the most poignant inscription, written on thousands of anonymous individual headstones scattered over Europe and beyond in Commonwealth War Graves cemeteries, is Rudyard Kipling's 'Known unto God'. This guide focuses on those easily seen while exploring the streets around Hyde Park Corner, The Mall, Victoria Embankment and Whitehall; each is well worth a pause for reflection. In addition there is an international memorial to all Victoria Cross and George Cross recipients inside Westminster Abbey.

Animals in War Memorial

Brook Gate, Park Lane on the edge of Hyde Park.

This memorial honours the millions of conscripted animals that served and suffered alongside British, Commonwealth and American forces in 20th-century conflicts. They include horses, mules, dogs, elephants, pigeons and canaries. Even glow worms are not forgotten as they were used by soldiers in the trenches in World War I to help them read maps in the gloom. Animal casualties number in their millions; eight million horses alone are thought to have died in World War I. The memorial consists of a 55 foot by 58 foot curved wall of Portland stone upon which the animals are depicted in bas-relief. Completing the memorial are two life-size, heavily laden mules struggling up steps towards a gap in the wall, beyond which are a bronze horse and dog.

The Battle of Britain Monument

Victoria Embankment close to Westminster Bridge.

Unveiled in spring 2005, this memorial is built into part of the Victoria Embankment wall between the RAF Memorial and Westminster Bridge. It is made up of two bronze friezes set in an 82ft-long granite structure. One depicts all the achievements of Fighter Command, while the other focuses on the people of London, featuring St Paul's Cathedral and an Anderson air-raid shelter. The central figures represent airmen scrambling for their aircraft. There is a plaque with the names of 2936 pilots and ground crew from Britain and 14 other countries. The plinth beneath the relief bears Winston Churchill's famous words: 'Never in the field of human conflict was so much owed by so many to so few.'

The Animals in War Memorial, unveiled in 2004

Belgium National Monument

Victoria Embankment Gardens.

In the autumn of 1918, before the end of the First World War, an official committee was established under two princesses of the Belgian royal family to erect a memorial in London as 'testimony of Belgium's deep gratitude towards Great Britain for the aid so generously bestowed upon Her during the war'. A woman representing Belgium, accompanied by two children bearing garlands and wreaths, is set in a recess of Portland stone. On either side are sculptures of Justice and Honour and above are carved the shields of Belgian provinces.

Canadian Memorial

The SE corner of Green Park, close to the junction of The Mall and Constitution Hill.

The Queen unveiled this recent memorial in 1994. It is unconventional in design, being a shallow pyramid made of dark red granite from Nova Scotia, divided in two to represent Canada and Britain. Water flows over the surface, which has a pattern of maple leaves to represent individual Canadians. Just to the east a compass rose is set into the paving aligned towards Halifax, Nova Scotia, the port from which most Canadians left for war. The memorial commemorates the one million Canadians who came to Britain to serve in both World Wars, and particularly the 110,000 who died.

Cavalry Memorial

The SE corner of Hyde Park between the Serpentine Road and Rotten Row.

Planned in 1920 to commemorate the cavalry from Britain and her Empire who fell in the First World War, it was originally erected at the Stanhope Gate entrance to Hyde Park but was moved in 1960 to its present location when Park Lane was widened. It is the magnificent armoured equestrian figure of St George with sword raised triumphantly having just slain the dragon. Interestingly, St George has been given Kaiser Wilhelm's upturned moustache.

The Cenotaph

Whitehall, between Downing Street and King Charles Street.

The national memorial to all those from the British Empire, Commonwealth and Allies who gave their lives in the two World Wars and subsequent conflicts. Here the Sovereign leads the nation at the annual wreath-laying ceremony and parade of veterans every November on Remembrance Sunday. Made of Portland stone, its every surface is subtly curved, with its raking verticals meeting at an imaginary point a thousand feet above the ground. It was unveiled on 11 November 1920 as part of the burial ceremony of the Unknown Warrior in Westminster Abbey. The power of the monument lies in its simplicity and brevity of inscription – 'The Glorious Dead'. Officers of the Armed Services in uniform walking past are obliged to salute.

Chindit Forces Memorial

The Victoria Embankment at the rear of the Ministry of Defence.

This memorial is dedicated to all those who fought in the Chindit columns, formed, trained and led by Major-General Orde Wingate to carry out operations in the jungle behind Japanese lines in Burma in 1942 and 1943. Chindits were recruited from the armed forces of Britain, Burma, Hong Kong, India, Nepal, West Africa and the United States. Chindits got their name from the mythical lion-like beast that guards Burmese temples called a 'chinthe'. A chinthe sits on top of the

memorial, the reverse of which commemorates Wingate, who was killed in an air crash in 1944.

Fleet Air Arm Memorial

On the north bank of the Thames in the Victoria Embankment Gardens, opposite the London Eye.

This unusual memorial is composed of a tall round pillar surmounted by a statue of a standing pilot holding up two angel's wings. It commemorates the sacrifice of all Fleet Air Arm personnel who lost their lives in World War II and in later conflicts.

The Cenotaph, dedicated to 'The Glorious Dead'

Guards Division Memorial

On the eastern edge of St James's Park overlooking Horse Guards Parade.

A very impressive broad Portland stone obelisk unveiled in 1926 commemorates the fallen of the Regiments of Foot Guards and other units that served

under them. Five bronze guardsmen, one from each of the Grenadier, Coldstream, Scots, Welsh and Irish Guards, stand side by side on the base of the memorial. Below each figure is the regimental badge, made from German guns captured by the then Brigade of Guards. The memorial also commemorates those of the Household Division who died in the Second World War and 'In the Service of their Country since 1918'. Some shrapnel damage inflicted during bombing raids in the Second World War has been deliberately left unrepaired.

The Gurkha Regiment's Memorial

Whitehall, at the junction of Horse Guards Avenue and Whitehall Court.

Unveiled in 1997, this commemorates the service and sacrifice of the Nepalese soldiers in the sixteen Gurkha Regiments that have served Britain since 1816. The pedestal is surmounted by a bronze figure of a Gurkha soldier with rifle and fixed bayonet. On the back of the pedestal are listed the Regiments and theatres of war in which they have served, including Bosnia in 1996.

Imperial Camel Corps Memorial

Victoria Embankment Gardens.

A memorial to the British, Australian, New Zealand and Indian troops of the Imperial Camel Corps who died serving in Egypt and the Middle East against the Ottoman (Turkish) Empire during the First World War. It is a smaller memorial than most and has a pedestal surmounted by a soldier riding a camel. The names of the fallen are listed on the pedestal.

Machine Gun Corps Memorial

Hyde Park Corner.

A strange design, in that a machine gun does not feature. It was unveiled in 1925 and consists of a large pedestal on which stands the naked figure of David holding Goliath's sword, just after killing the giant with his slingshot. The quotation from Samuel 18:7, 'Saul has slain his thousands, but David his tens of thousands', while perhaps being an appropriate allusion to the effectiveness of machine guns in the First World War, provoked considerable protest at the time.

The Malta GC Monument

Trinity Square Gardens, near the Tower of London.

This monument to the garrison and people of the island of Malta, who were collectively awarded the George Cross for their sustained gallantry during the siege of Malta during the Second World War, was unveiled by the Duke of Edinburgh on 15 August 2005, the sixtieth anniversary of the Japanese unconditional surrender. It consists of a large slab of granite from the tiny island of Gozo, north of Malta, with plaques telling the story of the siege. More than 7000 servicemen and civilians died defending the island, which saw Malta sustain some of the worst bombing of the war.

Monument to the Women of World War II

Central Whitehall, opposite the Cabinet Office.

This monument, standing 22 feet high and 16 feet long, was unveiled by the Queen on 9 July 2005 and commemorates the millions of women who worked for victory in World War II both in the Armed Forces and on the Home Front. Using the same typeface as that employed in wartime ration books, it represents all the practical contributions women made to the war effort, from building ships to running soup kitchens, from nursing to driving buses, from digging coal to growing food.

Royal Air Force Memorial

Victoria Embankment, just south of the junction with Horse Guards Avenue.

Unveiled in 1924, this is a tall obelisk-like memorial surmounted by a huge eagle with raised wings. It is dedicated 'in memory of all ranks of the Royal Naval Air Service, Royal Flying Corps, Royal Air Force and those air forces from every part of the British Empire' killed in the First World War. The RAF had been formed in 1918 by the merging of the RNAS and RFC. A later inscription commemorates RAF personnel who died in the Second World War.

Royal Artillery Memorial 1910

NE edge of St James's Park, alongside The Mall.

In 1905 a committee of Royal Artillery members organized the setting up of a memorial to their thousand comrades killed in the South African War of 1899–1902 (Second Boer War). The figure of Peace restraining a large horse is typical of the allegorical manner of much Edwardian sculpture. Only on seeing the bronze panels depicting garrison and mountain artillery, and the names of the fallen at each end of the wall, is the visitor certain of the purpose of this memorial.

Royal Artillery Memorial 1925

Hyde Park Corner.

The sculptor, C. Sergeant Jagger, had been awarded the Military Cross during the First World War and his experience of the brutality of war is much in evidence in the stone reliefs, and the recumbent bronze figure of a dead artilleryman covered by a greatcoat that partially overhangs the inscription, 'Here was a Royal Fellowship of Death'. The original memorial commemorates the 49,000 men of the Royal Artillery who gave their lives in the First World War. The three bronze panels mounted on a platform on the south side commemorate almost 30,000 artillerymen who died in the Second World War.

Royal Marines' Memorial

Admiralty Arch at the eastern end of The Mall.

Unveiled in 1903, this memorial commemorates all ranks of the Royal Marines killed in the South African War of 1899–1902 and the expedition to protect the foreign legations in Peking during the Boxer Rebellion of 1900. The heroic figure is of a Royal Marine with rifle and fixed bayonet protecting a fallen comrade. On the front of the memorial is the Royal Marines badge and on the reverse the names of the fallen.

The Tomb of the Unknown Warrior

Close to the west door of Westminster Abbey.

After the end of World War I it was decided to bury the body of an unknown British serviceman in Westminster Abbey as a symbolic gesture of gratitude to all those who gave their lives in the war. The black marble slab over the grave was quarried in Belgium, the inlaid brass inscription was made from spent cartridge cases collected from the trenches, the earth in the grave came from French battlefields and the coffin is made of English oak from King George V's Windsor estate. This is the only grave in Westminster Abbey that is never walked on. The inscription ends with the words:

FOR GOD
FOR KING AND COUNTRY
FOR THE SACRED CAUSE OF
JUSTICE AND
THE FREEDOM OF THE WORLD
THEY BURIED HIM AMONG THE
KINGS BECAUSE HE
HAD DONE GOOD TOWARD
GOD AND TOWARD
HIS HOUSE

The Victoria Cross and George Cross Memorial

Inside Westminster Abbey, near the west door, close to the Tomb of the Unknown Warrior.

Unveiled on 14 May 2003 by Her Majesty the Queen in Westminster Abbey, this is the first memorial to all, living and dead, who have been awarded either the Victoria or George Cross for quite exceptional gallantry on the battlefield, in the face of an enemy in the case of a VC or otherwise in the case of the GC. At the time of writing (2005), only fourteen VC-holders are still alive.

Other noteworthy memorials
The Artist Rifles *Royal Academy Loggia, Piccadilly*
The Battle of Britain Chapel *Henry VII's Chapel, Westminster Abbey*
The Old Contemptibles Chapel *crypt of St Martin in the Fields, Trafalgar Square*
The Royal Fusiliers *High Holborn*
The Royal Navy and Merchant Marine *Tower Hill*

THE ROMAN OCCUPATION

CAESAR'S LANDINGS

We were now faced with grave difficulties. Because of their size our ships could not be run ashore except where the water was deep; the soldiers were unfamiliar with the terrain, their hands were full and they were weighed down by the heavy weapons they carried; they had to jump down from their ships, get a footing in the waves and fight the enemy all at the same time.

The enemy, on the other hand, were standing on dry land or moving out just a little way into the water ... so they boldly hurled their javelins and spurred on their horses ... Our men were terrified by this. They were completely unfamiliar with this kind of fighting and did not show the same spirit and keenness as they usually did in battle on land.

And now, as our soldiers were hesitating, mostly because of the depth of the water, the aquilifer [eagle-bearer] of the Tenth Legion, after praying to the gods ... shouted out loudly, 'Jump down men, unless you want to betray your eagle to the enemy!'

With these words Julius Caesar described the first Roman landing on British soil in the late summer of 55 BC, which probably happened on the pebbled Walmer Beach just south of Deal, Kent. It succeeded, largely due to the leadership of the unknown aquilifer, but it was merely a probe of the defences, a reconnaissance in force, with two legions (about 10,000 men). Caesar returned the following year with three legions and 2000 cavalry in 800 ships. This time the landing was unopposed and almost certainly along the stretch of beach north of Deal. He pushed inland, fought a battle to cross the Stour at Canterbury, and then sent the 7th Legion to storm the stronghold on the heights of Bigbury some two miles from the ford.

The British tribes in the south-east were then united under the leadership of Cassivellaunus, King of the Catuvellauni (Hertfordshire, Buckinghamshire and Cambridgeshire). Cassivellaunus fought the Romans at the Thames crossing, quite possibly at the ford near Westminster, where the legionaries struggled across up to their necks in water. The Romans triumphed and pushed north through heavily wooded country against continuous hit-and-run attacks until confronted by a major fortified encampment 'in a densely wooded place' – probably the camp immediately east of Wheathampstead, Hertfordshire. The Romans made a determined assault, and British resistance collapsed. Caesar extracted hostages, an annual tribute and a cessation of hostilities. Within two months of landing he was back in Gaul, never to return. Ninety-seven years were to pass before legionaries returned to Britain.

THE CONQUEST

When the Emperor Claudius decided to invade Britain in AD 43, he had no plan for the occupation of the whole country. The Romans were forced into further advances by aggressive acts of the Britons themselves. An attack by Caratacus led to retaliation in AD 48 under Ostorius Scapula and a push beyond the Severn, and the seizure of Brigantia by Venutius in AD 69. Petillius Cerealis advanced north in 71, continuing into Scotland. The Romans' objective was to gain control of the rich lowlands and protect the Empire's frontier by means of friendly states. They achieved this in the north with the creation of the client kingdom of Brigantia under Queen Cartimandua, but were unable to do the same in Wales because of the hostility of the tribes in that area, enflamed by their war leader Caratacus and the strong influence of the Druids.

By the end of the first century the Romans were faced with the problem of defining their northern frontier. Changes in policy led to the construction of two walls (Hadrian's and the Antonine) and several campaigns in Scotland culminating with Agricola's victory at *Mons Graupius* in AD 83 (p. 157) somewhere in the Grampian Mountains, possibly near Inverurie, Aberdeenshire, where it is said that up to 10,000 Scots died. The problem of attacks and incursions from the Scots was not solved until Severus administered a final crushing defeat to them in the Caledonians in 208 and created a deep fortified zone in front of Hadrian's Wall.

THE ROMAN IMPERIAL ARMY

This Army was surely one of the most formidable fighting machines ever to march. In Britain it has left us the outlines or foundations of hundreds of its fortresses, forts and camps. It has also left us roads: long stretches of the A1(M) south of Peterborough and the A15 north of Lincoln hide Ermine Street, built by legionaries, often as straight as an arrow, from London to York. The A5 north-east from Milton Keynes to Tamworth lies over fifty miles of the old Watling Street, and the gently curving A6 from Leicester to Lincoln was once the famous Fosse Way. At Ackling Dyke in Dorset, halfway along the A354 between Salisbury and Blandford Forum, you can clearly see the main causeway (*agger*) flanked by drainage ditches.

Unconquered and
unoccupied tribal territory

✗ C

Inchtothil
(temporary)

Antonine Wall

Hadrian's Wall

York
VI Legion

Chester
XX Legion

B
✗

Watling Street

Leicester

Ermine Street

Iceni revolt
60AD

Gloucester

Icknield Way

Colchester

Fosse Way

St Albans

Caerleon
II Legion

London

Celtic trackway

✗ A
**Site of Caesar's
landing 55 BC**

☐ **Exeter**

Dorchester

KEY

Area under military control during Roman occupation

Area under civil control

■ Permanent Legionary Fortress and HQ

■ Fort or military camp (selection)

☐ Saxon Shore Forts, AD 300–400

Town sacked by Boudicca during the Iceni rebellion

Major Roman road

Celtic trackway used by the Romans

✗ Major battle

A Caesar's first landing, 55 BC

B Boudicca's final defeat in the Midlands, AD 60

C Caledonian tribes defeated in AD 83

Other Roman road

○ Major civil settlement

The Roman Army has left us fragments of its language. Our 'century' derives from 'centurion', the Roman officer commanding around one hundred men. A school 'prefect' was once a senior officer called a *praefectus*, while a 'signal' or to 'signify' originated from the Roman standard, the *signum*, and its bearer, the *signifer*, who signalled battlefield drill movements with his raised standard. However, the most spectacular reminder of the Roman Army, not just in Britain but throughout Europe, is surely the seventy-two miles of Hadrian's Wall (now a World Heritage Site; see feature pp. 116–19) that marked the northernmost frontier of the Empire for nearly three hundred years. Throughout this period the core of the Army was the legions, heavily armoured infantry, all Roman citizens, each about 5500 strong. They were augmented by scores of auxiliary units (often locally raised outside Italy) 500 strong, trained and equipped as cavalry, infantry or mixed units. At the centre, at Rome, was the Emperor, protected by the elite Praetorian Guard; as commander-in-chief he controlled some thirty legions that were deployed around the Empire to guard frontiers or watch potentially rebellious tribes. At times Britain merited four legions, but her usual garrison was three. They formed the governor's strategic reserve with permanent bases at Caerleon (Isca), Chester (Deva) and York (Eboracum). The legions also provided the engineers to supervise the construction of fortresses, bridges and roads, while the legionaries provided the labour.

A Roman legion was perhaps the equivalent of today's brigade battle group, a formidable force of all arms capable of operating independently for limited periods. The infantry were organized into centuries (companies) of about eighty men under centurions (commissioned officers). The second-in-command of a century was the *optio* (sergeant major) and the number three the *tesserarius* (sergeant). Each had its signifer with the standard. These sub-units were grouped into ten cohorts (battalions) each of six centuries. If a cohort was detached for any reason the senior centurion commanded. The legionary commander was the *legatus legions* (major-general). To assist him were six tribunes, the senior of whom (*tribunus laticlavius*) was the second-in-command of the legion. The other five were used as cohort or detachment commanders as required. The camp prefect (*praefectus castrorum*) was the third-in-command, invariably a former chief centurion between fifty and sixty years of age, who was the legion's administrative officer/quartermaster. Every legion also had its chief centurion (*primus pilus*) who commanded the first century of the first cohort, and an eagle bearer (*aquilifer*). The legion had a small unit of horsemen, about 120 strong, and its own field artillery. These were catapults (resembling giant crossbows) of varying sizes carried on carts drawn by oxen and firing stones or bolts. According to the Roman writer Vegetius each legion also had ten *onagri*, larger machines that could hurl heavy stones for siege work or defence of forts.

LEGIONARY FORTRESSES

These large military barracks covering 50–60 acres were the permanent home of a 5500–6000-man legion – a substantial military township. Eleven such fortresses are known to have been built in Britain, but most lie under modern towns and thus have only been partially explored. The earlier ones were timber-built – Exeter, Colchester, Chichester, Lincoln, Gloucester, Kingsholm and Wroxeter. Of the three later stone fortresses, York and Chester have been covered over and disturbed by medieval and later buildings. Caerleon, however, is worth a visit as most of it has been excavated, although the central area is occupied by a church and graveyard. There remains the fortress at Inchtuthil, Perthshire (p. 156), which was abandoned before completion, although excavations have provided us with a detailed layout. Except for the bathhouse, outside the fortress, and the walls it was a timber construction containing barracks for the ten cohorts, six each for Cohorts II–X, with larger accommodation for Cohort I. Each cohort had a granary/foodstore, the commander and each senior officer his own house, and there was a hospital and workshop for repair of weapons or armour.

Although the legions were the backbone of the Roman Army, in terms of numbers they only represented half its total strength. The auxiliaries (*auxilia*) included cavalry, light infantry, archers, slingers and mixed units. They were formed into cohorts, usually about 500 strong, under the command of a prefect. Initially formed from frontier populations to fight in their own area, they gradually became formalized with standard equipment and were often sent to serve in countries other than their homeland. These units were stationed along the frontiers to absorb the first shock of barbarian attack, to delay and give warning so that the legions, the strategic reserve, could group to meet the threat. A Roman Army on a major offensive would have numerous auxiliary cohorts under command. As a reward for long and loyal service (twenty-five years) the auxiliary soldier would be awarded Roman citizenship, which would pass to his sons. This carried considerable privileges and was a major inducement to join. When the apostle Paul was accused of defiling the Jewish temple in the same year Boudicca was rebelling against Rome in Britain, he invoked his right as a Roman citizen to be tried in Rome. The grant of citizenship was inscribed on two bronze sheets known as a *diploma* – another modern word adopted from the Roman military.

THE ICENI REBELLION, AD 60

The most famous British ruler to confront the Romans was the queen of the Iceni, a tribe inhabiting what is now Norfolk and Suffolk. There is a statue of Queen Boudicca in her chariot on the Victoria Embankment in London to remind the passer-by of her place in our history as a British resistance leader.

Just before the king of the Iceni, Prasutagus, died in about AD 59 he named the Emperor Nero as his co-heir along with his two daughters. Nero took the view that the entire personal fortune and estates of a client king became imperial property on his death, so Britain's procurator, Catus Decianus, descended on the Iceni with a small military escort and a horde of tax collectors and clerks to make an inventory of all Prasutagus's possessions before taking control of them. His widow, Queen Boudicca, was unsurprisingly appalled; but not only were her protests brushed aside, she herself was stripped and lashed like a criminal, while her daughters were raped. The Iceni (joined by the neighbouring Trinovantes) rose up in spontaneous rebellion and Decianus fled – all the way to Gaul.

The British governor, Suetonius, with the 14th and 20th Legions, was slaughtering the Druids and destroying their sacred groves on Anglesey when he was informed about the rebellion. By this time the rebels were moving on the unprotected towns of south-east Britain. Suetonius hoped the 9th Legion, being the nearest to the revolt at Lincoln, would delay if not confront the rebels while he hastened towards

them with the 14th and 20th. The 2nd Augusta, then at Exeter, were ordered to join him as soon as they could.

Colchester, garrisoned by retired veterans, was the first town to be swamped and destroyed. The commander of the 9th Legion, Petillius Cerealis, seriously underestimated the situation and rode out with a mounted escort of 2000 men straight into an ambush. Most of his men were killed, while he only escaped by abandoning the fight and galloping back to Lincoln. St Albans met the same fate as Colchester – buildings burnt and thousands of people put to the sword.

Meanwhile Suetonius and his two legions were marching back from Anglesey. He was increasingly concerned at the scale of the revolt and the lack of news from the 2nd Augusta, which should have been hurrying to meet him from Exeter. But when the message to march arrived the legate was away and command therefore devolved onto the *praefectus castrorum*, one Poenius Postumus, who refused to move, feeling that the uncertainty and responsibility were too great. Thus when Suetonius, who had ridden ahead of his marching men, reached London he had too few troops to defend it. He withdrew. Those who could march came with him, those who could not were left to die in the city's ruins.

When Suetonius rejoined his command, numbering little more than 10,000, the outcome of the impending battle was not promising. Boudicca led a vast horde of warriors accompanied by even greater numbers of women, children and camp followers. Suetonius chose a site protected on its flanks and rear by hills and thick woods. The fight was prolonged but volleys of Roman javelins coupled with

The well-preserved strongroom at Chesters

Richborough Fort, once the gateway to Roman Britain.

disciplined swordwork prevailed. The retreating British became entangled in the huge wagon-lager drawn up behind their army that accommodated the thousands of spectators. It is said that 80,000 British fell at a cost of 400 Romans, although halving the former figure and doubling the latter would probably be more accurate. Boudicca died, possibly by taking poison. When the news reached Exeter, Postumus did the honourable thing and fell on his sword.

Regrettably, the site of this great battle cannot be fixed with certainty. A possible location is the ridge south of the River Anker just on the outskirts of Mancetter village as you approach Atherstone on the A5 (Watling Street) from Nuneaton.

THE ROMANS DEPART

By the end of the third century the threats to Roman Britain had changed dramatically, with a constant stream of sea raiders from across the North and Irish Seas. Coastal defences now had to be provided, and the fleet adapted to meet this menace. The threat of Germanic raiders led to the building of a system of coastal forts from the Wash to the Solent. These became known as the Saxon Shore Forts, and in their first form, with their massive thick walls and bastions, resembled later medieval castles. The most important

was Richborough in Kent. After 360 the western Roman Empire began to collapse. More and more troops were withdrawn from Britain and other frontiers to defend Italy. In 367 Emperor Valentinian sent a large force to deal with a 'great barbarian conspiracy' that threatened to destroy Britain. Its success was only temporary as, during the final years of the fourth century, the pressures on Rome became too great for her rulers to be concerned with anything but self-preservation. In 409 Rome abandoned Britain. The following year the Goths stormed and sacked the Eternal City. But Britain, for so long a civilized Roman province, had already been slipping into economic decline. Forts were abandoned, industries shut down, roads and buildings went unrepaired. The so-called 'Dark Ages' had begun.

Well worth a visit
Ackling Dyke Roman road *p. 10*
Richborough Castle *p. 46*
Walmer Beach *p. 49*
Lunt Roman Fort, near Coventry *p. 66*
Deva Roman Experience, Chester *p. 95*
Senhouse Roman Museum, Maryport *p. 95*
Inchtuthil legionary fortress *p. 156*
Caerleon Roman Legionary Museum *p. 123*

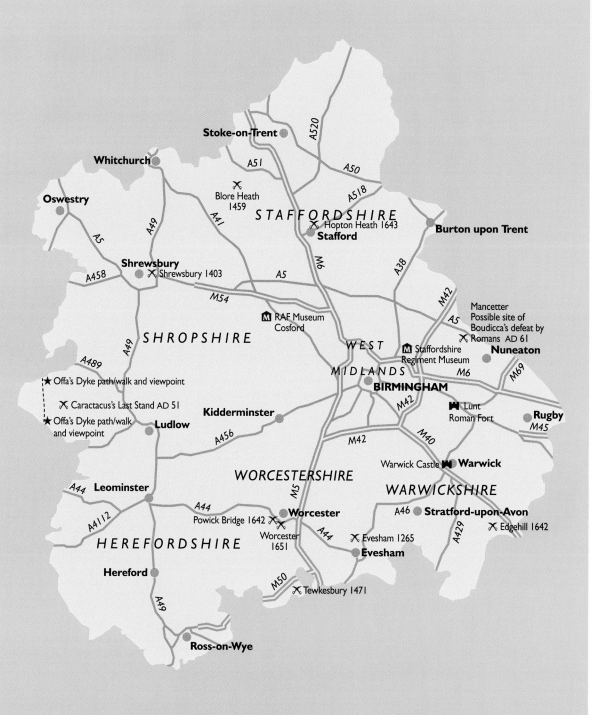

Stoke-on-Trent

A520

Whitchurch

A51

A50

Oswestry

Blore Heath
1459

A518

A41

STAFFORDSHIRE

Burton upon Trent

A49

Hopton Heath 1643

Stafford

A5

A38

Shrewsbury

A458

Shrewsbury 1403

A5

M6

A49

M54

M42

Mancetter
Possible site of
Boudicca's defeat by
Romans AD 61

A5

SHROPSHIRE

RAF Museum
Cosford

WEST

Staffordshire
Regiment Museum

A489

MIDLANDS

M6

Nuneaton

BIRMINGHAM

M69

A49

★ Offa's Dyke path/walk and viewpoint

Caractacus's Last Stand AD 51

Kidderminster

M42

Lunt
Roman Fort

Rugby

★ Offa's Dyke path/walk
and viewpoint

Ludlow

A456

M42

M40

M45

Warwick Castle

Warwick

A44

Leominster

WORCESTERSHIRE

WARWICKSHIRE

A44

A46

Stratford-upon-Avon

A4112

Powick Bridge 1642

Worcester

A429

Edgehill 1642

HEREFORDSHIRE

Worcester
1651

M5

A44

Evesham 1265

Hereford

Evesham

A49

M50

Tewkesbury 1471

Ross-on-Wye

WEST MIDLANDS

Blore Heath, Battle of, 1459 (Shropshire)

Free. Easy access. Farmland with some parking on roadside. Approximately 2½ miles east of Market Drayton on the A53 to Newcastle-under-Lyme. Most of the fighting took place in the area of the Cross, south of the road halfway up the slope to the Yorkist position.

A battle in the first phase of the Wars of the Roses, fought on 23 September 1459 between the Lancastrians under Lord Audley and the Yorkists under Lord Salisbury. Audley had around 9000 men, whom he drew up in a defensive position with alternating infantry and mounted divisions astride the A53 east of Market Drayton along a low ridge leading down to a small stream known today as Hempmill Brook. Salisbury, who was outnumbered two to one, declined to attack and deployed across the same road in a defensive position some 500 yards further east and opposite the Lancastrians. Stakes were planted in front of the Yorkist position and a trench dug in their rear.

Salisbury induced Audley to attack by feigning a retreat, then ordered a rain of arrows that defeated two mounted charges by the Lancastrians across the stream, killing many horses. Audley then led 4000 infantry forward and a desperate mêlée took place on the slopes of the Yorkist position. During this hand-to-hand struggle Audley was killed – the commemorative cross on the battlefield supposedly marks the spot. Shortly thereafter his army disintegrated.

Caractacus's Last Stand, AD 51 (Shropshire)

Easy access. Free. Farmland. Parking available. Twenty-five miles SW of Shrewsbury. Follow the A49 south through Church Stretton. Eight miles further on turn right onto the B4368 and stop at the junction with the B4385 in the village of Purslow. The River Clun is to the south with Caractacus's ridge behind it.

Caractacus was a successful British tribal leader who resisted the Roman advance across southern and central Britain during the years AD 47–51. The Romans fought seven campaigns against him before his final capture at a battle thought to be in Shropshire, near the Welsh border. He was taken in chains to Rome and paraded in a triumphal procession.

Although the site of this battle remains uncertain, the research of Colonel A.H. Burne and the detailed description of the action by the Roman historian Tacitus indicate the ridge immediately south of the River Clun, a mile south-west of the village of Clunbury in Shropshire. Here, it is suggested, some 15,000 British were drawn up along the ridge facing north, with Clunbury Hill on their right flank and the small river an obstacle in front. The present Purslow Wood did not exist. A hastily constructed palisade of earth and stones protected the front. The position was attacked by two legions and accompanying light troops all commanded by the Roman Governor Publius Ostorius. The legion attacks probably concentrated against the ridgelines, moving forward with shields raised against a rain of missiles. The flimsy barricade was pulled down and the British forced back in bitter hand-to-hand fighting, at which the Romans excelled. The line was broken and it is possible rearguard actions took place on Clunbury and Black Hills on either flank of the British line. The circumstances of Caractacus's capture are unknown but it could have been on Black Hill.

Evesham, Battle of, 1265 (Worcestershire)

Free. Access reasonable, but much of the battlefield is now under the modern housing of northern Evesham. Parking possible. Greenhill area of Evesham. There is a car park off the High Street, and a visit to the monument to de Montfort is worthwhile.

After the Battle of Lewes in 1264 (see p. 42) Simon de Montfort, Earl of Leicester, governed England in the name of King Henry III, holding the heir to the throne Prince Edward hostage at Hereford to ensure the king's compliance. However, Edward escaped and on 4 August 1265 de Montfort found himself with an army of 6000 trapped within the loop of the River Avon at Evesham.

The de Montfort memorial in front of the Abbey Tower of Evesham (Battlefields Trust)

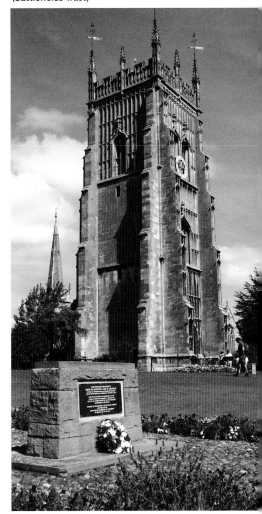

Edgehill, Battle of, 1642 (Warwickshire)

Free. Open fields. Some restriction on access to Ministry of Defence land. Seven miles NW of Banbury. Take the B4100 NW from Banbury and the B4086 at the fork at Warmington leading to Kineton. The battlefield is on your left after passing Knowle End.

The first major clash of the English Civil War, Edgehill took place on the open ground between the villages of Radwell and Kineton on 23 October 1642. On the evening of 22 October, King Charles I was resting his army of about 15,000 near the village of Edgecote, unaware that the Parliamentary army of roughly equal numbers under the Earl of Essex was only seven miles away at Kineton.

On the following day the King drew up his army along Edgehill. It was in two lines with the bulk of the infantry (three brigades) in the centre and cavalry on each flank. The cavalry regiments on the right were commanded by Prince Rupert and on the left by Lord Wilmot. The second line consisted of two infantry brigades. In front, positioned between the infantry, was the artillery. Essex took some time to march out of Kineton and it was not until noon that both armies faced each other about a mile apart. Essex was not prepared to assault so strong a position so there was a long pause during which an ineffective, long-range artillery duel took place. Charles then decided to attack, so the Royalist army descended the slope and both armies faced each other as shown on the map.

The action started with two spirited cavalry charges by the Royalist horse on both flanks, which hit the Parliamentary squadrons at a gallop and dispersed them towards Kineton. But the Royalist horsemen could not be contained or rallied and swept off the field in a wild pursuit, leaving the infantry of both sides with exposed flanks. The two leading lines closed to 'push of pike' although not before, unusually, the Royalist musketeers had fired off their muskets. Neither side gave ground but the surviving Parliamentary cavalry regiments under Balfour and Stapleton rode out from behind Meldrum's brigade and charged the Royalist left flank. Byron's brigade halted Stapleton but Balfour's troopers broke through Fielding's brigade. The Royalist line fell back, first on the left and gradually in the centre and right as well. The King's standard-bearer, Sir Edmund Verney, was killed and the standard taken, though it was recovered that evening.

Both armies were now utterly exhausted. By the time Rupert's horsemen drifted back and reformed on blown horses night was approaching, and with neither side inclined to renew the fight it became clear the battle had ended in a stalemate. The next day Essex withdrew to Warwick while the King prepared to march on London.

The northern side of Edgehill; viewed from the battlefield, just behind the Royalist lines near King's Leys (Battlefields Trust)

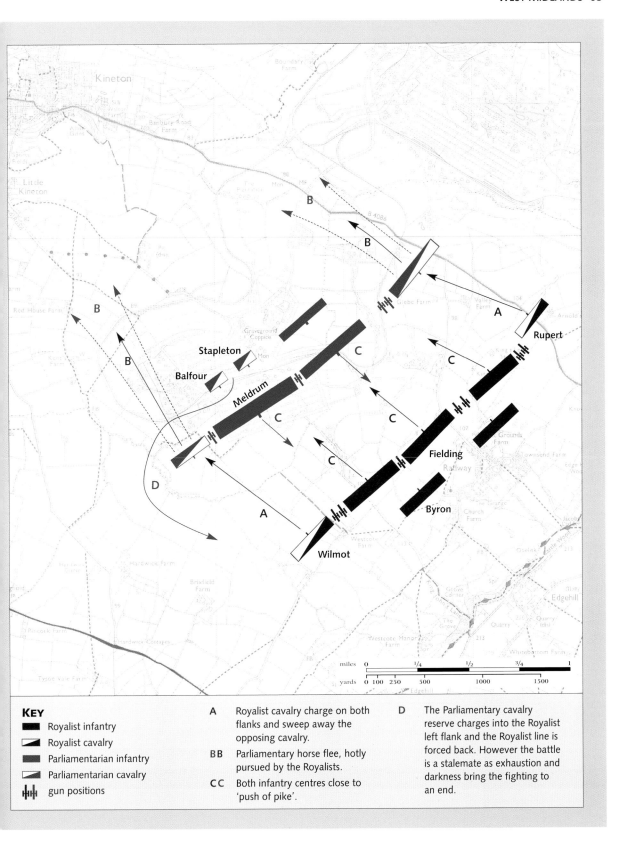

KEY

- ▰ Royalist infantry
- ◿ Royalist cavalry
- ▰ Parliamentarian infantry
- ◺ Parliamentarian cavalry
- ⥊ gun positions

A Royalist cavalry charge on both flanks and sweep away the opposing cavalry.

B B Parliamentary horse flee, hotly pursued by the Royalists.

C C Both infantry centres close to 'push of pike'.

D The Parliamentary cavalry reserve charges into the Royalist left flank and the Royalist line is forced back. However the battle is a stalemate as exhaustion and darkness bring the fighting to an end.

Edward, with some 8000 men, had deployed in two divisions on either side of the A4184 immediately south of the junction with the A4538 to Worcester on Green Hill. The trap was closed. De Montfort advanced up the hill to fight his way out. A brutal and prolonged mêlée ensued, much of it in sheeting rain. Edward's cavalry charged in on both wings and completed the encirclement. De Montfort was surrounded and cut down, 'his body cruelly mutilated'. The slaughter was unprecedented even for medieval warfare with some 4000 dead – 'such was the murder of Evesham, for battle it was not'.

Hopton Heath, Battle of, 1643 (Staffordshire)

Free. Open pasture, arable land except for the RAF depot that occupies a quarter of the battlefield. Parking in Hopton village. Three miles north of Stafford between the villages of Salt and Hopton. Easily approached from the A51 or from Stafford. A memorial is planned.

In March 1643, early in the English Civil War, Charles I dispatched a force under the Earl of Northampton to Staffordshire, which arrived in Stafford just before a Parliamentary force commanded by Sir John Gell and Sir William Brereton intent on taking the town.

The armies faced each other on Hopton Heath on 19 March with Northampton's 1200 Royalists, mostly mounted, drawn up where the RAF depot now is, and the Parliamentarians, with a mixed force of some 1500, deployed opposite on ground pitted with rabbit holes. Both sides fielded cannons; one huge Royalist piece known as 'Roaring Meg' that fired a 29lb ball allegedly did considerable damage. Northampton attacked and pushed back the enemy horse but failed to dislodge the infantry in the centre, being killed himself in the charge. His men regrouped for a second assault and this time the Parliamentarian cavalry fled but their infantry remained steady. Night brought an end to the fighting and the Parliamentarians withdrew during darkness. It was a hard-fought engagement with around 500 casualties, mostly Parliamentarian.

Lunt Roman Fort (Warwickshire)

££. Usual hours April–October weekends and bank holidays, 16 July–18 September Wed–Sun. Shop. Bookstall. Picnic area. Guided tours. School visits.
Tel. 024 7630 3567. At Baginton village south of Coventry off the A45 and A46 (follow tourist information signs). The fort is off Coventry Road.

Built and occupied by the Roman Army at the time of Boudicca's revolt, this ancient site includes the timber gateway, 350ft of ramparts, granary and Gyrus (cavalry training area), all faithfully reconstructed from archaeological evidence. The granary building contains a museum of Roman life, archaeological finds and a model of the fort in AD 64.

Mancetter, possible site of Boudicca's defeat by the Romans (Warwickshire)

Free. Open access. Parking possible off-road. The best educated guess puts the battlefield near Mancetter on the outskirts of Atherstone close to the A5 – the old Watling Street.

In AD 60 the Iceni tribe under Queen Boudicca rebelled against Roman rule. After sacking Colchester, St Albans and London, in AD 61 the massive army of Britons some 100,000 strong was confronted by two Roman legions (about 7000) and their auxiliaries (5000) under Paulinus. The mass of the Britons were drawn up in a vast semicircle with thousands of wagons at the rear crammed with women and children who had come to watch, while the Romans awaited attack on high ground. The Britons charged in chariots and on foot in one vast screaming mass. At 40 yards the Romans delivered a volley of thousands of javelins, then another before, in a solid wedge formation, the legionaries counter-charged with shield and sword. Boudicca's warriors broke and were slaughtered in their frantic rush to get through the wagons at their rear. Supposedly 40,000 Britons died, including countless women and children who were cut down without mercy. Boudicca was said to have taken poison. Perhaps 800 Romans perished.

Offa's Dyke (Shropshire)

Free. Open and wooded countryside. Somewhat remote areas but access possible via minor roads. It is possible to walk the entire length over some magnificent countryside with splendid views – best done in dry weather. Tourist offices provide a detailed guide with maps. It can also be seen from certain selected viewpoints. In Shropshire the best viewpoints are where it crosses the minor road three miles north of Knighton and where it crosses a path half a mile west of Mainstone.

The longest earthwork in Britain (120 miles), Offa's Dyke was built as a defensive frontier in the reign of Offa, King of Mercia (757–96) although never completed. It runs close to the present boundary between England and Wales, sometimes in the former, sometimes the latter. On the western side was a deep ditch with the 25ft rampart topped by a wooden palisade or stone wall. It may also have had towers, but there is no evidence of gateways. See also p. 20.

Powick Bridge, Battle of, 1642 (Worcestershire)

Free. Good access to bridge but the battlefield to north is largely built over. Parking possible. The SW suburbs of Worcester. The area north of the old Powick Bridge immediately west of the modern bridge carrying the A449 over the river. The bridge is worth a visit and could be combined with a visit to the battlefield of Worcester close by (p. 71).

Although only a skirmish, Powick Bridge was the first significant action of the English Civil War.

On 12 September the Royalist Sir John Byron left Oxford, having taken as much silver as his convoy could carry to finance the war, and now planning to hand it to the King at Worcester. The Parliamentary army was also making for Worcester under the Earl of Essex. On 22 September Essex had sent an advance guard of 1000 troopers and dragoons ahead to chase the treasure convoy. Their commander, Colonel Fiennes, had marched them all night so as they crossed the Powick Bridge over the River Teme on the 23rd they were exhausted. Awaiting them in Wick Field was Rupert with a similar force. The Royalists charged.

Mortimer's Cross, Battle of, 1461 (Herefordshire)

Free. Fields, farmland and small hamlet (inn at crossroads). Good access. Parking off-road. Fifteen miles north of Hereford on the A4110 road. The battlefield is easily explored and can be viewed from the bridge or from the rising ground 150 yards across the bridge to the east. The Monument Inn, with the 1799 pedestal in front, is at a fork in the road three miles towards Kingsland.

A small but interesting action fought during the Wars of the Roses, and unusual in that it was fought in midwinter (2 February), well outside the normal campaigning season. The Yorkists under the Earl of March (the future King Edward IV, perhaps England's greatest 'soldier-king') intercepted the Lancastrians, commanded by the Earl of Pembroke, who were marching into England from South Wales.

Edward chose his blocking position at Mortimer's Cross where the road from Ludlow crosses the River Lugg and the road coming north from Hereford. Strangely, he selected a position with his back to the river instead of using it as an icy defence. His force of around 6000 was deployed in the usual three divisions with Edward commanding in the centre, probably between the crossroads and the bridge. There, in the bitter cold amid flurries of snow, he awaited the arrival of Pembroke's force, which the Yorkists outnumbered. The Lancastrians, who had French and Irish troops in their midst, were similarly organized into three divisions. On arrival Pembroke ordered an attack.

The battle was really three small but separate actions. Despite a rain of arrows, the Earl of Ormond on the Lancastrian left charged and drove back the Yorkist right north of the bridge, forcing soldiers into the freezing water. In the centre Pembroke's attack made no headway against Edward's men-at-arms and archers. After much hacking and slashing at close quarters the Lancastrians fell back. Meanwhile, the Lancastrian third division, under Owen Tudor, moved to the right in an attempt to outflank his enemy's left. However, Edward's left division, thus far unengaged, attacked them in flank on the road to Kingsland and broke them up after a short fight. Owen Tudor was surrounded, captured and beheaded next day in Hereford. Edward's victory was complete, although Ormond and Pembroke escaped.

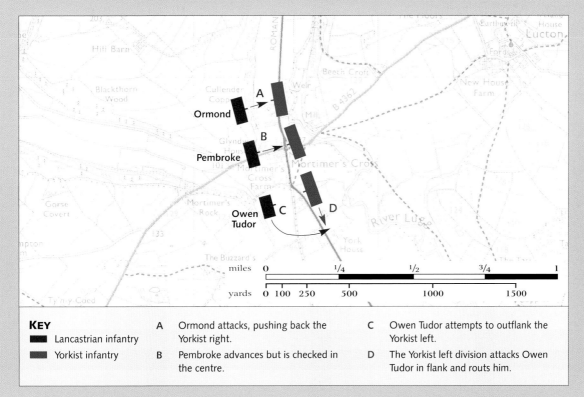

KEY

■ Lancastrian infantry

■ Yorkist infantry

A   Ormond attacks, pushing back the Yorkist right.

B   Pembroke advances but is checked in the centre.

C   Owen Tudor attempts to outflank the Yorkist left.

D   The Yorkist left division attacks Owen Tudor in flank and routs him.

Looking north-east across the battlefield from the viewing mound towards the church (Battlefields Trust)

Shrewsbury, Battle of, 1403 (Shropshire)

Free. Open farmland. Good access along roads and paths. Parking off-road possible. A mile north of Shrewsbury on the A49. The battlefield is on the left of the road. Viewpoints and parking are as shown on the map. It is an easy battlefield to explore as the minor road to Albright Hussey crosses the centre of the field where most fighting took place.

Shrewsbury, which features prominently in Shakespeare's play *Henry IV Part One*, was fought between King Henry IV and the rebel army of Sir Henry Percy, better known as Harry Hotspur. On the Royalist side was Prince Henry (later King Henry V). It was the first time that English bowmen in large numbers faced each other on a battlefield.

Hotspur had been marching south towards Shrewsbury, gathering recruits en route and hoping shortly to be joined by another rebel force under Owain Glyndwr from Wales. However, on arrival at Shrewsbury on 20 July Hotspur saw the royal standard flying over the town so turned away to encamp at Berwick on the Severn, probably near the present West Midlands Showground. He hoped his Welsh allies would appear over the nearby ford but he was to be disappointed. The next day he drew up his army along an east–west ridge to the

west of what is now the A49, some 1200 yards north of the village of Battlefield. Estimates of numbers vary wildly, but it is likely that Hotspur mustered around 7000 men-at-arms and 3000 archers who were deployed in front of the main line. The King's army was drawn up about 1000 yards to the south. He outnumbered the rebels by around 4000 men and had divided his command into two. Prince Henry had a division of around 3000–4000 men on the left flank while retaining personal control over the main body. Once again bowmen fronted the line.

The King advanced and halted about 500 yards from his enemy. A prolonged exchange of archery followed, and King Henry then moved forward again into a veritable arrow storm from the ridge ahead. It was too much for both bowmen and men-at-arms and the king's division fell back in some confusion. Hotspur, an experienced soldier, saw his chance and led his line forward down the slope. A brutal and bloody mêlée followed. Hotspur hacked his way towards the royal standard with his personal guard, but he was struck down and killed before reaching the King. The news of his death spread and coincided with Prince Henry launching his division in a well-timed assault on the rebels' right flank and rear. Hotspur's army fled in panic, hundreds of the fugitives being cut down by their pursuers. Some 2000 bodies remained on the battlefield to be buried in a mass grave said to be under St Mary Magdalene church, which was built five years later.

Hotspur's body was beheaded and cut into quarters. The head was displayed in York and the four quarters in Chester, Newcastle, London and Bristol. However, his widow eventually got the pieces back for a burial in York Minster.

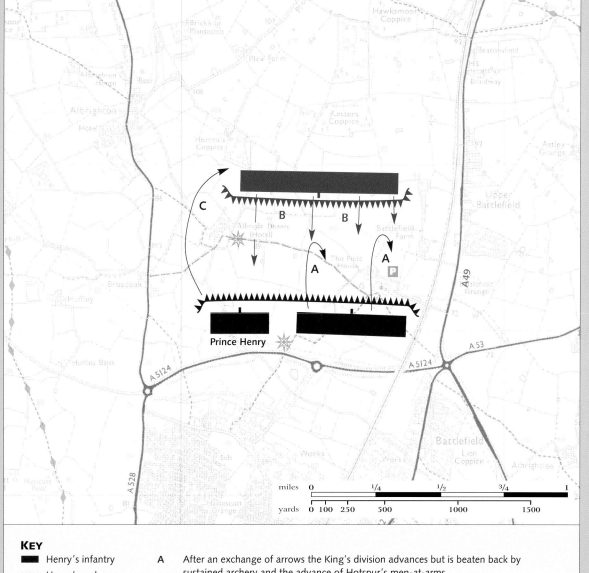

miles   0   1/4   1/2   3/4   1

yards   0   100   250   500   1000   1500

KEY

■ Henry's infantry

▲▲▲▲ Henry's archers

■ Hotspur's infantry

▲▲▲▲ Hotspur's archers

✴ Viewpoint

🅿 Parking

A After an exchange of arrows the King's division advances but is beaten back by sustained archery and the advance of Hotspur's men-at-arms.

B Hotspur advances and a mêlée results, with the King losing ground..

C Prince Henry attacks Hotspur's flank. Hotspur is killed and his army flees in panic.

The Parliamentarians ineffectively fired a few wheel-lock pistols before the enemy smashed into them. Despite better equipment Fiennes's men were routed and fled back over the bridge leaving some 150 casualties behind. The silver was saved, and the Royalist victory was excellent propaganda for the King's cause and the reputation of his cavalry under Prince Rupert.

RAF Museum Cosford (Shropshire)

£££. Usual hours. Shop. Refreshments. Picnic areas. School visits. Library. Research facilities. Lecture hall. Conference and dining facilities. Free parking. Tel. 01902 376200. Ten miles NW of Wolverhampton. Exit M54 at Junction 3. www.rafmuseum.org.uk/cosford/index.cfm

One of the largest aviation collections in Europe, with over eighty aircraft displayed including the *Vulcan* and *Victor* bombers, the huge *Belfast* freighter and enemy aircraft from the Second World War and the Falklands. There is a section devoted to British and German experimental and cur-

rent missiles. The British Airways Hall contains the nation's civil aviation history, and there is an interactive gallery illustrating science and technology.

The Staffordshire Regiment Museum (Staffordshire)

££. Tues–Fri 10 a.m.–4 p.m.; also weekends and bank holidays 1 April–31 October 12.30 p.m.–4.30 p.m. Shop. Picnic area. School visits. Free parking. Tel. 01543 434394. Three miles from Lichfield on the A51 to Tamworth, next to Whittington Barracks.

The museum displays the story of The Staffordshire Regiment from the Caribbean in the 1700s through the Crimean and two World Wars to the present day. A particular highlight is the 'Trench Experience', the only outdoor mock-up in Britain of a First World War trench system that includes barbed wire and an enemy machine-gun post. There are also collections of military vehicles, medals, uniforms and a bible that stopped a German bullet.

Warwick Castle (Warwickshire)

££££ – expensive, but really the castle caters for whole-day visits. Usual hours. Shops. Café and restaurant. Audio tours. Special events during the summer include jousting. School and group visits. Parking nearby. Tel. 0870 442 2371. www.warwick-castle.co.uk Warwick town centre, two miles from Junction 15 on the M40. Follow the signs.

The castle is a very busy tourist site. However, its attractions are many, not least the massive gatehouse and barbican and Caesar's and Guy's towers, built in the late 1300s. For those wanting a great day out there is much to see and do. A complete tour includes the armoury, with a thousand years of weapons and armour, climbing the towers, walking the ramparts, venturing into the dungeons and torture chamber, exploring the great hall and state rooms and walking in the sixty acres of gardens. It is very crowded on special events weekends and advance booking is advisable.

RAF Museum Cosford, which has one of the largest aviation collections in Europe

Warwick Castle – there's enough to do here to fill a whole day

Worcester, Battle of, 1651 (Worcestershire)

Free. Easy access, but much of the battlefield lies under the streets of the town. Parking in town. Worcester east of the Severn. Walking round the city is rewarding, including New Street where Charles's house can be seen and Sidbury Gate with its monument.

The last major conflict of the English Civil Wars, Worcester was a battle between the ruling Parliamentarians and the would-be Charles II, aided by his Scottish allies. Charles marched south from Scotland, entering Worcester on 23 August with some 13,000 men to rest and gather supplies.

Cromwell, with an army perhaps twice that of the Royalists, attacked on 3 September. The Parliamentarian General Fleetwood launched an assault via pontoon bridges of boats over the River Teme in the south-west near Powick Bridge, while Cromwell attacked from the east of the city. The Scottish troops in the south resisted stoutly and Charles, watching from the tower of Worcester Cathedral, launched an attack on Cromwell's eastern advance. The streets of Worcester were filled with struggling soldiers; the bitter fighting raged for some three hours. Despite the valour of the Scottish foot, 'fighting with the butt-ends of their muskets when their ammunition was spent', Charles's forces were pushed back, eventually breaking in a rush to seek refuge in the city through the Sidbury Gate. Charles made his escape to France, avoiding capture, so the story goes, by hiding in an oak tree. Casualties were heavy but the numbers are uncertain.

A628

D E R B Y S H I R E

Buxton

Chesterfield

Worksop

A1

N O T T I N G H A M S H I R E

A614

A6

M1

Newark 1644
✕
Newark-on-Trent
✕ Stoke Field 1487

A1

A46

Derby

A50

Nottingham

A42

A46

Queen's Royal
Lancers Museum

A1

LEICESTERSHIRE

✕ Bosworth
1485

M69

Leicester

A47

A6

A43

N O R T H A M P T O N S H I R E

M1

Naseby 1645
✕

Kettering

A14

A508

A45

Northampton
✕ Northampton 1460

A5

Edgcote 1469
✕

Towcester

A43

EAST MIDLANDS

Edgcote, Battle of, 1469 (Northants)

Free. Farmland, fields. Good access and viewpoints on high ground. Parking possible. Five miles north-east of Banbury. Take the A361 Daventry road out of Banbury and turn right at Wardington onto the minor road to Culworth.

Edgcote was a lesser-known engagement of the Wars of the Roses, the first in the Lancastrian uprising of 1469–71 against the Yorkist King Edward IV. The battle came when Edward's army under the Earls of Pembroke and Devon, marching to join the king at Nottingham, encountered the rebel army under Robin of Redesdale on 26 July. There are two alternative sites to the battle, one involving fighting along and across the River Cherwell around the Trafford Bridge that carries the minor Culworth–Chipping Warden road over the river, the other on the Danesmoor plain about a mile to the south. Pembroke's force was initially the stronger, numbering perhaps 8000–9000 men against around 7000. However, either the night before the battle, or in its early stages, Devon withdrew his force, which included most of the Royalist archers. Redesdale opened the fight with his archers, forcing Pembroke, who could not reply, to attack with his knights and men-at-arms. This assault was initially successful, forcing the rebels back. However, the timely arrival of some 600 Lancastrian reinforcements under a John Clapham turned the scales and Pembroke's army, thinking the new enemy was the Earl of Warwick with his entire army, fled. Pembroke was captured and executed the next day.

There is currently no monument but an interpretation panel and a waymark trail are being prepared by the Battlefields Trust.

Newark, Battle of, 1644 (Notts)

Free. Usual access to Newark town. Town walk recommended, starting at the castle. Small museum in Mill Gate. Newark-on-Trent.

English Civil War battle fought on 21 March 1644. On 6 March the Parliamentarian Sir John Meldrum had attacked the Muskham Bridge and defeated one of Sir Richard Byron's Royalist regiments garrisoned at Newark, thus gaining control of 'The Island' – that part of Newark enclosed by the River Trent. Messengers were sent to summon help from Prince Rupert, who arrived with over 6500 men on 20 March. Approaching from the south, Rupert undertook a night flank march around the town to cut off Meldrum's retreat to the north-east and encamped on Beacon Hill. His attack the next day was successful and Meldrum found himself surrounded on the 'Island'. Rupert resolved to starve him into submission but a Roundhead regiment mutinied and Meldrum surrendered.

Battle of Edgcote: Trafford Bridge, the scene of heavy fighting (Battlefields Trust)

Bosworth, Battle of, 1485 (Leics)

££ (Battlefield Centre), otherwise free. Enclosed farmland but good access. Centre opening hours April–October 11 a.m.–5 p.m., November–December Sundays only, March Saturdays and Sundays only. Shop. Refreshments. Special events. Battle Trail. Parking (£1). Tel. 01455 290429. Eleven miles west of Leicester and two miles south of Market Bosworth. The battlefield is part of a country park signposted off the A447 and A444.

This is perhaps the most contentious battlefield in England as there are three possible sites; ongoing research and archaeological work may result in the official battlefield site moving south-west to the area around New Barn and North Farm (see map). In the meantime, the account below and map rely on our current understanding of events.

In 1485 the young Henry Tudor, the Lancastrian claimant to the throne and then exiled in France, invaded England to seek the throne from the Yorkist King Richard III. On 22 August both armies made for Ambion Hill, west of Sutton Cheney in Leicestershire and the obvious commanding feature in the area. Henry had some 5000 men, including 2000 French mercenaries, many armed with handguns, with the balance of his troops Welsh and English; Richard, a far more experienced commander, led a force of 8000. Each army had about a third of its strength in archers, who still bore the main brunt of shooting though artillery was becoming more effective. Knights had complex plate armour with elaborate jointing. Men-at-arms were also well protected but their jointing was less effective.

Richard's leading division under the Duke of Norfolk arrived first and deployed facing south-west, followed by the King's division with Northumberland's men at the rear. Henry's forces, led by Lord Oxford and arriving from the south-west, were dispirited to find a long line of glittering horsemen and men-at-arms fronted by bowmen on the ridge they had hoped to occupy. They were also obliged to skirt around marshy ground to the south of the hill before Oxford could deploy his van to face the enemy. If Richard was to make a successful charge downhill, this would have been the moment to do it, while the rebels' main division was still straggling up past the marsh. The chance was not taken. Instead Oxford was given time to deploy his archers, backed by billmen, and to bring forward his cannons. The battle began with an almost simultaneous, and not very effective, exchange of artillery fire and flights of arrows.

But Bosworth was a battle decided as much by treachery as by tactics or fighting ability. Henry, concerned about his lack of numbers and the cosmopolitan nature of his force, was counting on the support of Lord Stanley (2000 men) and his brother Sir William Stanley (2000 men) but neither would commit themselves before the battle since Lord Stanley's son was in Richard's hands and they wanted to see who looked like winning before coming off the fence. The King was well aware of the doubtful loyalty of the Stanleys and indeed of several more of his barons, including the Earl of Northumberland commanding his left wing.

Looking north to the battlefield from Crown Hill at Stoke Golding (Battlefields Trust)

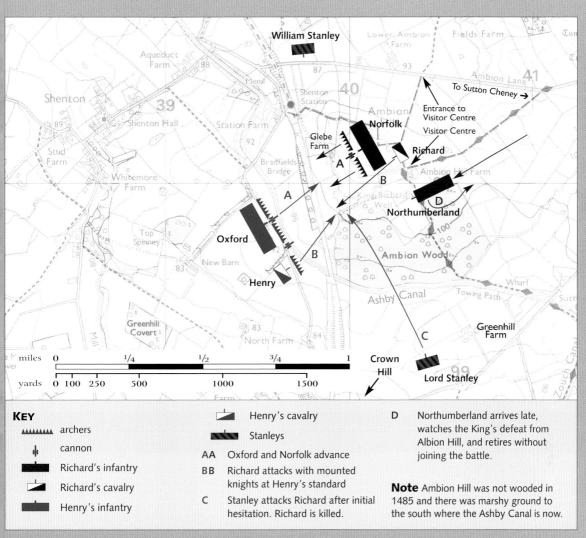

KEY

▲▲▲▲▲▲	archers
╬	cannon
▬	Richard's infantry
◥	Richard's cavalry
▬	Henry's infantry

◢ Henry's cavalry

◤◤◤◤ Stanleys

AA Oxford and Norfolk advance

BB Richard attacks with mounted knights at Henry's standard

C Stanley attacks Richard after initial hesitation. Richard is killed.

D Northumberland arrives late, watches the King's defeat from Albion Hill, and retires without joining the battle.

Note Ambion Hill was not wooded in 1485 and there was marshy ground to the south where the Ashby Canal is now.

The position of the Stanleys has never been established with certainty but it is quite possible Sir William had positioned himself north of Ambion Hill while Lord Stanley was to the south, perhaps around the present Greenhill Farm. Alternatively they could have joined forces. In any event they were well placed to watch events. Northumberland was hanging back and still west of Sutton Cheney when the forces of Norfolk and Oxford advanced on each other. This head-on clash took place around Glebe Farm. Richard, becoming aware of the Stanleys' treachery, ordered that Stanley's son be killed, but the execution party, fearing retribution, released their hostage unharmed. Richard, his crown around his helm, then led his mounted knights downhill to smash his way towards Henry's Red

Dragon standard. Knowing the King would never forgive his failure to act earlier, while Henry would be forever grateful for a timely intervention, Stanley at last ordered his trumpets to sound, dug in his spurs and led a charge into Richard's left flank. It was decisive, and it convinced Northumberland back on Ambion Hill to remain a spectator.

Richard, isolated and surrounded, died fighting having lost his horse, possibly in the marsh – the origin of Shakespeare's famous lines, 'A horse, a horse! My kingdom for a horse!' When Richard's death became known, his army melted away. There was little pursuit. Lord Stanley was handed Richard's crown and placed it on Henry's head, hailing him as King Henry VII. Richard's losses amounted to about 1000, Henry's to a mere 200.

Naseby, Battle of, 1645 (Northants)

Free. Open fields, farmland. Easy access by road but some restrictions for walking. Naseby village is six miles south-west of Market Harborough and best approached from the A508 via the minor roads through either Clipston or Haselbech villages.

Fought on 14 June 1645, Naseby was the decisive battle of the English Civil War, seeing the destruction of Charles I's army – only around 4000 Royalists escaped – and forming a crucial part in the chain of events that led to Charles's execution, Commonwealth rule and the subsequent restoration of a limited monarchy under Charles II. Perhaps only Hastings and the Battle of Britain in 1940 can be compared with Naseby in terms of its effect on how England is governed.

On 30 May, in order to draw Fairfax and his Parliamentarian army away from the King's headquarters in Oxford, a Royalist force stormed and sacked Leicester. This manoeuvre succeeded and Fairfax raised the siege of Oxford on 5 June to march north to confront the Royalists. The speed of his approach surprised the King, but at a council of war in the early hours of the 14th he decided to stand and fight, despite being heavily outnumbered.

As a result of early-morning reconnaissance by Fairfax and Cromwell (and Prince Rupert for the King)

both armies moved west. The King halted on Dust Hill two miles south of Market Harborough. There he deployed his army of around 9000 men, about half of whom were cavalry. Meanwhile Fairfax had formed his force of some 13,500 (6000 cavalry, 6500 infantry and 1000 dragoons) along Red Hill about a mile to the south. Both armies were drawn up in the conventional way with two or three lines of pike and musket-armed infantry in the centre and large bodies of cavalry on each flank. Cromwell commanded the cavalry on the Parliamentary right, while Rupert commanded the Royalist horse on their right. While the King kept some cavalry back in reserve in the second line, the only obviously significant tactic was the positioning by Fairfax of Colonel Okey's dragoons well forward, along the line of hedges (Sulby Hedges) on the left of the position. From there they were both protected by the hedge and able to fire into the flank of Rupert's force if they attacked.

The battle opened with an advance by the Royalist infantry down the slope, across Broad Moor and up the incline of Red Hill until they clashed with Fairfax's centre regiments, with 'push of pike'. Within a short while the Royalist pikemen began to push their opponents back over the crest and Rupert, seated on his horse near the present Prince

Broadmoor and Dust Hill viewed from the Parliamentary lines close to the battlefield monument (Battlefields Trust)

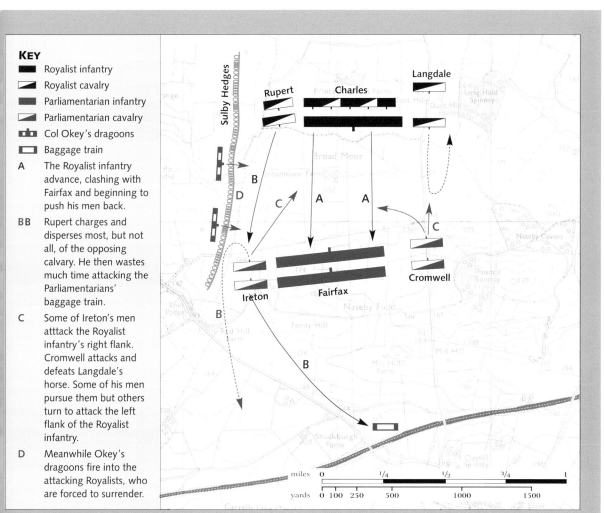

KEY

▬ Royalist infantry

◣ Royalist cavalry

▬ Parliamentarian infantry

◪ Parliamentarian cavalry

▭ Col Okey's dragoons

▭ Baggage train

A The Royalist infantry advance, clashing with Fairfax and beginning to push his men back.

BB Rupert charges and disperses most, but not all, of the opposing calvary. He then wastes much time attacking the Parliamentarians' baggage train.

C Some of Ireton's men atttack the Royalist infantry's right flank. Cromwell attacks and defeats Langdale's horse. Some of his men pursue them but others turn to attack the left flank of the Royalist infantry.

D Meanwhile Okey's dragoons fire into the attacking Royalists, who are forced to surrender.

Rupert Farm, saw his chance and led his 2000 horse in a spirited charge into the opposing cavalry under General Ireton. This sent the Parliamentary horse on the extreme left reeling with Rupert dashing after them in an enthusiastic pursuit. Unfortunately he then wasted an hour trying to overcome the enemy baggage guard before rallying and returning to the field, to find the situation had dramatically changed for the worse for the King.

Ireton, with commendable initiative, had ridden with the remainder of his cavalry onto the exposed right flank of the Royalist infantry. However, he was wounded and captured and it was only after Fairfax had reinforced his centre with reserve infantry that his greatly superior numbers began to tell. Meanwhile on the Parliamentary right Cromwell had led his horse in a successful attack against the outnumbered Royalist cavalry under Langdale. While some of Cromwell's men chased the fleeing enemy off the field, Cromwell turned his remaining squadrons in onto the struggling Royalist infantry's left. On the other flank Okey mounted his dragoons and attacked their right. These attacks were too much even for the King's veteran infantry – they were ridden down and forced to surrender. On his return Rupert's men, on exhausted horses, were unable to retrieve the situation.

Parliament had lost a mere 200 men. The King, although he escaped the field, had lost 1000 dead, 4500 captured, his artillery, his baggage, his private papers and, effectively, his throne.

Naseby is well worth visiting, as the new alignment of the A14 has not cut across the battlefield. A good view is obtained by following the Naseby–Sibbertoft road and standing by the Cromwell monument. However, the rights of way to explore on foot are limited.

Northampton, Battle of, 1460 (Northants)

Free. Open ground reasonable access with limited parking near Delapre Abbey (near the centre of the battlefield) one mile south of town centre. Take the A45 from M1 junction 15 to town centre, straight across at the next two roundabouts and then turn right before crossing the river into Ramsome Road. The battlefield is in the open ground beyond the end of the road.

A Wars of the Roses battle. The summer of 1460 saw King Henry VI's Lancastrian forces gathering in the Midlands in anticipation of an Irish invasion led by the Duke of York. In the king's absence London capitulated to York's son, Edward, Earl of March, who advanced north supported by the Earls of Warwick and Salisbury and Lord Fauconberg with some 7,000 men. As they approached Northampton on 10 July they found their path blocked by 5,000 Lancastrians under the Duke of Buckingham. He had taken up a strong position with the River Nene at his back and his flanks and front protected by a ditch, field fortifications and cannons. An attempt by Warwick to speak to the king under a flag of truce was rejected by Buckingham, but unbeknown to him one of his commanders, Lord Grey of Ruthin, had treacherously agreed to assist the Yorkists. The three divisions under Warwick, Salisbury and Fauconberg attacked simultaneously in pouring rain, which prevented the Lancastrians from firing their cannons.

Nevertheless the attackers had difficulty in struggling over the slippery defences until Grey's 'men met them and seizing them by the hand hauled them into the embattled field'. Within half an hour the Lancastrian army collapsed, Buckingham was slain and King Henry a prisoner.

The Queen's Royal Lancers' Regimental Museum (Northants)

Free, but entry to Belvoir Castle ££££. 11 a.m. to 5 p.m. April–September, Saturday – Thursday. Guided tours. School visits. Research facilities. Shop. Restaurant. Parking. Picnic area. Tel. 01476870262. www.qrl.uk.com
Belvoir Castle is 6 miles west of Grantham on the A1 and 12 miles from Melton Mowbray. Signposted from A1, A52, A607 and A46.

The museum, set in the beautiful rooms of Beauvoir Castle, tells the story of four cavalry regiments – 5th, 6th, 17th and 21st Lancers, now amalgamated into the Queen's Royal Lancers. Twenty superb displays feature arms, uniforms, medals, silver and personal artefacts. Actions covered include the American War of Independence, Waterloo, the cavalry charges at Aliwal (India), Balaklava (the famous Light Brigade), Ulundi (Zulu War) and Omdurman (Sudan). They also cover the Indian Mutiny, Boer War, both World Wars and the Gulf War. Pride of place goes to the bugle that was blown during the Charge of the Light Brigade and a 100-year old bar of chocolate from the Boer War.

Stoke Field, Battle of, 1487 (Notts)

Free. Easy access, mostly fields. Parking in East Stoke. Take the A46 south from Newark to East Stoke. Take the road to Stoke Hall from the village crossroads – this leads to the top of the ridge on which Lincoln deployed.

The final battle of the Wars of the Roses, Stoke Field was fought on 16 June 1487 between a rebel Yorkist force of about 8000 men, 2000 of whom were German mercenaries, under the Earl of Lincoln, and the royalists with 12,000 nominally commanded by King Henry VII, but actually under the Earl of Oxford. Lincoln crossed the Trent at Fiskerton and deployed with mostly unarmoured Irish on his left, the Germans in the centre and his division on the right protected by a bend in the river.

Oxford pressed forward with an advanced guard and took the full onslaught of Lincoln's division and the Germans unaided. After a two-hour struggle Oxford was forced back. On seeing this the Irish dashed forward, only to be met by two more English divisions whose well-drilled troops soon dispersed their ill-disciplined enemy. Trapped by the river at their backs, Lincoln's army was cut down, with casualties for both sides totalling 7000.

A fragment of ridge and furrow on the slope survives in good condition at the battle of Northampton (Battlefields Trust)

DEFENCE AGAINST INVASION

Britain's best defence against invasion has been provided by nature – the English Channel, which has delayed migration and deterred enemies since the beginning of history. The Channel functions as a huge moat made dangerous by shoals and currents, wind and tides. It requires a massive logistical effort to get an army across, and if the coast is defended then the difficulties for an invader are doubled. There is no more risky operation of war than an opposed landing on a hostile coast; Caesar's landing on the pebble beach at Deal over 2000 years ago almost failed when the British warriors confronted the legionaries as they waded ashore.

Control of the Channel has always been crucial for the defence of Britain. The Roman and Norman invasions succeeded because their landings were unopposed. Since 1066 three major attempts to invade Britain have failed. The Navy (helped by violent storms) defeated the Spanish Armada in 1588 and, over 200 years later, prevented the French, under Napoleon, from launching their vast invasion flotilla, assembled for years around Boulogne. Then, in 1940, the Royal Air Force shredded the German invasion plan in the skies above southern England. For a thousand years the defence of Britain's coastline has absorbed a high proportion of the country's military effort in terms of men and money. There have always been three strands to Britain's defence – the Channel itself, the Royal Navy (and latterly the RAF) and fixed coastal defences. All along our southern and eastern coasts in particular are scattered the remains of forts, castles, gun emplacements, Martello towers, bunkers, pillboxes, ditches, canals and anti-tank obstacles. Many have disappeared, many have been built over, many more removed. Nevertheless, we can still visit coastal sites today and see examples of all the defences listed above. Some like Dover Castle, much modified and extended, have been in use since they were built.

THE SAXON SHORE FORTS

The Romans built these ten forts in the late third century AD along the south-east coast to guard against increasing incursions and piracy by Germanic tribes including Angles, Saxons and Jutes. The only written source for them is a late-fourth-century document called the *Notitia Dignitatum* ('Worthy of Record'), which records the commander of these forts as the 'Count of the Saxon Shore'. Most were rectangular in shape, with walls up to 15ft thick and 25ft high and round towers projecting at intervals and at the corners. As originally built they stood on the shoreline but today the sea has advanced at some sites such as Walton Castle and Reculver, washing part or all of the

remains away. At others it has retreated leaving them landlocked, as at Richborough. After the Roman Army withdrew in 409 several sites acquired Anglo-Saxon churches and then Norman castles. The best-preserved example is Porchester in Hampshire.

Well worth a visit
Pevensey, Sussex *p. 44*
Portchester, Hampshire *p. 44*
Burgh Castle, Norfolk *p. 85*

THE 'DARK AGES'

From the departure of the Roman Army in 409 until the arrival of the Normans under William the Conqueror in 1066, Britain was subjected to countless raids and invasions. The Angles, Saxons and Jutes landed in ever growing numbers from across the North Sea. They liked what they saw and stayed, pushing the Romano-Britons westwards. This gradual encroachment continued until about the turn of the sixth century when the Saxon advance was halted and even pushed back by the efforts of the legendary King Arthur, whose court was supposedly centred on South Cadbury Castle. Although the stories of Arthur drawing the sword from the stone and his knights of the round table may be false, Britons, under a forceful and talented military leader, did give the Saxons a bloody nose at the Battle of Mount Badon in *c.*500 (p. 17). Some seventy-seven years later the Saxons finally triumphed over the Britons at the decisive Battle of Dyrham or Deorham (p. 14).

The next wave of invaders who swept in across the North Sea and Channel were the Vikings from what we now know as Scandinavia. Powerful and brutal, they came initially to pillage, rape and loot. The first to suffer a ghastly death were the unfortunate, defenceless monks at Lindisfarne in 793, and by 840 full-blooded assaults by thousands of warriors began. The islands of Orkney, Shetland and the Hebrides fell. In the south too the Saxons proved a soft target. By 875 the Vikings had overrun East Anglia, Northumbria and Mercia and forced the Wessex King Alfred to take refuge at Athelney, deep in the Somerset marches – where according to tradition he burnt the cakes! The Vikings had done what the Saxons had done to the Britons – driven them westwards. Even Alfred's victory at Ethandun (p. 13) in 878, although it checked the Viking advance and saved Wessex, could not drive them back. By the time the Normans arrived the Celts, Romans, Angles, Saxons, Jutes, Norsemen and Danes had successfully invaded England. The Normans were the last invaders to conquer Britain.

Offa's Dyke, near Edenhope Hill in Shropshire

The Dark Ages saw the building of numerous long defensive dykes or ditches, not to stop invaders from landing on the coast but as barriers to enemies advancing inland. The main ones are still highly visible over many miles of our countryside and most make for excellent walking. The longest and best known is Offa's Dyke, which runs from the Severn estuary for 120 miles, although there are gaps, northwards to the Dee estuary at Basingwerk, where there was a Mercian fort. Designed to deter raids from Wales into southern England, it was built on the orders of Offa, King of Mercia in the late eighth century. It marked and guarded the frontier, with a bank fronted to the west by a deep ditch, its bottom 25ft from the top of the bank, although whether it was guarded and patrolled regularly throughout its length is highly unlikely. Nevertheless, archaeologists have recently discovered traces of a wooden palisade in some parts and a stone wall in others. Perhaps it was the Anglo-Saxon equivalent of Hadrian's Wall. Whatever its main purpose, today its course makes for some wonderful walking through beautiful countryside.

A much shorter (and earlier) stretch of earth bank, built by the Saxons as part of a network of defensive banks and ditches in East Anglia and what is now Cambridgeshire, still presents an impressive barrier near Newmarket – indeed part of it overlooks the racecourse and makes a handy grandstand for passers-by. This is the Devil's Ditch or Dyke, which runs in a straight seven-and-a-half-mile line just east of Newmarket. Just six miles to the south-east is Fleam Dyke. In places its rampart still rises to 50ft above the bottom of the ditch and it is best seen at Mutlow Hill, an ancient Bronze Age barrow.

The Wansdyke, built in the fifth and sixth centuries, faces north and was probably intended to help the Britons stem the advance of the Saxons. It runs from Portishead on the Bristol Channel south to Bath and thence eastwards north of Devizes, along the line of the Wiltshire Downs, to just south of Marlborough through Severnake Forest to Chisbury Camp. Many stretches make for fine walks with superb views.

Well worth a visit

Offa's Dyke pp. 20, 66, 125
West Wansdyke p. 23
Devil's Dyke p. 86
Fleam Dyke p. 86

HENRY VIII AND ELIZABETH I: THE BIRTH OF THE ARTILLERY FORT

After the Dark Ages came the Norman conquest and the start of traditional English (and Welsh and Scottish) castle building (see pp. 128–31). The castle was the linchpin of military strategy for nearly 500 years, but by the time Henry VIII ascended the throne in 1509 gunpowder dominated siegecraft, and the castles' walls could not cope with the cannon. Henry VIII is usually remembered more for disposing of his wives and inadvertently founding the Church of England than for his military record. However, this does him an injustice, as he was an enthusiastic campaigner – especially against the French – and eager to be at the forefront of military innovation. Later known as the father of the Royal Navy, Henry not only poured money into shipbuilding but also added the naval dockyards of Deptford and Woolwich to that set up by his father at Portsmouth. He encouraged the design of larger and faster ships (the *Mary Rose* at Portsmouth is a fine example) and developed a permanent establishment of ships, men and a naval administration.

From 1539 Henry began to fortify the coast from Hull round to Milford Haven with a new style of artillery fort; the stones from the recently dissolved monasteries came in handy for their construction. Not castles in the old sense, they were certainly not designed as residences or refuges for the nobility; instead they were small and squat, built to house a permanent garrison of regular soldiers under a master gunner. Their low profile and thick walls made poor targets for ships at sea, while their heavy cannons could easily smash wooden hulls. These forts were usually circular with two, four or even six protruding, semi-circular bastions with guns on the roof and in the lower gallery. Some had a low central tower carrying a third tier of cannons. These forts were surrounded by moats, with the walls having small handgun openings through which they could engage any enemy that came in close.

The most spectacular of Henry's other military innovations was the setting up of a national armoury in the Tower of London. He had all the old equipment removed before restocking the Tower with huge quantities of up-to-date weapons. A survey of these stocks at his death revealed 20,100 pikes, 6700 billhooks, 3060 bows, 13,050 sheaves of arrows (at 24 a sheaf, so 313,200 arrows), 23,040 bowstrings, 7700 handguns, 64 brass guns and 351 iron guns of all sizes. Henry also established and built up a field artillery train – although he himself was an archer of considerable skill able to defeat the best bowmen in his personal guard. Finally, he established a royal armour factory to produce fine armour for himself or as gifts for foreign princes.

Queen Elizabeth I, like her father, recognized the Navy's crucial role in defence of the realm, and encouraged privateers to go on the offensive against Spanish treasure ships. Most schoolchildren, even today, know that it was under Elizabeth that Sir Francis Drake (helped by the weather) smashed the Spanish Armada in 1588. She improved and expanded Henry's coastal forts. In particular Upnor Castle was built on the Medway to protect the docks at Chatham, Carisbrooke Castle was updated, Berwick's defences strengthened and the smaller forts protecting Plymouth modernized.

Pendennis Castle, built by Henry VIII to defend Falmouth Harbour

Well worth a visit

Pendennis Castle, Cornwall *p. 20*
Portland Castle, Dorset *p. 20*
St Mawes Castle, Cornwall *p. 21*
Carisbrooke Castle, Isle of Wight *p. 35*
Deal Castle, Kent *p. 36*
Upnor Castle, Kent *p. 49*
Berwick-on-Tweed Barracks *p. 99*
Lindisfarne Castle, Northumberland *p. 107*

NAPOLEONIC DEFENCES

From 1793 until the Battle of Waterloo in 1815 Britain was almost continuously at war with Republican France. Until 1805, when the French and Spanish fleets were destroyed at Trafalgar, the threat of invasion from across the Channel was acute. All along the French Channel coast, but centred on Boulogne, Napoleon's army was readied and rehearsed for invasion. Over 150,000 men and hundreds of transport vessels were assembled awaiting favourable weather and the protection of the French fleet.

It seemed certain that the landings, if they came, would be in Kent and Sussex, so strenuous efforts were made to strengthen and improve defences, particularly in the south-east and along the south coast. The first line of fixed defences built consisted of 'Martello towers', numbered from one to seventy-four. They got their name from a stone watchtower on Mortella Point in Corsica that had held at bay two British warships and inflicted sixty casualties during a British attack on the island in 1794. Martello towers were small oval-shaped gun towers about 35ft high with exceedingly thick walls and a single gun firing from the roof. Some were surrounded by a ditch with a drawbridge, others were accessed by ladder. They were sited sufficiently close to be able to support each other with flanking fire. There was no invasion, so the towers never fired a shot in anger. Another series of twenty-nine towers was constructed along the Suffolk and Essex coasts but by the time they were finished it was ten years after Trafalgar and Napoleon was safely confined on St Helena. Of the south coast towers twenty-five remain, nine more or less in their original condition. Some of these are now private residences but towers nos. 3 and 24 are open to visitors.

The other main defensive work designed to help defeat a Napoleonic thrust for London from the south coast was the 30ft-wide Royal Military Canal, which was begun in 1804 and runs for 28 miles between Hythe and Winchelsea. It was used both as a barrier and for military barges. There was a towpath on the coastal side, and a rampart and military road on the landward side. Every 600 yards earthwork gun positions were constructed and at every bridge a guardhouse. Today the canal has a public footpath along its full length, making an excellent long-distance trail with numerous interpretation panels. It is also a haven for the wildlife of the Romney Marsh, and used by the Environment Agency to manage water levels across much of the marsh.

Well worth a visit
Fort Amherst, Kent *p. 38*
Martello Towers nos. 3 and 24 *p. 39*
Royal Military Canal *p. 48*
Harwich Redoubt, Essex *p. 86*

Martello Tower no. 3, now a local history museum

VICTORIAN DEFENCES

Prime Minister Palmerston initiated the building of a series of modern artillery forts in the 1840s to protect major ports. Within ten years seventy-six forts and batteries had been completed or were under construction, of which nineteen were land forts with the remainder sited to guard ports. There has never been a more intensive and extensive fort-building programme in so short a time in Britain. The main effort was around Plymouth, Portsmouth and Chatham. Portsdown Hill, north of Portsmouth, was studded with four major and three minor forts, of which Fort Nelson is the most interesting to visit. No fewer than eleven forts or batteries guard Plymouth, of which Crownhill Fort was the key. But they became known as 'Palmerston Follies' because of the huge expense involved, and with the rapid advance in steam-powered warships, the increased range of guns and the greatly improved destructive power of shells, many of the forts were almost obsolete by the time they were finished. In 1859 a Royal Commission into the Defences of the United Kingdom Fortifications was scathing of their value.

Well worth a visit
Crownhill Fort, Devon *p. 12*
Nothe Fort, Dorset *p. 20*
Fort Brockhurst, Hampshire *p. 38*
Fort Nelson, Hampshire *p. 38*

20TH-CENTURY DEFENCES

One of the Second World War's most far-reaching effects on people living in Britain was its transformation of the landscape with a vast programme of building. Over 20,000 pillboxes were constructed, together with hundreds of miles of defensive ditches, anti-tank obstacles, hundreds of airfields, ten of thousands of gun emplacements, radar stations, air-raid shelters, Observer Corps posts, military camps and other structures. Their purpose was the defence of Britain from invasion, air attack and flying bombs. By the late summer of 1940, as the Battle of Britain raged overhead, these defences were rapidly growing, their construction in the hands of a workforce numbering many hundreds of thousands.

The comprehensive strategic defence of Britain involved coastal defence, inland defence in depth, airfields and airfield defence, anti-aircraft defences and naval and harbour defences. The main feature of the

inland, or defence in depth, strategy was a series of stop lines designed to block and delay enemy forces if they succeeded in landing in strength, to allow the field army time to concentrate at the decisive point. The map shows only the more important of these lines. Many readers will surely know of at least one pillbox now filled with mud and rubbish standing forlornly in the corner of a farmer's field. Hundreds remain because, although farmers were offered a demolition fee of £5 per pillbox after the war, demolition was often more trouble than it was worth. According to John Hellis, the Field Co-ordinator for the Defence of Britain Project, the most complete surviving line runs from Seaton in Devon to Bridgwater in Somerset, with about 280 surviving pillboxes and machine-gun emplacements every few hundred yards. In places some are still in use. A few have been converted or incorporated into uses including stores, a pub cellar, a golf course tee (the roof), an ice cream kiosk and a public lavatory!

The 'Cold War' saw the development of underground nuclear command posts and seats of regional government such as that in the chalk cliffs under Dover Castle. Dover Castle is a remarkable example of a medieval castle converted into a Napoleonic fortress and further adapted during two World Wars and during the Cold War. In the Second World War the 45th Infantry Division considered even the ruins of the Roman Saxon Shore fort at Pevensey Castle a key defensive point.

Principal Stop Lines against Invasion in WW2

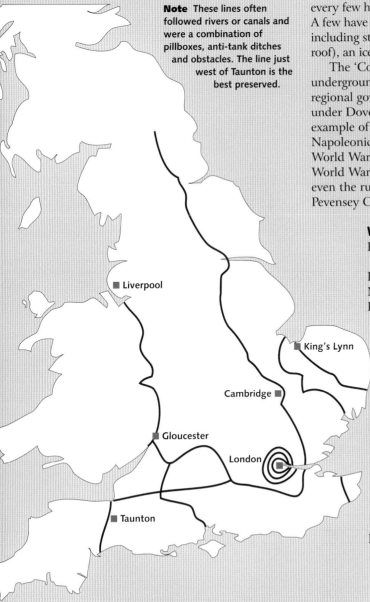

Note These lines often followed rivers or canals and were a combination of pillboxes, anti-tank ditches and obstacles. The line just west of Taunton is the best preserved.

Well worth a visit
Half-Moon Battery, Pendennis Castle, Cornwall *p. 13*
Dover Castle, Kent *p. 36*
Newhaven Fort, East Sussex *p. 44*
Kelvedon Hatch Nuclear Bunker, Essex *p. 87*
Tilbury Fort, Essex *p. 91*
Scotland's Secret Bunker, Fife *p. 147*

and the following Battle of Britain sites or museums
Battle of Britain Museum, Kent *p. 32*
RAF Manston History Museum, Kent *p. 46*
Spitfire and Hurricane Memorial Building, Kent *p. 48*
Tangmere Military Aviation Museum, West Sussex *p. 49*
RAF Museum Hendon *p. 53*
Battle of Britain Memorial Flight Visitors' Centre, Lincolnshire *p. 85*
Imperial War Museum Duxford, Cambridgeshire *p. 87*

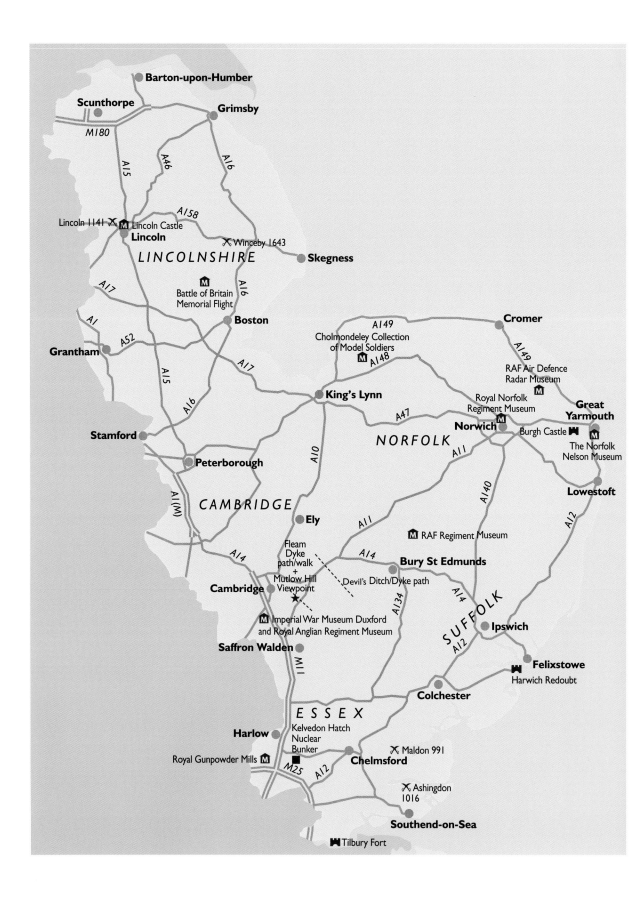

Barton-upon-Humber

Scunthorpe

M180

A15

A46

Grimsby

A16

A158

Lincoln 1141 ⚔ 🅜 Lincoln Castle
Lincoln
⚔ Winceby 1643

LINCOLNSHIRE

Skegness

A17

A1

A16

🅜 Battle of Britain
Memorial Flight

A16

Boston

A52

Grantham

A17

A15

A16

Cromer

A149

Cholmondeley Collection
of Model Soldiers
🅜 A148

A149

RAF Air Defence
Radar Museum
🅜

King's Lynn

A47

Royal Norfolk
Regiment Museum
🅜
Norwich

**Great
Yarmouth**
🅜
Burgh Castle ⚔

The Norfolk
Nelson Museum

Stamford

A1(M)

Peterborough

CAMBRIDGE

A10

A11

NORFOLK

A11

A140

A12

Lowestoft

Ely

A11

🅜 RAF Regiment Museum

Fleam
Dyke
path/walk
+
Mutlow Hill
Viewpoint
★

A14

A14

Bury St Edmunds

Devil's Ditch/Dyke path

Cambridge

🅜 Imperial War Museum Duxford
and Royal Anglian Regiment Museum

A134

A4

SUFFOLK

A12

Ipswich

Felixstowe
⛉
Harwich Redoubt

Saffron Walden

M11

Colchester

ESSEX

Kelvedon Hatch
Nuclear
Bunker
⚔ Maldon 991

Harlow

Royal Gunpowder Mills 🅜

M25

A12

Chelmsford

⚔ Ashingdon
1016

Southend-on-Sea

⛉ Tilbury Fort

EASTERN

Ashingdon (Assundun), Battle of, 1016 (Essex)

Free. Farmland. Limited access. Six miles north of Southend-on-Sea. There is some dispute as to the precise location, but it was probably halfway between the villages of Ashingdon and Canewdon.

A battle between the Danes under Canute (Cnut) and the English under Edmund. The Danes had completed a successful raid and, laden with booty, were making their way to their ships at Burnham-on-Crouch when Edmund caught up with them just east of Ashingdon. Canute turned to fight. Edmund began the battle by charging downhill at the head of his division. After advancing a considerable distance the English clashed with the Danish line, which had halted on a slight rise just east of the present Gadebrook Farm. Unfortunately for Edmund his right wing under Edric had declined to follow in support and thus exposed the English right flank, which was surrounded and perished to a man, although Edmund managed to retreat with the nucleus of his force. He died in 1017 and Canute was acknowledged as king of the whole country.

Battle of Britain Memorial Flight (Lincolnshire)

££ (for guided tours). Usual hours. Shop. Refreshments (May–October). Picnic area. Guided tours. Parking. Tel. 01526 342330. RAF Coningsby is south of the village and signposted from the A153 from Sleaford.

The Battle of Britain Memorial Flight operates a Lancaster, five Spitfires, two Hurricanes and a Dakota. It is possible to see these historic aircraft at their base at RAF Coningsby. These aircraft are not museum pieces and can be seen flying at a variety of air shows in the summer.

Burgh Castle (Norfolk) ⌗

Free. Open access. Parking nearby. Three miles west of Great Yarmouth, Norfolk. Signposted off the A143 and a five-minute walk from Burgh Castle church.

A Roman fort of the Saxon Shore. Although it only has three walls still standing, Burgh Castle is an impressive monument with walls up to 16ft high. The bastions, one of which has collapsed and rolled several yards down the hill, would have held light catapults or ballistas. The Normans constructed a motte in the centre but this was demolished in the 19th century.

The impressive remains of Burgh Castle

The Cholmondeley Collection of Model Soldiers: this painstakingly detailed scene is a recreation of the 1890 war in Algeria

Cholmondeley Collection of Model Soldiers (Norfolk)

£££. Open Wednesdays, Thursdays and Bank Holiday Mondays from Easter Sunday to 30 September, 2–5.30 p.m. Shop. Tea room. Parking. Tel. 01485 528569. Off the A148 King's Lynn to Cromer road.

Displayed in Houghton House, the collection consists of over 20,000 models, many arranged in battle scenes, together with individual models ranging from large china figures to tiny lead replicas. There are also a number of military paintings and prints on a variety of military subjects.

Devil's Dyke Path (Cambridgeshire)

Free. Open access. Two miles SW of Newmarket, from the village of Burwell SE to Ditton Green, skirting the southern end of Newmarket racecourse. For a quick visit it is easiest to see beside the racecourse.

A seven-mile-long, massive embankment thrown up by the Anglo-Saxons some 1450 years ago to defend against tribal invasions (see also p. 000), now preserved as a Site of Special Scientific Interest under Cambridge County Council. It makes for a splendid walk although there are two major gaps: one made in the Second World War to facilitate the take-off of heavily laden bombers from the nearby temporary airfield, the other to permit the passage of the A14.

Fleam Dyke Path (Cambridgeshire)

Free. Open access. It runs SE from the village of Fulham east of Cambridge. The best viewing point is Mutlow Hill close to the A11.

Another Dark Ages defensive embankment over three miles long (see also p. 80). It is still an impressive barrier with its 11ft ditch and 50ft embankment, which would have been topped by a palisade, providing a formidable defensive work.

Harwich Redoubt (Essex)

£. Usual hours, 1 May–31 August and Sundays throughout the year. Shop. Refreshments. Guided tours. Re-enactment over August Bank Holiday weekend. Tel. 01255 503429. Main Road, Harwich, Essex.

Built to keep Napoleon out of Harwich, this is the largest fort of its kind in the country and is being restored by the Harwich Society. Circular and surrounded by a moat, it took three years to build – the labour force being augmented by French prisoners. On completion in 1808 it mounted ten 24-pounder guns and housed a regiment of soldiers with sufficient stores, food and ammunition to withstand a lengthy siege. In the centre was a well. The redoubt now houses a fine display of large guns, uniforms and related exhibits.

Harwich Redoubt – this aerial view shows its circular layout

Imperial War Museum Duxford (Cambridgeshire)

£££. Usual hours. Shop. Bookstall. Refreshments. Picnic areas. Guided tours. Special events. Air shows. Parking. Tel. 01223 835000. duxford.iwm.org.uk Duxford, near Cambridge. Easily accessible and signposted from A14, A1, M1 and the north.

The IWM Duxford has probably the finest collection of military and civil aircraft in the world. In addition, the museum's land warfare collection is the best in Britain and includes the regimental museum of the Royal Anglian Regiment (see also p. 90). The American Air Museum is an amazing collection, standing as a memorial to the 30,000 US airmen who died on missions from Britain during the Second World War.

Kelvedon Hatch Nuclear Bunker (Essex)

££. Usual hours March–October, closed Mondays–Wednesdays November–February. Shop. Refreshments. Picnic area. Orienteering trail. Parking. Tel. 01277 364883. Kelvedon Hall Lane, Kelvedon Hatch, Brentwood. Access from the A414 Chelmsford to Ongar then the A1023 to Brentwood.

This Cold War nuclear bunker was built in 1952, using 40,000 tons of concrete to house a devolved central government and military commanders. Cunningly concealed 75ft below the Essex countryside, it could accommodate 110 tons of equipment and 600 personnel. The three storeys include government administrative rooms, a massive power and filtration plant, huge communications room, a BBC radio studio, scientists' centre, canteen, dormitories and sickbay. Fortunately the need to use it has never arisen.

Lincoln, Battle of, 1141 (Lincolnshire)

Free. Limited access. Limited parking. Although there is disagreement on the site, it is probably on the sloping ground leading down to the canal immediately west of the old city walls.

This battle between the forces of Ranulf, Earl of Chester, and King Stephen, the nephew of the deceased King Henry I, was a part of the strug-

Lincoln Castle, with a view of the spectacular cathedral behind

gle for succession after Henry's death in 1135, which had left only a daughter, Matilda, as heir. In February 1141 Stephen held Lincoln Castle and Ranulf marched up from the south to attack him. The rebels crossed the Fossdyke, a Roman canal linking the rivers Trent and Witham that is still in use, and deployed in three divisions with their backs to the canal. The King's army deployed from the west gate of the city and formed up with mounted troops on either flank and infantry in the centre. Ranulf's army advanced to the attack intent on a hand-to-hand mêlée. The royal right faltered and fled before blades had crossed. On the other flank the King's cavalry were initially more successful and, scattering some lightly armed Welsh, crashed into the main rebel cavalry force. However, at the crucial moment Ranulf's infantry centre was able to intervene and the remaining royal horsemen disintegrated in panic. The King fought on gallantly in the centre for some time, wielding first a sword and then a battleaxe. He was eventually struck down by a

stone and captured. It was total defeat and Lincoln was pillaged and burnt. Matilda became queen but only for a matter of months.

Lincoln Castle

££. Usual hours. Shop. Refreshments. Picnic areas in grounds. Guided tours (summer only). Special events. Heraldry centre. Tel. 01522 5111068. www.lincolncastle.com/lincoln_castle.htm Castle Hill, Lincoln.

This is one of Britain's better Norman strongholds, with a six-acre bailey that houses several former prison buildings and the modern Crown Court – the castle was a prison for more than 900 years, and some convicted felons were executed on the walls. There is a good circuit of the high walls and a wall walk as well as fine views from the Observatory Tower, and several exhibitions including one of the surviving copies of Magna Carta. An extensive calendar of special events runs throughout the summer. The only distraction is the magnificent nearby cathedral that dwarfs the castle and is a must for visitors.

Looking across the causeway to Northey Island (Battlefields Trust)

Maldon, Battle of, 991 (Essex)

Free. Open access. Parking possible. About two miles east of Maldon, the site is reached by taking the B1018 off the A414 and following it to the lane leading to South House Farm. Visitors must then proceed on foot down the lane across farmland to the river. The causeway is still there, widened to allow vehicles to cross, so it is easy to imagine the dramatic events of over a thousand years ago.

In August 991 a Viking raiding force under the leadership of Svein Forkbeard sailed up the River Blackwater and disembarked a substantial force onto the island of Northey, east of the modern town of Maldon. Northey was linked to the mainland by a tidal causeway and was therefore an ideal base from which to sally forth to loot and burn. On 10 August, before the tide had receded to reveal the causeway, the Saxon army approached and formed up opposite the crossing place. It was commanded by an elderly chieftain with snow-white hair, who stood some 6ft 9in tall and was called Byrhtnoth.

The two armies were now within shouting distance of each other. A Danish herald demanded that the Saxons avoid destruction by handing over tribute. Byrhtnoth refused, at the same time challenging the Danes to attack. There followed a long wait for the tide to fall. When the water was ankle deep the Danes rushed forward, only to be confronted by three Saxon warriors blocking the narrow passage. This negated the Vikings' advantage of numbers and would reduce any battle to an endless series of individual combats. The Danes shouted across for the Saxons to withdraw to allow their army over and thus allow a 'proper' battle. Byrhtnoth agreed, ordering his force to fall back a few hundred yards and form a long shield wall, presumably because he wanted the opportunity to destroy the raiders, not see them sail away to attack somewhere else.

Forkbeard then launched his assault in a wedge formation after an ineffective archery duel. The close combat that followed was brutal and bloody. Byrhtnoth was in the thick of the fight, head and shoulders above the warriors hacking and thrusting around him. He was first wounded by a spear thrust, and then again by a javelin, which a warrior beside him named Wulfmaer pulled out and threw back. Byrhtnoth drew his sword but a blow sliced through the muscle and sinews of his arm rendering further fighting impossible. As the ancient Anglo-Saxon poem of the battle describes it, 'his golden-hilted sword fell to earth; he could not use his hard blade nor wield a weapon'. His enemies crowded round and hacked him to death, finally cutting off his head as a gruesome trophy.

The loss of their chieftain demoralized many, but not all, of the Saxons. While a considerable number fled the field, a resolute group surrounded Byrhtnoth's headless body and fought on with great courage and ferocity. This 'last stand' prolonged the battle for several hours. By the time the last Saxon was cut down the Danes had suffered considerably and were exhausted. Nevertheless, the victors were granted some £10,000 in tribute. Byrhtnoth's body was recovered and buried in Ely Cathedral, a lump of wax replacing the head. His skeleton was discovered in 1796, enabling his exceptional height to be verified.

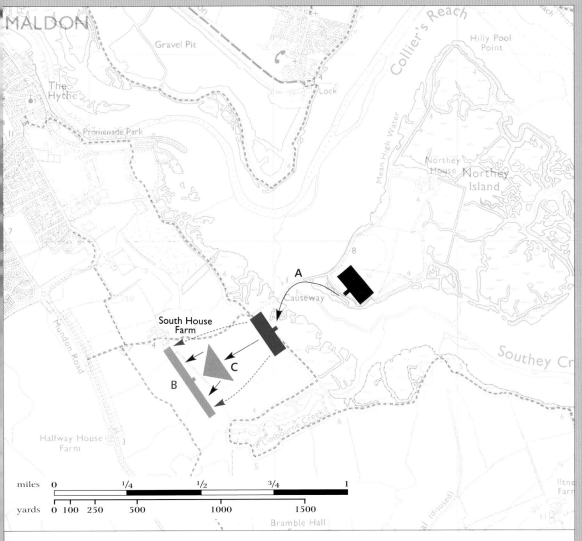

KEY

- Danes (under Sven Forkbeard)
- Saxons (under Byrhtnoth)

A   With the tide low the Danes attempt to attack across the causeway but find their progress blocked by a few Saxons.

B   On Forkbeard's request the Saxons withdraw to allow the Danes across so that a 'proper' battle can be fought.

C   The Danes attack the Saxon shield wall in a wedge-shaped formation. Byrhtnoth is killed and some Saxons flee, leaving others to fight to the last.

Norfolk Nelson Museum

£. Usual hours. Shop. Education room.
Outdoor play area. Car parks nearby.
Tel. 01493 850698.
www.nelson-museum.co.uk
26 South Quay, Great Yarmouth.

A small museum devoted to the life and times of Lord Nelson. The Naval Room illustrates Nelson's life from his Norfolk childhood, through his battles to his death at Trafalgar. Interactive activities explain knots, flags and navigation. The Merton Room shows the visitor how he looked, describes and illustrates his various wounds and illnesses and tells the story of his passionate and adulterous relationship with Emma, Lady Hamilton. In the 'Below Decks Experience', among the hammocks and mess tables, you see and hear something of how a seaman on the *Victory* lived. There is also a room devoted to civilian life under 'Mad King George', where you can try on wigs and clothes worn in Nelson's time.

RAF Air Defence Radar Museum (Norfolk)

££. Usual hours every Tuesday and Thursday April–end October, all Bank Holiday Mondays and every second Saturday each month all year. Shop. Refreshments. Picnic area. Guided tours. Parking. Tel. 01692 633309.
www.radarmuseum.co.uk RAF Neatishead, Norwich. Off the A1062 near Horning; follow RAF Neatishead and museum signs.

This museum traces the history of radar and air defences from 1935. It is housed in the original 1942 Radar Operations building and features sixteen exhibit rooms that include the Battle of Britain, 1942 Ground Controlled Interception, Military Communications Systems, a Cold War Operations Room, the Royal Observer Corps, Space Defence, Bloodhound Missiles and original Mobile Radar Vehicles. The guided tour lasts two hours.

RAF Regiment Museum (Suffolk)

Free (donations welcome). Visits by members of public by prior arrangement (01359 269561 ext 7824). Shop. Guided tours. School visits. Parking. RAF Regiment Depot, RAF Honington, Bury St Edmunds.

Presents the story of RAF ground defence of installations and airfields, from the RAF's armoured-car companies of the 1920s to the present day. There are displays illustrating the history of associated overseas forces – the RAF Levies (Iraq), the Aden Protectorate Levies and the RAF Regiment (Malaya). Major display items include the origins of the Regiment and the Second World War, uniforms and ceremonial, weapons, desert defensive positions, low-level defence, armoured cars, medals, Falklands and Gulf War, Belize and Northern Ireland.

Royal Anglian Regiment Museum (Cambridgeshire)

Entry is included in charge for Imperial War Museum, Duxford. Usual hours. Shop. Restaurant. School visits. Parking. Tel. 01223 835000. Imperial War Museum, Duxford, six miles south of Cambridge, signposted off the M11 at Junction 10.

This museum is an integral part of the Land Warfare Hall at the Imperial War Museum, Duxford (p. 87), giving particular emphasis to the East and Royal Anglian Regiments since the amalgamations of the eight county Regiments during 1958–60. The collection is impressively displayed, illustrating the history, traditions, uniforms, organization and records of the Regiment's operations around the world, including Malaya, Aden, Northern Ireland, the Gulf, Bosnia and Iraq. There are several comprehensive displays of weapons and equipment of the infantry soldier over the last fifty years.

Royal Gunpowder Mills (Essex)

££. Usual hours 30 April–early October. Shop. Refreshments. Picnic area. Guided tours (prearranged). Special events. School visits. Parking. Tel. 01992 767022.

An operations room at the RAF Air Defence Radar Museum

Displays at the Royal Anglian Regiment Museum

www.royalgunpowdermills.com/index.htm
Beaulieu Drive, Powdermill Lane,
Waltham Abbey. Leave M25 at Junctions
25 or 26 to Waltham Abbey.

Set in 75 acres of parkland with twenty-one historic buildings, the Royal Gunpowder Mills were the centre for explosives research and production from 1660 to the 1990s. The visitor sees a fascinating mix of the history of gunpowder manufacture, exciting science and lovely surroundings. There is an introductory film and interactive displays and a large collection of muskets, rifles, pistols and machine guns. 'The Munitionettes' is a photographic display of the role of women in gunpowder production during the First World War. A viewing tower enables visitors to get a panoramic view of the site and its abundant wildlife. A complete visit takes three or four hours.

The Royal Norfolk Regiment Museum (Norfolk)

£. Usual hours Tuesday–Saturday. Shop.
Refreshments. School visits. Parking
nearby. Tel. 01603 493649. Situated in
the Shirehall, central Norwich, opposite the
castle.

The museum tells the story of the part played by Norfolk soldiers in shaping 300 years of military history. The displays contain excellent, easily understood, interpretive panels and an important photographic collection. Additional features include a video about the Regiment in India and an extensive medal collection, including two VCs. There are also sections devoted to the everyday life of a soldier and a colourful display of drums.

Tilbury Fort (Essex) ⌗

££. Usual hours. Shop. Special events.
School visits. Tel. 01375 858489.
Half a mile east of Tilbury off A126.
Follow brown and white signs.

This fort is the finest example of 17th-century military engineering in England. Exhibitions, the powder magazine and bunker-like casements demonstrate how the fort protected the City of London. Visitors can fire an anti-aircraft gun and listen to tales of the fort on an audio tour. The best time to visit is during the summer when special events such as an artillery firing day, gladiator fights and military vehicle rallies take place. Contact the fort for an events diary.

A recent Battle of Britain memorial flight

THE BATTLE OF BRITAIN

The Battle of Britain took place when the German Luftwaffe attempted to win air superiority over southern England as an essential prerequisite for invasion by German naval and land forces – their Operation Sealion. The German high command intended to launch 13 divisions (90,000 men and 650 tanks) to make landings on a 200-mile front from Ramsgate to Weymouth. The key to German success lay in the Luftwaffe destroying the RAF's fighter force. Conversely, Fighter Command needed to hamper bombing and inflict losses, preferably before the target was reached. Goering, the commander-in-chief of the Luftwaffe, could put 1392 bombers and 1290 fighters in the air. The RAF had 704 serviceable Spitfires and Hurricanes, backed by a reserve of half that number of aircraft, but of no pilots. Aircraft could be replaced reasonably quickly but pilots could not; it was very hard to find suitable young men for the role.

The Battle of Britain was divided into four phases, each marked by a change in German tactics and targets.

Phase 1: Mid-July–12 August
A month of attacks on British coastal convoys and air battles over the Channel.

Phase 2: 13–23 August
This began with Goering's 'Eagle Day', a continuous series of four massive attacks with 200 aircraft each on coastal radar stations and airfields. The key to the RAF's beating off these assaults lay in the survival of the radar stations. Every German move was plotted by radar or spotted by the Observer Corps, traced on the map tables of control rooms and passed by radio to the squadrons in the air. Not only did the radar stations survive but within days of the attacks starting Goering declared, 'It is doubtful whether there is any point in continuing attacks on radar stations, since not one of those attacked has been put out of action.' This decision was a significant blunder.

Phase 3: 24 August–6 September
This was the really critical period, in which RAF fighter airfields in south-east England were the main German targets. For two terrible weeks the fury of the battle was seen daily in the dogfights above the fields and towns of southern England. But on the night of 24–5 August it was not fighter aircraft duelling in the sky that changed the course of the battle but German bombers dropping their first bombs on London. In response Churchill ordered a retaliatory raid on Berlin. Over one hundred aircraft set out but only twenty-nine found the German capital – enough for Hitler to broadcast hysterically, 'If they attack our cities, we will rub out their cities from the map …' Goering gave orders to switch from attacks on fighter airfields to massive daylight bombing raids on London and other cities. It was another decisive blunder – the turning point of the battle.

Phase 4: 7–30 September
The 'Battle of London' began on 7 September. Goering sent over the largest bomber force he could effectively escort – 372 bombers and 642 fighters – in two massive attacks in quick succession. The commander of Fighter Command, Air Marshal Dowding,

ordered a change of tactics. Instead of getting heavily involved with intercepting the Germans' high-level fighter escort, and thus allowing most of the bombers through, only a few Spitfire squadrons would be deployed against these enemy fighters. The remainder, and all the Hurricanes, would attack the bombers. These tactics worked. If there was one day that marked the high point of the struggle it was 15 September, when Goering mounted his biggest assault on London with five fighters for every bomber in the hope of saturating the defences. Given early warning by radar stations, Dowding was able to call up reinforcements from other sectors.

Throughout that day the people of London and Kent gazed up in amazement and fascination at the deadly drama overhead. Hundreds of aircraft criss-crossed the sky. The scream of engines, the rattle of cannon and machine gun fire were clearly audible. Planes dived and climbed, banked and rolled, twisted, turned and somersaulted. Some trailed black smoke, some hurtled into the ground with violent explosions and sheets of orange flame while others disintegrated in mid-air. Parachutes opened. Home Guard soldiers with rifles and farmers with shotguns or pitchforks ran to rescue or arrest the downed airmen. For those who fought and those who watched it was a day they never forgot. By the end of the afternoon the German formations had been broken up, scattered and hunted home.

Although the air offensive continued for another six weeks the Luftwaffe was a broken reed. By the end of the month the 'Few', the pilots of the Spitfires and Hurricanes, mostly young men straight from school, with minimum training, had won the Battle of Britain. Overall, during the two and a half months these pilots 'killed' some 1408 enemy aircraft at a cost of 697 British fighters.

THE SUPERMARINE SPITFIRE

When the designer of the Spitfire, Reginald Mitchell, was told in 1936 what the aircraft was to be called he grumbled, 'It's the sort of bloody silly name they would give it.' The Spitfire is undoubtedly one of the most famous aircraft ever built, its graceful lines combined with outstanding handling qualities making it the 'dream machine' of its day. At first pilots used to flying in open cockpits felt claustrophobic with the canopy closed and often flew with it fully open. Nor could they always remember it had a retractable undercarriage – something that caused a number of exciting and expensive landings. Its start to the war was not auspicious. The first time a Spitfire opened fire, at what became known as the 'Battle of Barking Creek' on 6 September 1939, it shot down two British Hurricanes. There were over 400 variants built during the war, the final one in

1947. Its last offensive sortie was against Communist terrorists in Malaya in 1951. It was never used in Korea but maintained a 'Temperature and Humidity Flight' operational until 1957.

The MK1 that fought in the Battle of Britain had a maximum speed of 362mph at 20,000ft but a diving speed of 450mph. Its initial climb rate was 2500ft per minute, which meant it took nine minutes to reach 20,000ft. It had a combat range of 395 miles and was armed with eight .303 Browning machine guns, four mounted on each wing. Their fire was synchronized to converge at a distance of 250 yards. Firing was in short bursts as it could carry only 14 seconds' worth of ammunition (2660 rounds). As with the Hurricane, its main German adversary in the battle was the Messerschmitt 109E (Me 109E). The Spitfire was much more manoeuvrable, although the 109E could out-climb and out-dive it and the German's cannon had a longer range than its machine guns.

The Battle of Britain Memorial Flight (p. 85) still puts Spitfires (and Hurricanes) into the air and they are always a big draw at major air shows.

THE HAWKER HURRICANE

For some reason the public associate the Spitfire and its pilots most with winning the Battle of Britain, but in fact there were more Hurricane squadrons than Spitfire squadrons and the Hurricane shot down more enemy planes in the battle than all other aircraft and ground defences put together – estimated at four-fifths of the 'kills' during July–October 1940. This is not so surprising as 1715 Hurricanes flew with Fighter Command during the battle. The Hurricane and Spitfire look similar to the layman but when the two are seen alongside each other the differences are clear. The Hurricane has an angular, stubby fuselage compared with the sleeker, noticeably slimmer line of the Spitfire, and rounded rather than pointed wing tips.

The Hurricane came into operational service in 1937, a year before the Spitfire, and was the first RAF fighter able to fly at over 300mph. Its big advantage over the Spitfire was its ability to survive considerable damage and still get home. It had a maximum speed of 328mph at 20,000ft with an initial climb rate of 2300ft per minute, and like the Spitfire it had eight wing-mounted .303 Browning machine guns. Altogether some 15,000 were built, 3000 of which were sent to the Soviet Union for service on the Eastern Front.

Well worth a visit

Tangmere Military Aviation Museum *p. 49*
RAF Museum, Hendon *p. 53*
RAF Museum, Cosford *p. 70*
Imperial War Museum, Duxford *p. 87*

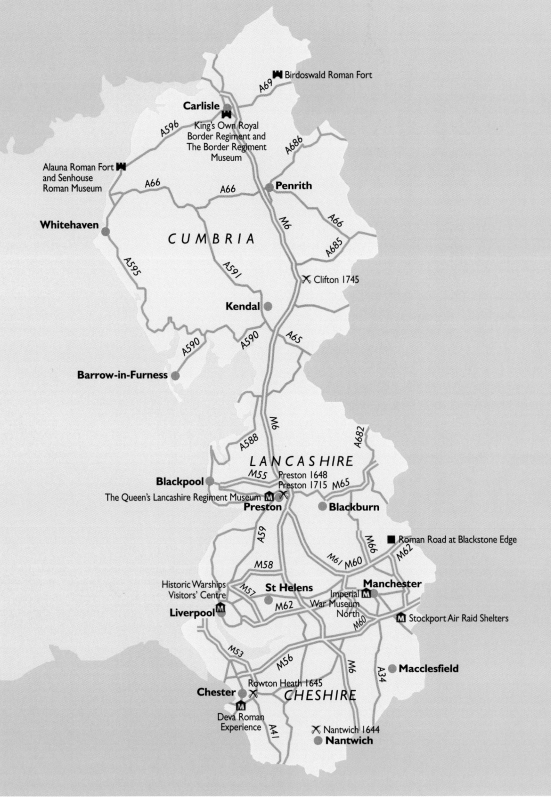

Birdoswald Roman Fort

Carlisle
King's Own Royal
Border Regiment and
The Border Regiment
Museum

A69

A596

A686

Alauna Roman Fort
and Senhouse
Roman Museum

A66

A66

Penrith

A66

M6

A685

Whitehaven

C U M B R I A

A595

A591

Clifton 1745

Kendal

A590

A590

A65

Barrow-in-Furness

M6

A588

A682

L A N C A S H I R E

Blackpool

M55

Preston 1648
Preston 1715

M65

The Queen's Lancashire Regiment Museum

Preston

Blackburn

A59

Roman Road at Blackstone Edge

M66

M62

M58

M61

M60

Historic Warships
Visitors' Centre

M57

St Helens

Manchester

Imperial
War Museum
North

Liverpool

M62

M60

Stockport Air Raid Shelters

M53

M56

M6

A34

Macclesfield

Rowton Heath 1645

Chester

C H E S H I R E

Deva Roman
Experience

A41

Nantwich 1644

Nantwich

NORTH-WEST

Alauna Roman Fort and Senhouse Roman Museum (Cumbria)

£. Usual hours; April–June Tuesday, Thursday–Sunday and July–October daily; November–March closes 4 p.m. Refreshments. Parking. Tel. 01900 8166168. The Battery, The Promenade, Maryport. Clearly signposted from the town centre.

This fort was the headquarters of Emperor Hadrian's coastal defence system. The adjacent Senhouse museum, housed in an old Victorian gun battery with spectacular views of the north Cumbrian coast, contains a unique collection of Roman altar stones taken from the fort. Displays include some excellent reconstructions of Roman military equipment and a soldier's life on the Wall.

Birdoswald Roman Fort (Cumbria) ⌗

£. Shop. Refreshments. Picnic area. Guided tours. Exhibition centre. School visits. Parking. Tel. 01697 747602. www.english-heritage.org.uk/birdoswald/index.htm Well signposted eight miles east of Brampton off the A69.

Perhaps the finest fort on the Wall, encompassing a five-acre site that was built to guard the Roman bridge over the River Irthing. There is an exhibition that displays the fort's history and the life of the garrison together with the story of the Border Reivers (raiders) and recent discoveries. A tour includes remains of the massive gateway, ovens, granaries, workshop/store and part of the Wall. Close by, at Gilsland, is a well-preserved milecastle with 10ft-high walls.

Border Regiment and King's Own Royal Border Regiment Museums (Cumbria)

£ (entry to castle). Shop. Guided tours. School visits. Research facilities. Tel. 01228 53277. Queen Mary's Tower, The Castle, Carlisle. Within easy reach from the M6 Junctions 43 and 44.

The museum for both these regiments is housed in Carlisle Castle, which can boast military occupation for over 900 years. Preserved within the walls are barrack blocks and other military buildings dating from the 19th century. The castle was the depot of the Border Regiment from 1873 to 1958. Outside the museum is a 1940 25-pounder field gun and a Ferret Scout Car. Inside, the museum is on two floors with displays of uniforms, weapons, equipment, medals, silver, pictures, memorabilia, dioramas, video presentations and anti-tank guns.

A legionary stands guard at the Deva Roman Experience

Deva Roman Experience (Cheshire)

££. Usual hours. Shop. Refreshments. Guided tours. School visits. Tel. 01244 343407. Pierpoint Lane, off Bridge Street, Chester.

Deva is a Roman fortress built almost 2000 years ago that now lies beneath the busy streets of modern Chester. A fascinating and unusual tour begins with the dark hold of a Roman galley. The visitor then enters through the gates to relive the sights, sounds and smells of everyday Roman life as well as exploring an archaeological dig. There is a museum with a large display of Roman finds.

Historic Warships Visitors' Centre (Merseyside)

££. Usual hours, but open only at weekends from 5 January to 16 February. Shop. Refreshments. Guided tours. Parking. Tel. 0151 6501573. East Float Dock, Dock Road, Birkenhead. Leave M53 at Junction 1, follow the signs to 'All Docks' then follow tourist information signs.

The collection consists of HMS *Plymouth*, an anti-submarine frigate, HMS *Onyx*, the only non-nuclear submarine to participate in the Falklands conflict, and HMS *Bronington*, the minesweeper once commanded by Prince Charles. Visitors can explore these ships and see how the crews spent their time at work and rest in very confined spaces. Also at the centre is the U534 Museum, which relates the story of this German submarine, U-boats generally and the Battle of the Atlantic using interactive computer displays, artefacts from U534, scale models and display boards.

The Imperial War Museum North: the interior is just as impressive as the exterior

Imperial War Museum North (Manchester)

Free. Usual hours. Shop. Restaurant. Café. Picnic area. Guided tours. Special events. Family weekend events and activities. Special exhibitions. Parking (chargeable). Tel. 0161 8364000. north.iwm.org.uk The Quays, Trafford Wharf Road, Trafford Park, Manchester. Leave M60 at Junction 9 or M602 at Junction 2 and follow signs for Trafford Park.

This new museum chronicles the conflicts in which British and Commonwealth forces have been engaged since 1914, bringing to life their experiences of war with hundreds of objects ranging from a large Russian T34 tank and a Harrier jump jet to works of art, photographs, uniforms, diaries, letters and medals.

The highlight of any visit is the transformation of the main exhibition area into a huge auditorium where visitors can experience an hourly 360-degree audio-visual display made up of three fifteen-minute presentations entitled 'Why War?', 'Weapons of War' and 'Children and War'.

Nantwich, Battle of, 1644 (Cheshire)

Free. Easy access, open fields and farmland. Parking possible off-road in some places and in Acton. A mile NW of Nantwich and in the fields immediately north and east of Acton. Best approached via the A534 from Nantwich.

Towards the end of 1643, a 5000-strong Royalist army under John Byron (later Lord Byron) subdued all of Cheshire except for Nantwich. In December Sir Thomas Fairfax, with a force of 3000 infantry, 1800 cavalry and 500 dragoons, set off to relieve the town. On 25 January Byron had deployed on high ground at Acton. When the Parliamentarians arrived they declined to attack, instead making a detour to the east. This provoked an attack by some Royalist regiments on the enemy rearguard. Then the Royalist right wing advanced to attack the head of Fairfax's column, which overstretched the Royalist line. The Parliamentarians turned to their right and a close-quarter mêlée took place among the fields and hedgerows immediately north-east of Acton between the A51 to the north and A534 to the south. The hedges proved a severe obstacle to movement, control and use of cavalry. The result was a win for Fairfax, who drove Byron's men towards Acton church. Their defeat was completed by the arrival in their rear of Parliamentary reinforcements from Nantwich. Some 1500 Royalists surrendered and several hundred died.

Preston, Battle of, 1648 (Lancashire)

Free. Access easy, but the battle was fought in the town and it is difficult to trace troop movements. Parking in town. Preston, in particular near the A6 bridge south over the Ribble.

This battle marked the end of the second phase of the English Civil War. On 17 August 1648, Parliamentarians led by Oliver Cromwell defeated Royalist forces under the Duke of Hamilton and General Langdale. Hamilton commanded a far larger force than Cromwell (18,000 to 8000) but his adversary was a much more experienced and astute general. Cromwell succeeded in attacking the Royalists as they were separated and in the process of negotiating the Ribble Bridge. There was heavy fighting and both sides had some successes and by nightfall the battle was undecided. Both armies were exhausted and soaked by pouring rain, and Hamilton decided to retire under cover of darkness along the road to Wigan. The next day Cromwell set off in pursuit and there were a series of clashes all the way to Winwick where the Royalists made a final stand. Some of the heaviest fighting took place around Winwick Church. However, although not destroyed, the Royalist forces dispersed and the battle of Preston was over.

Preston, Battle of, 1715 (Lancashire)

Free. Access easy, but the battle was fought in Preston town so much is now built over. Parking available in town. Central Preston. The streets round the market square, especially Church Street, Fishergate and Friargate, are on the same sites as in 1715. The main barricade in Church Street is thought to have been near the church.

A battle in the first Jacobite uprising, aimed at gaining the throne of James II's exiled son, fought on 13 November 1715. Some 2000–3000 rebels under a number of Scottish leaders barricaded themselves in Preston to meet the English forces, also about 3000 strong, under General Willis. The barricades were erected across Church Street, Fishergate, Lancaster Road and Friargate. Houses near these blocks were loopholed for musketeers and each barrier had a subsidiary barricade further out to delay any approach. The centre of Preston became a temporary fortress but no attempt was made to block the Ribble Bridge south-east of the town. When the English force arrived Willis crossed the bridge and sent a strong body of dragoons round to the north to make a demonstration from that direction. The main body then attacked from the south and east. The Cameronian infantry regiment successfully stormed the Church Street barricade, but the Fishergate one was held. Nevertheless, by nightfall the defenders had been pushed back with considerable loss. The next day the rebels surrendered.

The Queen's Lancashire Regiment Museum (Lancashire)

Free. Usual hours Tuesday–Thursday or by appointment. Shop. Guided tours available at £2 per person. School visits. Parking. Tel. 01772 260362. Fulwood barracks, Watling Street Road, Preston. NE of Preston on the B6245.

This museum houses the largest military heritage collection in this region, with extensive historical material including collections of photographs, film and sound, uniforms, badges, medals, weapons and equipment relating to many of Lancashire's famous regiments.

Rowton Heath, Battle of, 1645 (Cheshire)

Free. Easy access, mostly fields on either side of the A41 from Chester. Parking possible in Rowton or off-road in places. Two miles east of Chester on the A41. The first action took place either side of the road west of Waverton village, the second again on either side of the road at Rowton.

An English Civil War battle, fought on 24 September 1645 between almost entirely mounted forces. Sir Marmaduke Langdale with about 2000 Royalist horse confronted Colonel Sydenham Poyntz with a similar number of Parliamentarian cavalry. After Naseby, King Charles's only hope lay in gathering support from Ireland and Scotland and he was marching north to meet up with the Scots when he was distracted by calls to raise the siege of Chester. While Charles remained in Chester with some infantry, Langdale was dispatched with some 2000 horse to attack the approaching Poyntz and a confused and scattered fight took place on Rowton Heath. Both sides summoned reinforcements. About 300 Parliamentary musketeers arrived first together with more cavalry. Poyntz renewed his attack and drove Langdale back to the walls of Chester. Some very confused hand-to-hand fighting took place in the lanes outside the city in which the Parliamentarians got the upper hand, killing some 600 and capturing 800 Royalists. The King escaped but it was the final action of the first Civil War.

Stockport Air Raid Shelters (Cheshire)

££. Usual hours. Open bank holidays except Christmas, Boxing Day and New Year's Day. Shop. Guided tours. Evening Explorer Tours. Special events. Educational visits. Parking in Stockport. Tel. 0161 4741940. 61 Chestergate, Stockport. By road leave the M60 at Junction 1. The shelters are five minutes' walk from the bus station and ten minutes from the rail station.

A labyrinth of specially built tunnels under part of the town centre provided shelter – and a way of life – for Stockport and Manchester families during the Blitz, often accommodating 7000 people nightly. Visitors can now explore these reconstructed/refurbished shelters on self-guided tours or with a guide. On the first Wednesday of every month Evening Explorer Tours take place between 7 and 9 p.m. at a cost of £4.95 per head. Booking is essential.

Stockport Air Raid Shelters

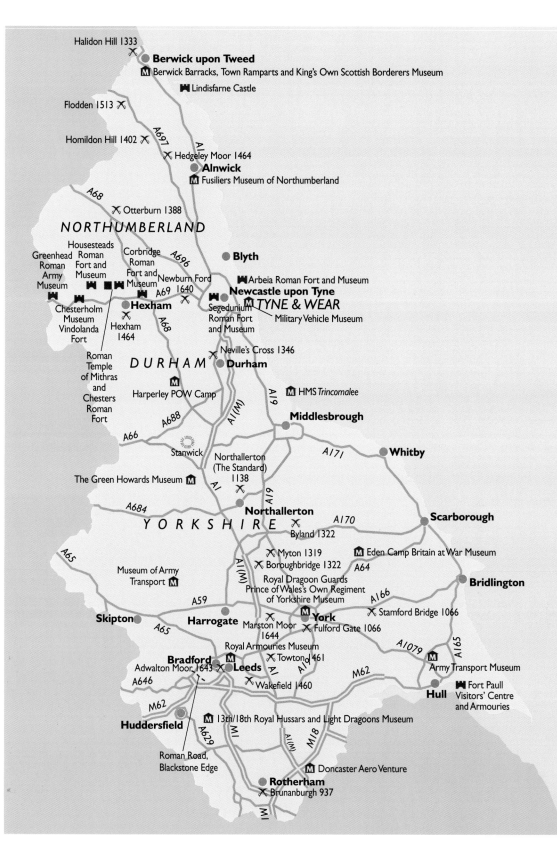

Halidon Hill 1333
● **Berwick upon Tweed**
Ⓜ Berwick Barracks, Town Ramparts and King's Own Scottish Borderers Museum

◼ Lindisfarne Castle

Flodden 1513 ✕

Homildon Hill 1402 ✕

A697

A1

✕ Hedgeley Moor 1464
● **Alnwick**
Ⓜ Fusiliers Museum of Northumberland

A68

✕ Otterburn 1388

NORTHUMBERLAND

● **Blyth**

Housesteads
Greenhead Roman
Roman Fort and
Army Museum
Museum

Corbridge
Roman
Fort and
Museum

A696

Newburn Ford
A69 1640

◼ Arbeia Roman Fort and Museum
Newcastle upon Tyne
Ⓜ **TYNE & WEAR**

◼◼ ◼◼◼

● **Hexham**
✕

Segedunium
Roman Fort
and Museum

Military Vehicle Museum

Chesterholm
Museum
Vindolanda
Fort

Hexham
1464

A68

Roman
Temple
of Mithras
and
Chesters
Roman
Fort

DURHAM

✕ Neville's Cross 1346
● **Durham**

Ⓜ
Harperley POW Camp

A19

Ⓜ HMS *Trincomalee*

A1(M)

Middlesbrough

A66

A688

Stanwick

A171

● **Whitby**

The Green Howards Museum Ⓜ

Northallerton
(The Standard)
1138
✕

A1

A19

A684

Y O R K S H I R E

● **Northallerton**

A170

● **Scarborough**

✕ Byland 1322

A65

Museum of Army
Transport Ⓜ

A1(M)

✕ Myton 1319
✕ Boroughbridge 1322

A64

Ⓜ Eden Camp Britain at War Museum

A166

● **Bridlington**

A59

Royal Dragoon Guards
Prince of Wales's Own Regiment
of Yorkshire Museum
✕

✕ Stamford Bridge 1066

Skipton ●

A65

Harrogate ●

Marston Moor
1644

Ⓜ **York**
✕ Fulford Gate 1066

A1079

A165

Ⓜ
Army Transport Museum

Royal Armouries Museum
✕ Towton 1461

Bradford Ⓜ
Adwalton Moor 1643 ✕ **Leeds**

A1

M62

● **Hull**

◼ Fort Paull
Visitors' Centre
and Armouries

A646
✕ Wakefield 1460

M62

Huddersfield

A629

M1

Ⓜ 13th/18th Royal Hussars and Light Dragoons Museum

A1(M)

M18

Roman Road,
Blackstone Edge

Ⓜ Doncaster Aero Venture

● **Rotherham**
✕ Brunanburgh 937

M1

NORTH-EAST

Adwalton Moor, Battle of, 1643 (West Yorkshire)

Free. Reasonable access. Some open fields. Four miles south-east of Bradford. The battlefield is in the open ground within the triangle of the A650, A58 and A62 immediately east of Drighlington.

An English Civil War battle in which the Royalists under the Earl of Newcastle with some 10,000 men defeated a Parliamentarian force of only 4000 under Lord Fairfax. On 30 June 1643 Newcastle drew up his army on the ridge of Adwalton Moor four miles south-east of Bradford, facing west. Fairfax, with his much inferior force, deployed opposite the Royalists on the edge of the moor but refused to attack. Newcastle advanced but was driven back in some very intense fighting. However, as the fighting reached more open ground the Royalist cavalry on the flanks was able to join the action. This, combined with superior numbers, ensured the Parliamentarian rout, and Newcastle went on to take Bradford and Leeds.

Arbeia Roman Fort and Museum (Durham) (World Heritage Site)

Free. Usual hours. Shop. Refreshments. Research facilities. School visits. Parking. Tel. 0191 4561369. Baring Street, South Shields, Tyne and Wear – a ten-minute walk from South Shields metro and bus station.

A splendidly informative site, combining the excavated remains of a Roman military supply base with reconstructions of the commanding officer's house, the west gate and a barrack block. The west gate features a display of the history of the site, a model of the fort and an armoury. The commanding officer's house has been partially rebuilt and fitted out with authentic furniture. The barrack block shows how Roman soldiers lived, eight men to an apartment, and features beds and the soldiers' equipment. The museum contains displays of finds excavated at the site including weapons, jewellery, armour, tools and household objects. There is also a Roman Garden of herbs and plants the Romans used as food and medicine. In the 'Time Quest', for which there is a small charge, there is a hands-on gallery that includes the opportunity to excavate real Roman artefacts.

Army Transport Museum (East Yorkshire)

££. Usual hours. Shop. Refreshments. Picnic area. Guided tours. School visits. Research archives. Lecture hall. Play area. Parking. Tel. 01482 860445. Flemingate, central Beverley, North Humberside.

Two acres of army road, rail, sea and air exhibits displayed in two indoor exhibition halls. The exhibits range from horse-drawn vehicles to the last remaining giant Blackburn Beverley transport aircraft. During the summer vehicle demonstrations are given outside.

Berwick-on-Tweed Barracks and Town Ramparts (Northumberland) ⌗

££. Usual hours. Shop. School visits. Research facilities. Parking (in town). Tel. 01289 304493. On the Parade, off Church Street in Berwick town centre.

Built between 1717 and 1721, these were the earliest purpose-built barracks in the country. They were the depot of the King's Own Scottish Borderers from 1881 to 1964 and still house its Regimental HQ and museum (see p. 106). The buildings have been restored and contain an exhibition of the history of the British infantry from 1660 to 1880. Visits can be made to the reconstructed barrack and schoolrooms.

Berwick was for centuries in a no man's land between England and Scotland, changing hands some thirteen times. The town's defences were rebuilt in the 1550s and what remains today makes Berwick the finest fortified town of early modern England. A walk along the ramparts, often 20ft high, makes a rewarding experience, with the massive Windmill bastion particularly worth seeing.

Boroughbridge, Battle of, 1322 (North Yorkshire)

Free. Easy access. Parking nearby in Boroughbridge. Central Boroughbridge. Leave the A1/M at junction 18. Visitors standing on the new bridge that carries the B6265 over the river are on the exact site of the 1322 bridge – the centre of the fighting. The ford can be found by walking along the riverbank for about 800 yards. The site of the Battle of Myton (see p. 107) can also be found nearby.

A battle fought on 16 March 1322 between Edward II's forces under Sir Andrew Harcla and rebel barons commanded by Thomas, Earl of Lancaster, who felt he had been denied his rightful place as the king's adviser and rose up in revolt. The clash came at the bridge and at the ford some 800 yards to the east over the River Ure at Boroughbridge. Edward's army with around 4000 men deployed their archers, defending the bridge on the north bank with their spearmen guarding a ford half a mile downstream. Lancaster, with some 3000 men, left Lords Clifford and Hereford to attack across the bridge while he took his mounted troops to assault the ford.

The assault on the bridge was broken up by a hail of arrows – inevitably on so narrow a frontage with such a concentration of fire. At the crucial moment a man who had hidden under the bridge killed Hereford and then Clifford was wounded. At the ford the cavalry had also failed to make headway and Lancaster withdrew his men; he was captured the next day and beheaded. Most casualties (the exact numbers are not known) occurred at the fight for the bridge.

Brunanburgh, Battle of, 937 (South Yorkshire)

Free. Difficult access as the possible battlefield is mostly under the M1 and A630 south of Rotherham. Much disputed, but possibly just south-east of Junction 33 on the M1 south of Rotherham.

A large and important battle, with both armies mustering as many as 18,000–20,000 men each. It was fought between the English King Athelston and the invading Scots with allied Norsemen from Ireland and Scandinavia. The Scots, commanded by Olaf, the son-in-law of the Scottish King Constantine, came by sea up the Humber and then marched south for London, gathering men from northern Britain on their way. Athelston blocked their path by occupying a ridgeline between the present Brindsworth and Catcliffe, south of Rotherham. Olaf attacked but could make no headway and was eventually forced back and routed. There was a relentless pursuit and much slaughter, largely along the banks of the River Don.

Byland, Battle of, 1322 (North Yorkshire)

Free. Reasonable access, open moors. Parking possible. Seven miles north-east of Thirsk.

A little-known battle fought on 14 October 1322 between Robert the Bruce of Scotland and the army of King Edward II of England under the Earl of Richmond. Robert the Bruce had laid waste large areas of north-west England around Carlisle and Preston before marching across the Pennines to Northallerton. He drew up his large army on Roulston Scar and sent a detachment to attack the English on the nearby ridge. Richmond counter-attacked but his horsemen were restricted by the narrowness of the valley. The dense Scottish band of pikemen easily saw off the attackers, who were cut down mercilessly when more lightly armed highlanders descended on their flanks. Bruce then sent Sir Walter Stewart to Rievaulx Abbey, where Edward II was staying, in an attempt to capture him.

Bruce followed up his first success by marching, largely unseen, onto Shaws Moor where the English were encamped. The Scots then launched a wild charge down the slope and the demoralized English broke and fled. The Earl of Richmond surrendered. But the King was able to escape from the Abbey by galloping away with a handful of followers.

Chesters Fort and Museum (Northumberland) ⌗

££. Usual hours. Shop. Refreshments. Parking. Tel. 01434 681379. Five miles north of Hexham. Signposted off the A6079 onto the B6320 and then the B6318.

One of the best-preserved Roman cavalry forts on Hadrian's Wall, Chesters accommodated 400–500 troops. Many parts are still visible, including the barrack blocks, a finely preserved bath-house, the remains of the headquarters building and the commanding officer's house. The Clayton Collection Museum contains a large display of carved stones, altars and sculptures found from all along the Wall.

Corbridge Roman Fort and Museum (Northumberland) ⌗

££. Usual hours; 1 November–28 March Wednesday–Sunday, 10 a.m.–1 p.m. and 2 p.m.–4 p.m. Shop. Refreshments. Parking. Twenty miles east of Newcastle on the A69.

Situated just south of the Roman Wall on the principal route into Scotland, Corbridge was one of the earliest military sites, built in AD 80 and originally built for a cavalry unit and later replaced by an auxiliary infantry cohort. It subsequently became a prosperous garrison town and supply base during Severus' campaigns in the north. The main military remains to be seen include granaries, the Stanegate road, temples, a water tank, aqueduct and the headquarters building with its interesting underground strongroom.

The museum contains displays of weapons, armour, sculptures, inscriptions of the II, VI and XX Legions, and finds illustrating Roman life in the town.

Doncaster Aero Venture (South Yorkshire)

££. Usual hours, Thursday–Sunday only. Shop. Bookstall. Refreshments. School visits. Parking. Tel. 01302 761616. www.aeroventure.org.uk Doncaster. Follow the signs to the racecourse and Doncaster Leisure Park then follow the brown propeller signs to the museum.

The collection is housed in the remaining hangar of RAF Doncaster and consists of eleven complete aircraft, eight cockpits and forty engines together with a large assembly of artefacts and memorabilia.

Eden Camp (North Yorkshire)

£££. Usual hours, 14 February–23 December. Shop. Restaurant. Bar. Picnic area. Educational visits. Children's assault course. Parking. Tel. 01653 697777. www.edencamp.co.uk Eighteen miles north of York. Signposted off the A64 from York and the A169 from Pickering.

An amazing 'Britain at War' museum which has won multiple awards. Allow three hours for a full visit. The museum is constructed in twenty-nine huts of an original prisoner of war camp built in 1942, each now featuring an aspect of wartime Britain. There are many reconstructed scenes, using movement, lighting, sound, smells and smoke machines to transport you back in time. Exhibits in huts include The Rise of Hitler, The Home Front, The U-Boat Menace, The Blitz, Women at War, Bomber Operations, Civil Defence, and Prisoners of War.

Fort Paull (East Yorkshire)

£££. Usual hours. Shop. Restaurant. Bar. Picnic areas. Re-enactments. Children's assault course. Parking. Tel. 01482 882655. Four miles east of Hull, signposted off the A1033.

A unique, National Heritage award-winning Visitors' Centre, Museum and Armouries combined, illustrating the history of warfare in England, which provides a full day out for the family, inside a coastal fortress built on the orders of Henry VIII in 1542. The fort saw service in Henry's reign, the English Civil War, the Napoleonic Wars and both World Wars.

A Hurricane fighter, one of the many Second World War aircraft at Eden Camp

Among the displays is a death mask of the German Luftwaffe commander Field Marshal Goering and a replica of the Crown Jewels. Underground passages lead to the fortress vaults, which contain historical scenes constructed with lifelike waxwork models plus a military hospital, gun and bomb stores and radio rooms. There is also a comprehensive display of weapons, classic military vehicles, armoured cars and working mechanisms.

Fulford Gate, Battle of, 1066 (North Yorkshire)

Free. Access difficult as the battlefield is under the southern suburbs of York. Fulford is on the southern outskirts of York on the A19 just before its junction with the A64.

Fulford Gate was fought on 20 September 1066 by the army of the English earls in an attempt to repel Harald Hardrada's invading army of Norsemen, which had sailed up the River Ouse. Instead of waiting for King Harold, who was marching north to join them, the English advanced out of York and met the invaders at Fulford, then an open and wet field. Although at first successful the English were outflanked on their right and the army rolled up against a large water-filled ditch to the east of the road. Many were cut down and others drowned.

Often dismissed as a minor affair, Fulford was in fact a battle of great importance. Had Harold been able to communicate with the earls and tell them to wait in York, their combined armies would probably have routed the invaders and then might have gone on to repulse William at Hastings, changing the course of British history.

The Fusiliers Museum of Northumberland (Northumberland)

Free – included in entrance to castle. Usual hours, except Fridays, Easter–October. Shop. School visits. Tel. 01665 602152. The Abbot's Tower, Alnwick Castle, Alnwick.

Set in the glorious surroundings of Alnwick Castle, this museum covers the history of the old 5th Regiment of Foot, later the Royal Northumberland Fusiliers, from its formation in the 1670s until amalgamation in 1968. It is an impressive, well laid-out museum with the ground floor displaying Colours and medals of the various battalions. The first floor covers uniforms and equipment of the 19th century, contemporary records, prints and paintings, while the second floor is devoted to the 20th century.

Flodden, Battle of, 1513 (Northumberland)

Free. A big battlefield, largely unspoilt with open fields and easy access. Parking possible. Branxton Hill lies immediately south of Branxton village, which stands just over a mile west of the A697 Wooler to Coldstream road. The battlefield is signposted from the main road and leads to the monument on the English position on Piper's Hill, which is a good viewpoint from which to see much of the field.

In 1513 King Henry VIII invaded France, which had ancient ties with Scotland – the so-called 'auld alliance'. As a result Louis XII of France asked James IV of Scotland for assistance. James agreed, and with a large army of some 40,000 men, including five huge cannons firing 60lb shot and a French contingent of 5000, crossed the border at Coldstream into northern England. After investing castles at Etal, Norham and Ford, James encamped on Flodden Edge. On hearing of the invasion, the Earl of Surrey assembled around 26,000 men at Newcastle and marched north, at Alnwick sending the Scots a challenge to battle that they accepted. The English army marched up on 7 September only to discover the enemy had taken up a formidable position on Flodden Edge that extended for a mile and rose 500 feet above the plain.

The centre of the battlefield, looking north-west from Branxton Hill (Battlefields Trust)

Concerned by the strength of this position, the Scots' superior numbers and the fact that they could easily withdraw back across the border, Surrey decided on a bold but risky flank march to get behind the Scottish position and attack them from the rear. At dawn on 8 September the English marched north in driving rain, keeping to the east of the River Till. After eight miles they successfully crossed the river by Twizel Bridge and Heaton Mill, then finding themselves some four miles to the rear of the Scots. On 9 September James was forced to turn his army around to face the unexpected threat. He then unwisely abandoned his position on Flodden Edge to move a mile north to redeploy on Branxton Hill, facing north. Meanwhile the English were struggling forward through boggy ground and took a long time getting into position. The Scots, formed in four divisions with a reserve, awaited attack. The battle opened with an artillery duel in which the English gunners gained the upper hand. This unsettled the Scottish Borderers on the left flank and they swept downhill, crashing into and driving back the English right under Sir Edmund Howard. Seeing this success, James ordered his two centre divisions forward in support. As they advanced they were met by a storm of arrows and the crash of cannons. The Scottish division under Crawford made little impression in the hand-to-hand fighting but James's division forced the English line back over 300 yards.

Meanwhile, behind the English centre, Lord Dacre commanding the reserve of 1500 mounted men, crashed into the victorious Borderers who were busy looting the dead, thus coming to the aid of the English right. Then came the turning point of the battle. On the English left Sir Edward Stanley led his division in an outflanking move that brought most of his men within easy range of the Scottish right division under Lennox and Argyll. These men found themselves under a galling flanking fire from Stanley's archers. It was devastatingly effective and most of the Scots at the receiving end fled before Stanley's follow-up charge came in. The Scottish right disappeared. In the centre the Scots were slowly being crushed by weight of numbers as the English on the flanks closed in. Despite being reinforced by the French and the reserve force under Bothwell they were pushed back. The final blow that destroyed all resistance was Stanley rallying his men and charging into the rear of the King's division. The English tactics had been much superior and the English bill superior to the Scottish pike.

King James was cut down, as were twelve earls, fourteen lords and 10,000 men, at a cost to the English of around 1500. Scottish power had, for the moment, been broken.

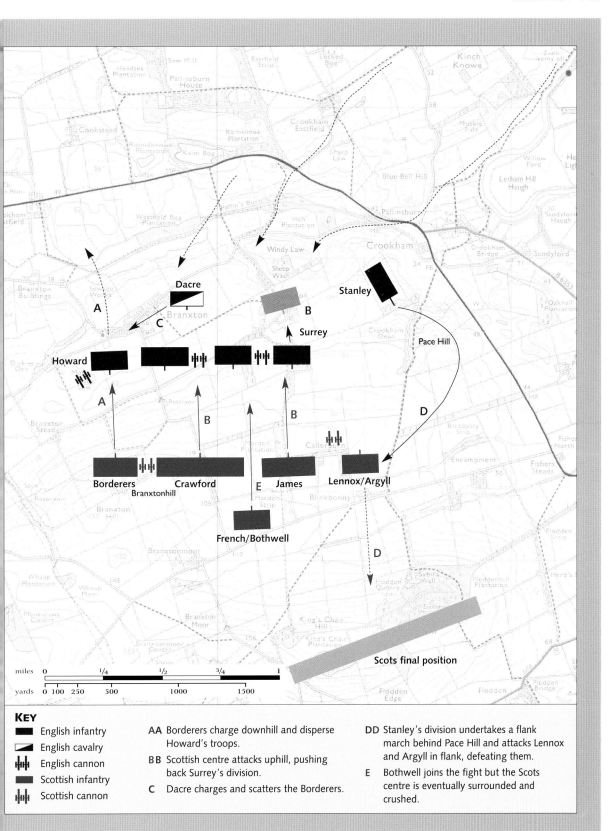

miles 0   1/4   1/2   3/4   1
yards 0   100   250   500   1000   1500

KEY

▬	English infantry
◪	English cavalry
⌗	English cannon
▬	Scottish infantry
⌗	Scottish cannon

AA Borderers charge downhill and disperse Howard's troops.

BB Scottish centre attacks uphill, pushing back Surrey's division.

C Dacre charges and scatters the Borderers.

DD Stanley's division undertakes a flank march behind Pace Hill and attacks Lennox and Argyll in flank, defeating them.

E Bothwell joins the fight but the Scots centre is eventually surrounded and crushed.

The Infantry Will Advance – a stirring depiction of the Green Howards at the Battle of the Alma in 1854

Greenhead Roman Army Museum (Northumberland)

££. Usual hours mid-February–mid-November. Shop. Refreshments. Picnic area. Sound guide. School visits. Lecture hall. Parking. Tel. 01434 344277. In the central section of the Wall some four miles west of Haltwhistle, at the village of Greenhead. Approached from either east or west on the A69.

This museum is at the Roman fort of Carvoran and is run by the Vindolanda Trust. Devoted to the Roman soldier and his way of life, it brings the garrisons of the Wall to life with reconstructions including the inside of a barrack room and artefacts of various kinds illustrating military life.

The Green Howards Regimental Museum (North Yorkshire)

££. Usual hours Monday–Friday February–November, also Saturday April–October. Shop. Refreshments next

door. Guided tours. Sound guide. School visits. Research facilities by appointment. Town parking. Tel. 01748 822133. Holy Trinity Church, Richmond town centre.

The museum collection, housed in a converted church, spans over 315 years of travel, campaigns and war. Archive film displayed on touch-screen monitors depicts the Western Front and the Green Howards in the Second World War, with colour film illustrating incidents over the past fifty years. The pride of the museum is the Medal Room, with over 3000 medals dating back to 1815 together with badges, buttons and gorgets dating back to 1750.

Halidon Hill, Battle of, 1333 (Northumberland)

Free. Farmland, fields – often muddy. Easy access. Car park. Two miles out of Berwick-upon-Tweed along the A6105. There is a monument on the northern side of the road, a viewpoint and County Council battle map. On a clear day the view from Halidon Hill is splendid.

A battle in the war between the English under King Edward III and Edward Balliol and the Scots commanded by Sir Archibald Douglas. Douglas, who was unsuccessfully attempting to raise the siege of Berwick with a series of raids, was forced to confront the English on 19 July 1333. The King had his army of some 10,000 drawn up in the usual three divisions on Halidon Hill, which was fronted by marshy ground. The Scots mustered around 15,000 and had no option but to attack if they were to relieve Berwick. As the Scots struggled forward through the bog many fell under the rain of English arrows from the bowmen in the centre. Despite initial superior numbers the attackers were much depleted by the time they reached the English line, and they were pushed back with comparative ease. The pursuit was ruthless and prolonged. The Scottish losses included Douglas and around 4000 men while those of the English amounted to a mere 100 as they had kept their formation throughout the fighting.

Harperley Prisoner of War Camp (Durham) ⌗

£. Usual hours. Shop. Restaurant. Guided tours. Special events. Aquatics centre. Children's play area. Parking. Tel. 01388 767098. On the A689, 200 yards from the roundabout intersecting the A68 near Crook, County Durham.

This POW camp, purpose-built during the Second World War to house German and Italian prisoners, consists of forty-nine huts of which twenty-two are being turned into a museum. A guided tour is well worthwhile. Among the highlights are the theatre where prisoners put on shows for local people and the surviving ten wall murals painted by a homesick prisoner and depicting typical German scenes. The restaurant serves wartime 'specials', although in considerably improved conditions.

Hedgeley Moor, Battle of, 1464 (Northumberland)

Free. Easy access. Open fields. Off-road parking. Three miles south of Wooler on the A697. The battlefield is immediately south of the junction of the A697 and B6346.

A Wars of the Roses battle fought on 24 April 1464, in which the Yorkists with some 2000 men under Lord Montagu confronted a smaller force of Lancastrians whose three detachments were under Lords Hungerford and Ros and Sir Ralph Percy. Hungerford and Ros did not like the odds and departed with their men before the battle started. Percy was made of sterner stuff and stayed to fight – unwisely, as it turned out. As the Yorkists closed in to surround the much-depleted Lancastrians, Percy made a spirited charge at what he thought was the weakest part of the enemy line. His horse gave a tremendous leap – at what became known as 'Percy's Leap' – but was wounded in the process and Percy, now dismounted, was mortally injured. His men were systematically slaughtered on the marshy part of the field.

It is worth a stop to see the plaque and the walled enclosure with two boulders marking Percy's Leap. Percy's Cross is in the garden of a cottage some 500 yards to the south, on the east of the road.

Hexham, Battle of, 1464 (Northumberland)

Free. Easy access. Open fields. Off-road parking possible. Two miles south-east of Hexham. The battlefield is in a field known as Hexham Levels immediately west of the junction of the B6306 and B6307.

A Wars of the Roses battle fought on 15 May 1464, soon after Hedgeley Moor (above). The Lancastrians had now rallied under the Duke of Somerset with the forces of Lords Hungerford and Ros. On 14 May Somerset encamped with his back to the Devil's Water stream, about a mile and a half south-east of Hexham. The next day the Yorkists, under Lord Montagu, arrived in greatly superior numbers and attacked. The Lancastrian centre gave way and, seeing this, the troops on either wing turned to flee. Some escaped but many were cut down trying to cross the stream. Somerset was captured and his spurs were struck off, his coat of arms torn off and he was strapped to a hurdle before being dragged to a scaffold and beheaded. Ros and Hungerford were later caught and lost their heads at Newcastle.

Harperley Prisoner of War Camp: these huts housed German and Italian PoWs

HMS *Trincomalee:* the last of the Nelson-age frigates, berthed at Hartlepool Historic Quay

Scots as they were drawn up on Homildon Hill. Percy sent the bulk of his bowmen up to the summit of the steep Harehope Hill, opposite the Scots but within range of his longbows. The remainder of his force, mounted men, were hidden from the view of the Scots in a field known as Red Riggs, now marked by the Bendar Stone. The English archers on Harehope Hill outranged the Scottish bowmen and rained arrows down on their enemy, who could not reply. The Scottish spearmen advanced and were also cut down. Then Douglas launched his mounted knights but they too could not face the firepower of the bowmen. The main force under Percy now attacked to complete the slaughter. Douglas was wounded in the eye and captured while his men were chased to the River Tweed and many shot down as they crossed.

Housesteads Roman Fort and Museum (Northumberland) ⌗

££. Usual hours. Shop. Refreshments. Picnic area. Museum. Parking. Tel. 01434 344363. Two and three-quarter miles north of Bardon Mill on the B6318. Well signposted.

The finest Roman fort on the Wall, Housesteads covers five acres in a commanding position on the Whin Sill escarpment; it once housed an infantry cohort of about 800. The remains include four gates, the commandant's house, barracks, granaries, hospital and latrines. The museum has an impressive collection of artefacts together with a reconstruction of the fort. Housesteads is an excellent place from which to begin walks along the Wall.

HMS *Trincomalee* (Durham)

£££. Usual hours. Shop. Refreshments. Ship's tours. Sound guide. School visits. Children's fun trail. Parking. Tel. 01429 223193. www.hms-trincomalee.co.uk Hartlepool Historic Quay – follow the brown tourist signs.

The last of the Nelson-age frigates, built in 1817 and superbly restored, is berthed within Hartlepool Historic Quay, the oldest British ship afloat. Visitors get an interactive experience of life aboard a British frigate two centuries ago. A tour includes the captain's cabin, the quarterdeck, cramped mess deck, powder magazine, bread locker and hold.

Homildon Hill, Battle of, 1402 (Northumberland)

Free. Farmland, fields. Easy access. Parking possible off-road. Two miles west of Wooler on the A697 – the Bendar Stone is in the middle of a field north of the road. The visitor may look in vain for Homildon Hill, but will find Humbleton Hill, which is the same place. Opposite, to the north-west, is Harehope Hill.

The Scots with some 10,000 men under Sir Archibald Douglas marched into England in September 1402 while the English King Henry IV was busy dealing with rebels in Wales. The English forces in the north under Lord Percy moved to intercept, reaching the

King's Own Scottish Borderers Museum (Northumberland)

££ (included in entrance to Berwick Barracks). Shop. Research facilities. Parking in town. Tel. 01289 307426. On The Parade in Berwick-on-Tweed town centre.

Illustrates the history of the Regiment since 1689, with displays including uniforms, prints, paintings, silver and medals. There is a comprehensive collection of German, Japanese, Russian and Chinese weapons and trophies from the Second World War and subsequent campaigns. A rare exhibit is the original 'Backs to the wall' message of Field Marshal Haig in 1918.

Lindisfarne Castle (Northumberland) ❧

££. Usual hours March–October, closed Mondays. Shop. Refreshments. Parking Lindisfarne village. Tel. 01289 389244. On Holy Island, well signposted from the A1 south of Berwick-on-Tweed. It can only be approached by vehicle or on foot along a three-mile causeway that is closed two hours before and three hours after high tide – tide tables are displayed at the causeway.

Originally an artillery fort built by Henry VIII, converted by Sir Edwin Lutyens into a splendid country house perched on a rocky promontory with some magnificent views. Well worth the ten-minute walk from the village. Also worth visiting is the nearby ruin of Lindisfarne Priory with its surviving 'Rainbow' arch.

Military Vehicle Museum (Northumberland)

£. Usual hours. Shop. Research facilities. Parking near entrance in Claremont Road. Tel. 0191 2817222. www.military-museum.org.uk In Exhibition Park just north of Haymarket, Newcastle-upon-Tyne.

A museum of military vehicles and equipment created by the North East Military Vehicles Club and housed in a historic building. Over forty vehicles are on display together with a growing collection of over sixty cabinets of artefacts of wartime service life since 1900.

Myton, Battle of, 1319 (North Yorkshire)

Free. Open fields. Easy access. Parking possible in Myton-on-Swale. Two miles east of Boroughbridge off the A1. From the bridge north of Myton-on-Swale a good view of the site of the slaughter is possible. See also the nearby Battle of Boroughbridge (p. 99).

A battle, or rather a massacre, of the English by the Scots in the Scottish Wars of Independence. It took place on 20 September 1319 with the English under Melton, Archbishop of York, and the Scots commanded by the Earl of Moray and Lord James Douglas.

King Edward III had laid siege to Berwick and in response Moray and Douglas (both veterans of Bannock-

burn) marched through the north of England with several thousand men, laying waste to all in their path. Their real objective was to capture Edward's twenty-one-year-old queen from the court at York and hold her hostage. The Archbishop of York raised a scratch force of untrained civilians and straggled off to meet the Scots at Myton. In order to conceal the size of their force the Scots set light to three haystacks as they deployed. When the smoke cleared the English were appalled at the array confronting them. The Scots gave a tremendous roar and charged. The English rabble turned and fled without exchanging a blow. The Scottish mounted men cut off the retreat to the Myton Bridge and the resultant massacre and drownings in the River Swale accounted for some 4000 men.

Neville's Cross, Battle of, 1346 (Durham)

Free. Part open field, part under housing. Parking possible on some roads. Western outskirts of Durham. The open part of the battlefield leading to Baxter's Wood is immediately west of the A167 north of the bridge over the railway.

The battle was fought on 17 October 1346 between the English under Sir Ralph Neville with some 12,000 men and the Scots under King David II with around 15,000. The English deployed on a ridge just north of the railway line astride the A167 with their left on Baxter's Wood. There they awaited the Scottish attack. A ravine forced the Scots to crowd in on the centre, thus providing a splendid target for the English bowmen. On the flanks the English horsemen charged and pushed back their opponents and thus exposed the Scottish centre, forcing a retreat. King David was captured and imprisoned in the Tower.

Newburn Ford, Battle of, 1640 (Northumberland)

Free. Easy access to area of ford over River Tyne. Mainly open fields. Parking possible near bridge. Newburn is on the A6085 on the eastern outskirts of Newcastle. The ford is immediately west of the Newburn–Ryton bridge with the barricades and fighting taking place south of the river.

Fought on 28 August 1640 between the small English army (5500) of King Charles I under Lord Conway and the far larger invading Scottish army (20,000) under Alexander Leslie.

The Scottish force was marching south towards Newcastle-upon-Tyne but, rather than attack the city's strong northern defences, Leslie decided to cross the Tyne at Newburn ford and attack from the south. The far inferior English force of 4000 foot, 1500 cavalry and 4 cannons, formed behind some hastily constructed barricades, blocked Leslie's passage. The action started with an artillery exchange, with the English unable to reply effectively to a light cannon the Scots had installed on top of Newburn church. The Scots then advanced into the river. The defenders of the barricades gave desperate but ineffective musket fire for a few minutes before abandoning their defences. English resistance collapsed and an unknown number of fleeing soldiers were cut down.

This small action forced Charles to recall Parliament, which he had dissolved eleven years previously. It was the forerunner of the English Civil War later that decade.

Otterburn, Battle of, 1388 (Northumberland)

Free. Easy access, open fields and paths. Parking possible off-road. Half a mile west of Otterburn on the A696. There is a monument north of the road just east of the school.

Fought on 19 August 1388 as part of the frequent border wars of this time between the English under Sir Henry Percy (known as Hotspur) and the Scots commanded by Sir James Douglas. Both armies numbered around 10,000 men.

Hotspur had sworn to recapture his lance pennant, snatched by Douglas in a recent skirmish outside the gates of Newcastle. Douglas taunted him by saying he would await the English at Otterburn. On the night before the battle Douglas was encamped outside the small town astride the A696 near the present school. Hotspur launched a night attack with Sir Thomas Umfraville

Looking north towards the Royalist position from the monument, with Moor Lane on the right (Battlefields Trust)

Marston Moor, Battle of, 1644 (North Yorkshire)

Free. Fields and farmland. Easy access. Parking possible off-road by the monument. Six miles west of York alongside the B1224 about a mile along the minor road leading to Long Marston.

The largest battle of the English Civil War, fought on 2 July 1644 between the Royalists under Prince Rupert and the Allied (Parliamentary) Army under Lord Fairfax. That summer three large Parliamentarian forces, the Eastern Association under Manchester, the Scots under Leslie, Earl of Leven, and the Fairfaxes, some 25,000 men in total, besieged Royalist York.

Prince Rupert advanced with around 16,000 men to raise the siege. When Rupert reached Knaresborough Castle Fairfax broke off siege operations and concentrated his army around Long Marston village to confront the Royalists. Rupert drew up his force north of the Long Marston–Tockwith road with a ditch and bank running for much of its one-and-a-half-mile frontage. He placed cavalry under Byron on his right and Goring on the left, while he retained a strong reserve behind the infantry centre. Opposite, spread out in full view on the forward slope of the Marston ridge

south of the road, the Allies deployed. The Scottish mercenaries occupied the right centre; to their left were two English infantry groups under Lord Fairfax and Manchester. On the left was half the cavalry under Cromwell while the remainder on the right were under 'Fiery Tom' Fairfax, the commander-in-chief at Naseby a year later.

Rupert awaited attack. When it had not materialized by 7 p.m. he ordered food brought forward. But within half an hour the allied army advanced across the road towards the Ditch. On the right flank Tom Fairfax's horsemen crossed the Ditch and were instantly charged by Goring's horse. Most of Fairfax's men were dispersed and pursued off the field by the bulk of their Royalist antagonists. However, although wounded, Fairfax rallied a force of some 400 men. On the other flank Cromwell's cavalry crossed the Ditch to engage Byron's horsemen. After a short mêlée in which Cromwell was wounded, Byron's first line fled. Rupert then led forward his cavalry reserve to stabilize the situation on the right. However, after a prolonged fight the Royalist troopers were driven off in the direction of York.

Cromwell, together with Fairfax's 400 men, now turned on the Royalist infantry centre, in particular the massed ranks of the musketeers and pikemen of the famous Whitecoat Regiment and Greencoat Brigade. These units had occupied an enclosure and held out for over an hour against repeated attacks, launched by the Parliamentary horse and dragoons. Then, out of ammunition and refusing to surrender, most were cut down where they stood. The battle was over. Rupert fled north and York quickly fell. Some 6000 men died, mostly Royalists.

Much of the battlefield can be explored. A walk up the track south of the monument leads up to the Allied position. Continue across the field to the three trees ringed by a fence, Cromwell's Plump; this is the highest point of the ridge and affords good viewpoints over the battlefield towards the Royalist position. Back at the monument take Moor Lane, known as 'Bloody Lane', and continue for 200 yards beyond the Ditch to reach the centre of the battlefield.

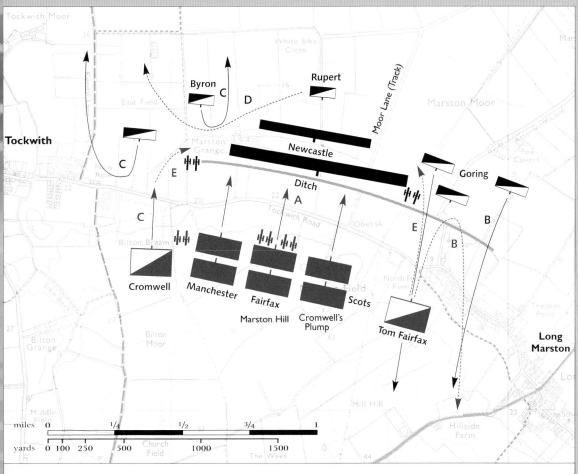

KEY

- ▬ Royalist infantry
- ◤ Royalist cavalry
- ♯♯♯ Royalist cannon
- ▬ Parliamentarian infantry
- ◤ Parliamentarian cavalry
- ♯♯♯ Parliamentarian cannon

A The Parliamentarians advance up to and over the ditch.

BB Goring charges Tom Fairfax's cavalry who are mainly driven from the field, with Goring's men in pursuit.

C Cromwell attacks Byron's cavalry, scattering them off the field.

D Rupert's reserve advances to stabilize his right, but after a fierce meleé his men give way.

E Cromwell and Tom Fairfax attack the Royalist infantry on each flank. The Royalists are forced back but some make a prolonged stand in an enclave (possibly White Sike Close) before being cut down.

Northallerton (The Standard), Battle of, 1138 (North Yorkshire)

Free. Easy access, open fields. Off-road parking possible. Approximately three miles north of Northallerton, just to the east of the A167. It is an easy field to view from the road or from the higher ground of Standard Hill and Standard Hill Farm (north). A visit to the gloom of Scot Pit Lane is essential. There is a large stone monument to the east of the main road on which can be seen the symbol of the archbishop's standard. The monument marks the approximate left wing of the English army.

Fought on 22 August 1138 between the English under Thurstan, the Archbishop of York, and a Scottish army under King David I. When King Henry I died in 1135 he left the English crown to his daughter Matilda. However, Matilda's cousin Stephen laid claim to the throne with the backing of many barons. Her uncle, King David of Scotland, supported Matilda's claim and in July 1138 he began to advance into northern England. The task of defending the kingdom for Stephen fell to Thurstan, Archbishop of York. The alternative name for this battle is The Standard, which refers to the archbishop's huge standard that was placed in the centre of his army. It was a ship's mast topped by a small vessel containing consecrated Holy Communion wafers, the whole contraption carried on a four-wheel cart.

The two forces met three miles north of Northallerton. The English deployed in three lines on the southernmost of two hills. In front were the archers, backed up by spearmen with a mounted force in the third line as reserve – Standard Hill Farm was just in the rear of the army. The Standard was positioned in the centre of the second line. The army of around 10,000 occupied a frontage of about 800 yards. The Scots, with about the same number, formed up opposite, some 600 yards to the north on another hill with a division of West Highlanders on the left, the mass of wild, poorly equipped Galwegian Picts in the centre and young Prince Henry, King David's son, with the cavalry on the right. In the rear the King commanded a small reserve of mounted men.

The Picts started the action by making a charge downhill straight into a storm of arrows from the English bowmen. As the distance closed and the hail of arrows continued the attackers were shot down in scores. Their advance was checked and a long phalanx of disciplined spearmen took over the defence of the hill as the archers retired. Prince Henry, on seeing the Picts fall back with heavy losses, led his mounted men forward round the English left flank to attack the baggage wagons and led horses. However, the archbishop, very much a general as well as a man of God, charged the enemy

horse and a fierce hand-to-hand clash occurred immediately north and west of the southern Standard Hill Farm. It was a desperate and bloody engagement but one in which the English slowly gained the advantage. Eventually, the Scottish cavalry were pushed back and seeing this the rest of King David's army turned to run. In the chaos at the end, both the king and his son escaped.

Many hundreds of dead from both sides were buried in Scot Pit Lane, a heavily tree-lined lane some 300 yards to the rear of Standard Hill Farm (south). This lane links the A167 to the minor road running north from Brompton.

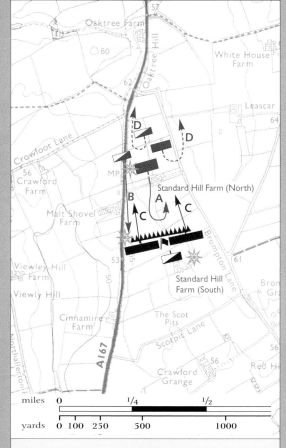

| miles | 0 | | ¼ | | ½ |
| yards | 0 100 250 | | 500 | | 1000 |

KEY

▬ English infantry		A	The Picts attach but are defeated by archers
◢ English cavalry			
▲▲▲▲ English archers		B	Prince Henry attempts to outflank the English left
▬ Scottish infantry			
◳ Scottish cavalry		C	The English advance
⚑ The Standard		D	The remainder of King David's army turns to run

attempting a wide outflanking march to the north while he advanced frontally. Douglas advanced to meet the frontal attack but sent another force on a short outflanking move to charge downhill onto the English right. The Scots counter-attack was successful, although Douglas was killed by three spear thrusts. Hotspur was wounded and captured and the English fled.

The Prince of Wales's Own Regiment of Yorkshire Museum (York)

£. Usual hours Monday–Saturday. Shop. Parking nearby. Tel. 01904 658824. www.yorkshirevolunteers.org.uk/pwo.htm 3 Tower Street, York. In the centre of the city opposite Clifford's Tower about ten minutes' walk from the station. It is in the same building as the museum of the Royal Dragoon Guards (see below).

The collection consists of uniforms, badges, medals, pictures, photographs and trophies laid out to show the story of the old regiment (1658–1958).

Roman Road, Blackstone Edge (Greater Manchester)

Free. Parking possible nearby but some walking involved. Six miles north-east of Rochdale on the A58 and 2½ miles east of Littleborough. It can be reached by a path from the A58 to Halifax road.

The finest example of a Roman military road (although some scholars dispute its origins). The road, 16ft wide, attacks the steep gradient straight-on and is in some parts entirely intact. The beautifully tooled cobbles lie between strong kerbs and surround a mysterious central groove – possibly intended to steady the break poles of laden wagons. Follow the road to the top of the hill and, turning right, walk the half mile to the fantastically contorted rocks called Robin Hood's Seat. The road was probably part of the Roman Army's communication system for controlling the central Pennines linking the fort at Manchester with the one at Ilkley on the other side of the Pennines.

Royal Armouries Museum (Leeds)

Free. Usual hours. Shop. Refreshments. Picnic area. Group tours. Special events. Parking. Tel. 0113 2201999. www.royalarmouries.org Armouries Drive, Leeds. Well signed on all roads leading into Leeds. A ten-minute walk from the rail station.

An award-winning collection of arms and armour in five galleries that tell the story of the development of arms and armour in war, the tournament, hunting and self-defence from earliest times to the present. A typical visit would take four to five hours including watching live demonstrations of jousting in the tilt yard, hand-to-hand combat or falconry, or of an armourer, leatherworker or gun-maker at work, all supported by films and interactive displays.

Royal Dragoon Guards Museum (York)

£. Usual hours Monday–Saturday. Shop. Parking nearby. Tel. 01904 642036. www.rdgmuseum.org.uk 3a Tower Street, York. In the centre of York opposite the Clifford Tower. It is in the same building as the museum of the Prince of Wales's Own Regiment of Yorkshire (above).

An interesting display of uniforms, medals, badges, weapons, pictures, standards and photographs telling the story of the 4th/7th Dragoon Guards from 1665 until its amalgamation with the 5th Royal Inniskilling Dragoon Guards to form the Royal Dragoon Guards. Displays illustrate campaigns in India, South Africa, Flanders, North Africa, Italy, Burma, Malaya and Aden.

A set of Indian elephant armour in the Royal Armouries Museum

Towton, Battle of, 1461 (North Yorkshire)

Free. Easy access to view the farmland and fields over which the fighting took place. Parking in Towton or Saxton and off-road in some places. One mile south of Towton village, which stands on the A162 Pontefract to Tadcaster road. The battlefield lies between the A162 and the B1217. A cross stands close to the B1217, supposedly marking the spot where Dacre was killed; he is buried in Saxton churchyard. From this monument there is a good view of the battlefield.

Towton was the largest battle of the Wars of the Roses, with the Lancastrians under the twenty-four-year-old Duke of Somerset mustering 30,000 and the Yorkists under Prince Edward some 25,000. After the death of Richard, Duke of York at Wakefield (p. 115), his son, Edward, was victorious at Mortimer's Cross (p. 67) and marched to London, where the nobles declared him King Edward IV. But meanwhile Queen Margaret's Lancastrian forces had defeated the Earl of Warwick at the second Battle of St Albans (p. 48) and succeeded in freeing Henry VI. Both kings knew their claim to the throne would be decided in battle. They met at Towton on 29 March 1461.

Somerset had drawn up his Lancastrian army on the ridge just south of Towton with his right flank resting on, or just west of, today's B1217 and his left on the A162; to his front was the low ground of Towton Dale and North Acres. He had also placed a small ambush party of archers in Castle Hill Wood some 1000 yards away to the south-west, almost opposite the enemy position. To the south, only 700 yards away, were the Yorkists on another ridge with their flanks resting on the same roads. Both sides had a frontage of about 1000 yards with bowmen in the front line. At 9 a.m. on Palm

Looking north along the Saxton–Towton road towards the Lancastrian position (Battlefields Trust)

Sunday, with the church bells ringing, snow falling, and very poor visibility, the two armies advanced simultaneously on each other.

With the lines about 300 yards apart, the Yorkists halted and shot several volleys of heavy arrows which, with a following wind, caused some loss to the Lancastrians. Thinking the range was shorter than it was, Somerset's bowmen replied with lighter arrows into the wind, most of which fell short. The Yorkists advanced again, salvaged the useable enemy's arrows and shot them back. Both lines of archers then closed for a hand-to-hand struggle. They quickly became exhausted and the main armies advanced to become locked in close combat in the low ground of Towton Dale. At some stage the Lancastrian archers in Castle Hill Wood opened fire and caused some faltering in the Yorkists' second line. By 3 p.m. the battle was still raging, although by then many on both sides were close to exhaustion and pauses in the fighting took place. During one brief rest one of the senior Lancastrian commanders, Lord Dacre, sat down and removed his helmet, only to be hit in the face by an arrow shot by a local Yorkist supporter hidden in a nearby tree.

At about this time a possible Yorkist defeat was turned into a victory by the timely arrival of reinforcements on the right flank under the Duke of Norfolk. His appearance proved too much for the Lancastrians, who began to slip away. Fear is infectious and soon Somerset's army was in flight. Many men drowned in the Cocke stream and others fell fighting in the appropriately named 'Bloody Meadow'. The pursuit was sustained and ruthless. It is claimed that some 20,000 Lancastrians died and around 8000 Yorkists.

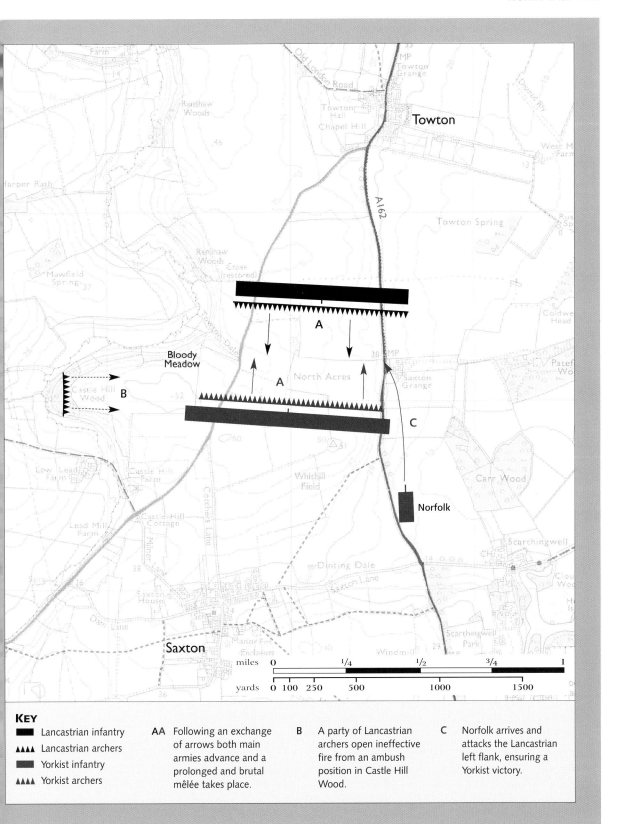

KEY

■ Lancastrian infantry
▲▲▲▲ Lancastrian archers
■ Yorkist infantry
▲▲▲▲ Yorkist archers

AA Following an exchange of arrows both main armies advance and a prolonged and brutal mêlée takes place.

B A party of Lancastrian archers open ineffective fire from an ambush position in Castle Hill Wood.

C Norfolk arrives and attacks the Lancastrian left flank, ensuring a Yorkist victory.

13th/18th Royal Hussars and Light Dragoons Museum (Yorkshire)

£. Usual hours. Sundays 12–5 p.m. November, December and March Sundays only; closed January and February. Shop. Refreshments. Lecture room. Parking. Tel. 01226 790270. Cannon Hall Museum, Park and Gardens are off the A635 between Barnsley and Denby Dale. Brown and white tourist signs from Barnsley, on the A635 and from Junction 38 on the M1.

This regimental museum, called 'The Charge', is part of the Cannon Hall Museum belonging to the Cannon Hall Park and Garden complex. Exhibits are located in four rooms and a corridor, with the accent on uniforms and equipment from the Peninsular War to the present day. Tours are enhanced with audiovisual displays.

Segedunum Roman Fort and Museum (Newcastle upon Tyne) (World Heritage Site)

££. Usual hours March–September. Shop. Refreshments. School visits. Lecture hall. Library. Research facilities. Parking. Tel. 0191 2955757. www.segedunum.com Wallsend, Tyne and Wear. From Newcastle take the metro from either Monument or St James Park to Wallsend. The site is a minute's walk from the metro and bus station.

A must for anyone interested in the Roman Army and Hadrian's Wall, Segedunum Fort, Bath and Museum combines the excavated remains of the fort with spectacular reconstructions and hands-on museum displays to show what life in Roman Britain was really like. The remains represent the most extensively excavated site of the Roman Empire and the reconstructed bath-house is the only one of its kind in the UK. No other site on Hadrian's Wall can match the views from the 100ft tower. Highlights include the Roman Gallery, which explores the life of a Roman soldier at the fort with the aid of a model and interactive virtual tour, and the Industry Gallery which traces the site's history after the Roman occupation. Visitors to the bath-house can explore the changing room and progress through a series of cold, warm and hot rooms. There is also an 80m section of the original Wall together with a reconstructed section that gives an impression of how the Wall would have looked 1800 years ago.

Stamford Bridge, Battle of, 1066 (Yorkshire)

Free. Reasonable access, some built-up areas near bridge but open fields where the main action took place. Parking in village. Stamford Bridge eight miles east of York on the A166. The site of the footbridge can be found 300 yards upstream of the road bridge, and the Battle Flats on the east of the village are accessible.

A battle fought on 25 September 1066 between the English under King Harold and the invading Vikings under Harald Hardrada of Norway. While watching the coast of Kent for an expected invasion from Normandy, Harold heard of the Vikings' landing and march on York. He had no alternative but to hurry north to engage them. With around 4000 men he advanced to attack his enemy encamped at Stamford Bridge eight miles east of York.

The Vikings were surprised by the English approach and hastily left a rearguard to defend a narrow wooden footbridge (300 yards upstream from the present road bridge), while their main force withdrew over the river to form a shield wall on what is now known as Battle Flats, some 400 yards east of the bridge. Harold marched up the A166, charged the bridge guard and overwhelmed it – although there is a story that a giant Norseman wielding a huge axe delayed things for half an hour. Harold then launched another fierce onslaught on the shield wall of the main Viking position. A prolonged hacking and slashing mêlée ensued in which the English triumphed despite Viking reinforcements arriving from their ships. Hardrada was killed and all except a handful of his force destroyed.

That night Harold heard that William of Normandy had landed at Pevensey. He marched south, covering 260 miles in twelve days to fight and die at Hastings.

Stanwick Iron Age Fort (Yorkshire) ⌗

Free. Open any reasonable time. Parking nearby possible. Take the A66 from Scotch Corner on the A1 and then turn right onto the B6274. This road cuts through the outer rampart. Turn right opposite Fawcett church and right again after 100 yards – at the end of the houses there is a sign to 'Stanwick Camp'.

A massive stronghold covering some 700 acres, making it the largest prehistoric stronghold in Britain. It was built in the first century AD by the Brigantes tribe. Today it provides an excellent glimpse of what hill-fort defences looked like, as an excavated section of the ditch and rampart are open to view.

Temple of Mithras, (Northumberland) ⌗

£. Usual hours. Parking nearby. museums.ncl.ac.uk/archive/mithras/frames.htm On the Wall, at Carrawburgh Fort two miles west of Chesters Fort. Best approached from the A69 at Hexham along the A6079 and combined with a visit to Chesters.

The cult that had the largest following within the Roman army was that of Mithras, a Persian god of light and truth introduced by the army of occupation into Britain. According to legend Mithras had captured and killed in a cave the primeval bull, the first creature created on earth, and from his slaying sprang the benefits of mankind. Worshippers had to pass initiation tests of courage and endurance before being allowed to progress from one grade to another, through Raven, Bridegroom, Soldier, Lion, Persian and Courier of the Sun to Father. A novice was tested by having to lie down in a 6ft-long pit next to a fire, as though in a grave. He was then covered with stone slabs and subjected to the heat of the fire and cold of the pit, before being allowed into the inner sanctuary to take the oath, which bound him never to reveal the rites and ceremonies of the cult.

The tiny temple at Carrawburgh has been excavated and still retains something of its dark mysteries, with the three altars at the far end.

The earthworks at Stanwick, Britain's largest prehistoric stronghold

Vindolanda Roman Fort and Chesterholm Museum (Northumberland) (World Heritage Site ⊞)

££. Usual hours, closed mid-November–mid-February. Shop. Coffee shop. School visits. Parking. Tel. 01434 344277. Well signposted off the A69 between Hexham and Haltwhistle.

There are extensive remains and things to see at Vindolanda – fort, civil settlement, reconstructions and museum. The remains of the fort are part of a third- and fourth-century construction to house the 4th Cohort of Gauls, a mixed infantry and cavalry regiment raised in France. A tour, including an introductory talk, can take up to two hours. There is much to see, including burial tombs, the unit's bath-house, entrance gates, headquarters building, commanding officer's house, latrines and the civil settlement, the latter the most extensive such site on the Wall. The museum is full of fascinating artefacts found on the site, including a lady's slipper and a fragment of a letter on a wooden writing tablet.

Wakefield, Battle of, 1460 (West Yorkshire)

Free. Easy access to viewpoint at Sandal Castle. Mostly open fields but some urban development. Parking near Sandal Castle. Sandal Castle ruins stand two miles south of Wakefield and can be reached via the A61 Wakefield–Barnsley road. Turn off at the signposted castle road and climb the castle hill. The view of the battlefield to the north and west is excellent.

A battle in the Wars of the Roses, fought on 30 December 1460 between the Lancastrians under the Duke of Somerset and the Yorkists commanded by Richard, Duke of York. The Lancastrians with some 18,000 men hugely outnumbered the Yorkists' 5000 installed in Sandal Castle. The Lancastrians formed up about two miles south of Wakefield but out of sight of the castle. Somerset sent a small detachment up to the castle to show itself to the defenders. Perhaps Richard thought they were reinforcements arriving, or perhaps he was tempted to attack so small a force; whatever the reason, the Yorkists sallied forth from the castle. This was the signal for the main Lancastrian army to advance in three divisions from its concealment in nearby woods. Instead of retiring, Richard launched an all-out assault on his enemy's centre. Inevitably with the huge disparity in numbers the Lancastrian wings closed in on Richard's flanks and the slaughter began. Some 2000 Yorkists were cut down including Richard, whose head was later displayed on York's city walls adorned with a paper crown.

THE WALLS: HADRIAN'S AND THE ANTONINE

HADRIAN'S WALL

This wall, 72 miles long from Newcastle upon Tyne in the east to Bowness-on-Solway in the west, is probably the finest military monument in the whole Roman Empire. It was no ordinary wall. Rather it was a complex system of fortifications that served as a defensive barrier against northern barbarians and facilitated the control of civilian movement in both directions. It enabled tolls to be collected, imports and exports to be checked and suspicious persons interrogated. When completed the military zone consisted of four components: the wall itself, with a v-shaped ditch in front (north); a series of forts, milecastles and turrets along the wall to house its garrison; a ditch and earthworks to the south called the vallum; and a road linking the forts called the 'military way'.

The wall was born in around 122, when Emperor Hadrian visited Britain and gave orders for its construction. Detachments of legionaries, and even some sailors from the British Fleet, began building straight away. A legion contained engineers, surveyors, masons, carpenters and glaziers – all the skilled personnel to plan and supervise the labour force of

An impressive view of Milecastle 39 and the Wall on either side. Note the two entrances in the north and south walls to allow easy access in both directions.

soldiers – although it is possible local civilians were involved in transporting some materials. Soldiers from the permanent bases at York, Chester and Caerleon all took their turn. Leaving the comfort of their fortresses for a tour of duty building the wall in wild winter weather cannot have been a popular posting. With its associated forts, it took fourteen years to complete.

The original plan was for a continuous stone wall, fronted by a ditch, from Newcastle forty miles west to the River Irthing (just west of Haltwhistle), and a wall of turf blocks and timber from there to the Solway. The wall was 15ft high, 7½–10ft wide up to the rampart walk, with a parapet and merlons adding another 6ft. In front was a 20ft berm (space), a 10ft deep and 30ft wide ditch with a sloping outer (northern) lip (see diagram). At intervals of a Roman mile (1620 yards) were milecastles, constructed of stone or earth, turf and

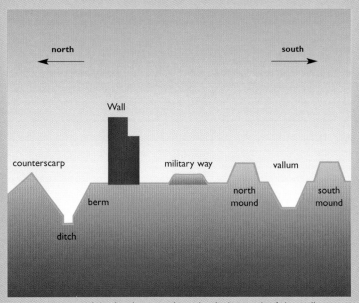

The arrangement of the fortifications, from the ditch – north of the Wall – to the military way and the vallum which lie to the south.

timber on the turf portion of the wall. These were small fortlets with gates to the north and south and a barracks for up to a maximum of thirty-two men and stores. Between each milecastle were spaced two turrets, or watchtowers.

The original scheme was not carried out in full. About AD 124 the chain of forts on the Stanegate, the main Roman road to the south and parallel to the wall, seem to have been abandoned and replacement forts integrated into the wall itself. When completed fifteen such forts, each capable of housing a cohort of 500 or sometimes 1000 soldiers, studded the wall throughout its length. At the same time the continuous earthwork, the vallum, was built. It ran the entire length of the wall and was carefully constructed as a barrier intended to channel access to the military zone of the wall from the south. The ditch was 10ft deep with a flat bottom 8ft wide and 20ft wide across the top – a substantial obstacle. On either side was a berm and then a mound or bank of earth 6ft high. Causeways opposite the forts provided the vallum's only crossing points. At places the wall had to cross

rivers. Examples can be seen at Chesters and Willowford. The Tyne had to be crossed at two points – Newcastle and Corbridge. Small streams were carried through the wall by culverts.

On completion of the wall the soldiers spent their lives in the fifteen forts that formed part of it rather than in the thirteen built earlier that lined the Stanegate just to the south. From these forts detachments, based in the milecastles under a centurion, would patrol the ramparts and turrets and check all movement through the wall. It was, like all soldiering then and since, tedious work very rarely interrupted by short periods of intense excitement. No two wall forts were exactly the same although the basic layout only varied slightly. They were, effectively, much scaled-down fortresses, resembling in shape a squarish playing card with the same rounded corners.

WHO GARRISONED THE WALL?

Contrary to popular belief, although legionaries built the wall they did not provide its garrison. Rather they were held back at their bases to form the strategic reserve. Tactical defence and control on the wall was the responsibility of auxiliary units. Each fort was built to accommodate a single auxiliary unit. There were six different types and sizes of auxiliary units and all are attested to on the wall. The most common was the 500-strong mixed infantry and cavalry regiment, closely followed by the 500-man infantry unit. There were also several 1000-strong mixed and infantry regiments. Cavalry units were rare, reflecting the more static role of the garrison. The only British cavalry regiment of 1000 men was the *Ala Petriana* at Stanwix, near Carlisle. Its commander was the senior officer based on the wall – although not necessarily in direct command over all garrison units. During the 300 years the wall was in use, some 65 different cohorts and locally raised irregular units (*numeri*) formed its garrison, and that of northern frontier forts. Most

Housesteads, the best-preserved fort on Hadrian's Wall

served on or near the wall for many years. An extreme example was the cavalry regiment *Ala 1 Hispanorum Asturum* (originally raised in Asturia, northern Spain), which was stationed at Benwell from 205 to 367. In 162 years, generation after generation of men from northern Britain would have enlisted, served their time and earned Roman citizenship. There was a cohort of Hamian archers raised in Syria that during Hadrian's time was stationed at Benwell, then went for a period to Bar Hill on the Antonine Wall before returning to Benwell around 163.

VISITING HADRIAN'S WALL

The wall is a World Heritage Site and as such attracts many thousands of visitors each year, by car, coach, bicycle or on foot. Hadrian's Wall Path was opened in May 2003 so it is now possible for walkers to follow the wall from end to end along an unbroken, signposted trail. This path covers 81 miles and is ideal for a week-long holiday. For day trips more than forty short walks have been created. If visiting in the winter

walkers are advised to follow circular routes or to visit any of the twelve managed sites that are open during winter months. An essential for a long walking visit is a copy of the National Trail Guide entitled *Hadrian's Wall Path* by Anthony Burton (Aurum Press), which contains a description of the route alongside OS strip maps. To plan your visit ahead contact the Haltwhistle information helpline (Tel: 01434 322002, e-mail haltwhistle@btconnect.com) for leaflets, information on where to stay and available public transport.

Well worth a visit
Birdoswald Fort *p. 95*
Arbeia Fort and Museum, South Shields *p. 99*
Chesters Fort and Museum *p. 100*
Corbridge Fort and Museum *p. 100*
Greenhead Roman Army Museum *p. 104*
Housesteads Fort and Museum *p. 106*
Segedunum Fort and Museum *p. 114*
Temple of Mithras *p. 114*
Vindolanda Fort and Museum, Chesterholm *p. 115*

THE ANTONINE WALL

In AD 142 the Emperor Antoninus Pius decided to move the frontier of Roman Britain northwards from Hadrian's Wall. To mark this new frontier another wall 37 miles long was built from Bridgeness on the Firth of Forth to Old Kilpatrick on the Firth of Clyde – the narrowest part of Britain – supervised by the Governor of Britain, Lollius Urbicus. Unlike Hadrian's Wall to the south, this Antonine Wall was constructed of turf. There were three parts to this defensive barrier: first a v-shaped ditch to the north 40ft wide and 12ft deep, then the wall itself, consisting of a rampart of turf, originally some 12ft high, set on a 14ft-thick stone base; finally a military road about 15ft wide, cambered, with a gravelled surface on a stone base. This ran some 50 yards to the rear of the wall. Nineteen forts were built of timber just south of the wall at two-mile intervals. A few smaller fortlets and signalling platforms have also been found; there is archaeological evidence that they were built on the foundations of forts constructed by Agricola when he came north in AD 80–1.

The Antonine Wall was, like Hadrian's, constructed by legionaries, as evidenced by inscriptions on stone distance-slabs, but afterwards garrisoned by cohorts of auxiliaries. It was occupied twice during its short life as the northernmost frontier of empire. The first period lasted about thirteen years, until the troops were withdrawn to deal with insurrections in the south. The second occupation was for a mere three years (160–3). After this it was again abandoned and never reoccupied. During the time it was operational it was much more heavily garrisoned than Hadrian's Wall as its length was far shorter and it had more forts.

Because the wall was built of turf, little has survived, although the ditch is clearly visible, particularly at Watling Lodge just west of Falkirk. The best-preserved fort excavations are at Rough Castle (p. 147), near Bonnybridge eight miles south of Stirling. An Antonine Walkway Trust has established the area of the wall around Bar Hill (p. 114) and Croy Hill as a visitors' centre for walking or cycling to picnic areas and viewpoints.

Well worth a visit

Antonine Walkway Trust area which includes Bar Hill
    and Croy hill-forts, Kilsyth *p. 143*
Kinneil Fortlet, Bo'ness *p. 145*
Rough Castle, Falkirk *p. 147*

Rough Castle, one of the few surviving forts on the Antonine Wall

WALES

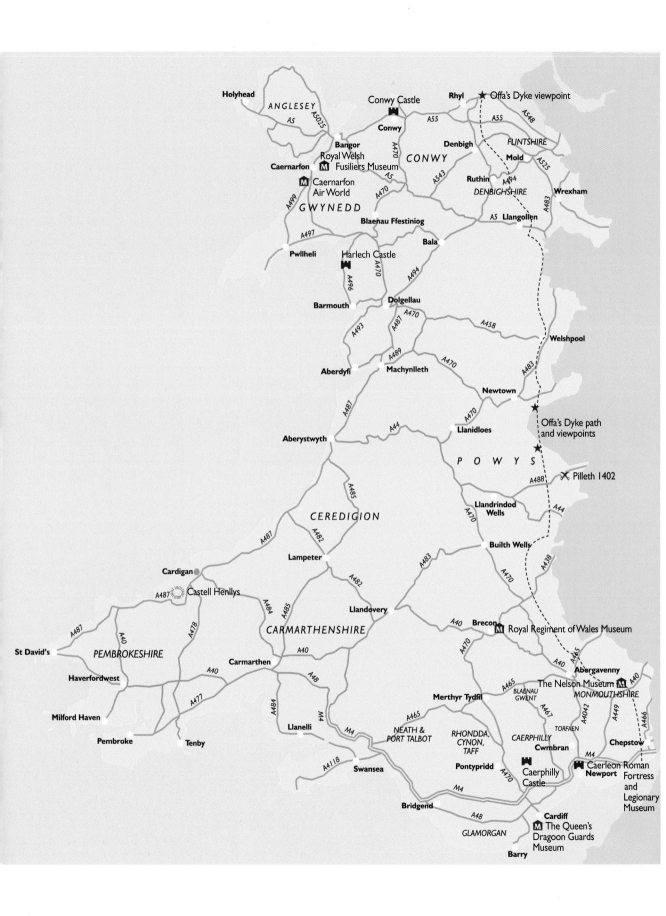

WALES

A copper Winged Victory, on display at the Caerleon Roman Legionary Museum

Caerleon (Isca) Roman Fortress and Legionary Museum (Gwent) (Cadw)

££ (Roman baths only). Museum, barracks and amphitheatre free. Usual hours. Gift shop. Cafés/restaurants nearby. Picnic area. School visits. Parking by baths and amphitheatre. Tel. 01633 423134 (museum) or 01633 422518 (baths, barracks and amphitheatre). A mile NE of Newport. Take the B4596 from Junction 25 on the M4.

One of only three permanent Roman fortresses in Britain, Caerleon was built in AD 75 to accommodate the 5500 heavy infantry of the II Augusta legion, whose base it was for some two hundred years. The Romans created not just a military fortress but also a town. Visitors can explore the only uncovered legionary barracks foundations in Europe, complete with latrines, cookhouse and centurions' rooms, and a full-scale reconstruction of a barrack room. Outside the west gate is Britain's most complete amphitheatre – where picnicking is

allowed. The baths contain a visitor centre, display and audiovisual explanation of the whole site. The museum contains a fascinating display of Roman artefacts, armour and weapons showing how Roman soldiers lived, fought and died.

Caernarfon Air World (Gwynedd)

£££. Museum usual hours 1 March–1 November; winter by request; pleasure flights daily throughout year weather permitting. Gift shop. Restaurant Easter to end of season. Coffee shop daily throughout year. Picnic area. Cinema. School visits. Children's adventure playground. Tel. 01286 830800. www.air-world.co.uk Four miles SW of Caernarfon. Turn off the A499 to Dinas Dinlle – signposted.

The premier aviation attraction of North Wales, this is a great indoor hands-on attraction where visitors can sit in cockpits, take the controls in a Varsity Trainer and wander round full-sized planes. There are sections and exhibitions featuring the Dambusters, Welsh flying VCs, the first RAF Mountain Rescue Service and the Fleet Air Arm. Aerial tours of ten or twenty minutes are available over Caernarfon Castle, Menai Straits, Beaumaris Castle, Snowdonia and Bardseys Island.

Caerphilly Castle (Caerphilly) (Cadw)

££. Usual hours. Shop. Picnic area. Special events in summer. Exhibitions. Parking. Tel. 02920 883143. In the centre of Caerphilly, five mile north of Cardiff and ten miles west of Newport.

A rescue helicopter at Caernarfon Air World

Caerphilly Castle, the largest in Wales

This fortress covers some thirty acres and dominates the town of Caerphilly. It is the largest in Wales, with the most extensive water defences of any British stronghold. Built in the late 13th century by the Anglo-Norman lord Gilbert de Clare, it was a high point in medieval military architecture and a classic example of the concentric 'walls within walls' defensive system, particularly famous for its 'leaning tower'. Buy a guidebook and take your time – it is an exciting experience. Special events include the firing of siege engines, arms and armour demonstrations, falconry and medieval re-enactments.

Castell Henllys Iron Age Fort (Pembrokeshire)

££. Usual hours from Easter until end of season. Shop. Picnic areas. Guided tours. Visitor centre. School visits. Education Centre. Children's activities. Parking. Tel. 01293 891319.
www.castellhenllys.com Signposted off the A487 between Newport and Cardigan.

As a resource for understanding life in an Iron Age hill-fort Castell Henllys is second to none. Buildings such as roundhouses, a smithy, granary and chieftain's house have been carefully reconstructed, and visitors can explore historic trails and enjoy woodland walks and riverside paths below the fort.

Castell Henllys Fort, reconstructed to give a fascinating insight into Iron Age life

Conwy Castle (Conwy) (Cadw)

££. Usual hours. Shop. Guided tours. Exhibitions. Special events. Parking. Tel. 01492 592358. www.conwy.com Central Conwy, three miles south of Llandudno.

Conwy Castle stands sentinel on its rock over the town, river and valley. Soaring curtain walls and eight huge round towers give it an intimidating presence. Conceived and built in only four years (1283–7), it is one of Edward I's famous castles, one of his 'iron ring' of fortresses built to contain the unruly Welsh. The views from the battlements are superb and include the ring of town walls, a mile long and guarded by twenty-two towers – one of the finest in the world. An hour or more exploring the interior and battlements armed with a guidebook is a thoroughly rewarding experience. Special events include the Welsh Warband, the Wales Actors' Shakespeare Tour and medieval living history and combat events.

Harlech Castle (Gwynedd) (World Heritage Site; Cadw)

££. Usual hours. Shop. Special events. Parking nearby. Tel. 01766 780552. Harlech, on the coastal A496.

The ten castles built in north and central Wales by Edward I from 1277 onwards are visually, militarily and technically unrivalled. Built in just seven years from 1283 to 1290, Harlech is spectacularly sited on a huge rock gazing out to sea and over Snowdonia, giving it immense defensive strength. Its battlements are a continuation of a near-vertical cliff face. The massive inner walls and towers still stand almost to their full height, making the views some of the best in Wales. A long siege during the Wars of the Roses inspired the stirring song 'Men of Harlech', and it endured another lengthy siege during the Civil War, before finally surrendering to Cromwell's forces in 1647. A tour of the castle includes (in summer) a walk down the fortified steps that lead to the sand dunes at its foot.

The Nelson Museum (Monmouth)

££ (accompanied children free). Usual hours. Shop. Exhibitions. Educational groups. Parking nearby. Tel. 01600 710630. Priory Street, Monmouth town centre.

Housed in the former Market Hall, the museum contains a wide variety of ship models, swords, prints, pictures, books, letters, silver, ivory and wood carving, all concerned with the life and times of Lord Nelson.

Offa's Dyke Path (see also pp. 20, 66)

Free. Open and wooded countryside. Somewhat remote areas but access possible via minor roads. It is possible to walk the entire length over some magnificent countryside with splendid views – best done in dry weather. Tourist Offices provide a detailed guide with maps (Offa's Dyke Long Distance Path). It can also be viewed from certain selected viewpoints.

The impressive exterior of Conwy Castle

Wales has at least four good places at which to view Offa's Dyke and/or join it for a lengthy or short walk. They are, starting in the north:

• Prestatyn, four miles south of the town at the minor crossroads east of the village of Cym

• Oswestry, four miles NW of the town on the B4579, at the sharp bend in the road a mile west of the village of Selattyn

• Hay-on-Wye, six miles NW of the town on the B5494 east of the village of Newchurch

• Hay-on-Wye, three miles south of the town on the minor road by Hay Bluff peak and anywhere south along Black Mountain ridge line.

Pilleth, Battle of, 1402 (Powys)

Free. Open fields. Easy access from minor roads. Take the B4355 south from Knighton, then the B4357 to Whitton. At Whitton turn right onto the B4356 and the battlefield is on your right.

This battle took place on 22 June 1402 between the forces of the great Welsh guerrilla fighter Owen Glendower and the English under Edmund Mortimer. Glendower with around 3000 men, including numerous archers, took up position on the hill above Pilleth church called Bryn Glas. Mortimer, whose more heavily armoured men slightly outnumbered his opponent, advanced up the hill. When halfway up, the Welsh shot a storm of arrows into the advancing enemy and followed it up with a wild charge. The rush down the steep slope was unstoppable and the English were swept away, losing some 800 men in slaughter. Mortimer was captured. Today there is a conspicuous clump of trees marking the spot where bones from a mass gravesite were discovered.

The Queen's Dragoon Guards Museum (Cardiff)

Free (included in entry to Cardiff Castle). Usual hours. Shop. Refreshments. Picnic area. Guided tours. School visits. Research facilities. Parking. Tel. 02920 222253. Cardiff Castle, city centre. (This museum is currently closed for refurbishment but is likely to reopen in mid-2007.)

Offa's Dyke, still dominating the surrounding countryside

The South Wales Borderers confront the Zulus at Rorke's Drift, in a painting displayed at the Royal Regiment of Wales Museum

The exhibits include a colourful display of uniforms of Dragoon Guards from 1685 to the present day. There are items worn at Waterloo and a splendid collection of medals, badges, weapons, silver, standards, drums and photographs. There is also a TV monitor display of the regiment in action in the two World Wars and uniforms and equipment used in the Gulf War in 1991 and in Iraq in 2005.

The Royal Regiment of Wales Museum (Powys)

££. Usual hours Mon–Fri, also weekends in summer. Shop. Guided tours. School visits. Library. Research facilities. Tel. 01874 613310. www.rrw.org.uk The Barracks, Brecon.

This is one of the finest military museums in the country – an essential for any visitors to Brecon interested in military history. The Royal Regiment of Wales was formed in 1969 by the amalgamation of the South Wales Borderers and The Welch Regiment. There is a particularly fascinating display of weapons, while the medal room contains over 3500 medals in a dazzling exhibition with the 16 Victoria Crosses owned by the Regiment forming the centrepiece. Another big attraction is the Zulu War Room with its displays of the famous stand by the South Wales Borderers at Rorke's Drift, when the Regiment gained ten VCs, accompanied by a film describing these events.

The Royal Welch Fusiliers Museum (Caernarfon Castle)

Free (admission is included in castle entrance of £££). Usual hours. Shop. Refreshments close to castle. Parking behind castle. Tel. 01286 673362. Caernarfon Castle.

Occupying five floors in two towers within the castle, this enjoyable museum contains exhibits and six audiovisual presentations depicting the history of Wales's oldest infantry regiment. There are numerous displays of uniforms, dioramas, weapons, models, medals, paintings and military memorabilia from Marlborough's wars through the American War of Independence, Napoleonic Wars, the Crimea, Indian Mutiny, Boer War and the great conflicts of the 20th century.

NORMAN AND MEDIEVAL CASTLES

Because this Guide covers such a comprehensive spectrum of Britain's military history, and because many books on British castles are already available, only a select few are described in detail here. Readers wanting more complete coverage should refer to *Daily Telegraph Castles and Ancient Monuments of England* and a guide similarly entitled for Scotland by Damien Noonan (both published by Aurum Press).

For centuries castles and similar fortifications were an essential part of the structure of British society. Iron Age man built huge earthworks and ditches to keep out enemy tribes and wild animals. The Romans as an occupying power built scores of forts. As recently as the Second World War, castles many hundreds of years old, such as Pendennis in Cornwall and Dover in Kent, have been modified to give them a role in the defence of this country, housing gun batteries, radar early-warning systems, communications centres or military headquarters. Some might even consider the underground command bunkers, like the one in Fife (p. 147), a type of nuclear age castle.

However, most people's idea of a castle is based on those that began to be constructed in Britain soon after the Norman Conquest of 1066, several of which (after many additions and adaptations) are still in use today, most famously the Tower of London (p. 51) and Windsor Castle. A castle is a fortified military residence whose primary initial purpose was to hold down a conquered country. They served as residences for kings and nobles; they represented power and wealth and as

Pevensey: first a Roman fort, then the earliest Norman castle

such intimidated local populations – as well as providing them with places of refuge in times of conflict.

By the time William the Conqueror died in 1087 he had stamped his authority over much of England as well as venturing into both Wales and Scotland. Dividing up his new territory, William retained a quarter of the land for himself, gave a quarter to the Church and distributed the remainder as a reward to his loyal supporters who had fought under his banner of conquest – they later became known as barons and knights. They held the land for the king as tenants-in-chief and in return provided him with taxes and soldiers as required, exercising their authority from castles.

The first Norman versions were simple affairs, known as 'motte and bailey' castles. The motte was the mound on which a tower (or keep) was built, a huge pile of compacted earth up to 250ft in diameter, often interspersed with layers of stone. The flat top was surrounded by a wooden palisade and a wooden tower in the centre served as the residence of the lord. Soon wooden towers were replaced by stone, like the White Tower at the Tower of London.

The bailey was a larger area of land adjoining, or sometimes surrounding, the motte. It was enclosed by a smaller mound with a wooden fence on top and protected by a deep ditch or moat around the outside. Inside were the domestic buildings – stores, soldiers' quarters, a chapel, stables and a well. It was from this simple structure that the elaborate stone castles, with their huge towers and gateways joined by thick curtain walls, developed over the next three hundred years. The castle became not just a defensive fortification but a place in which many people lived and worked in peaceful times, centred on the bailey, the defences of which were much expanded and improved.

Before visiting a castle, stand for a moment a short distance away from the walls, look up and consider how an attacker might seek to overcome such impressive defences. Later, while climbing the spiral stairways inside the towers or walking the ramparts, imagine yourself a soldier of the garrison – how would you beat off determined attacks? The main methods of assaulting and defending a castle are described below.

METHODS OF ATTACK
The escalade
This was a quick attack using long ladders carried forward by scaling parties, only possible if the base of the walls could be reached. The attack would be supported by covering fire from archers and crossbowmen who usually stood behind large shields,

called 'pavises', their aim being to clear the enemy off the wall-walk to give the ladder parties a chance to climb up. These ladder men had a tough time. Climbing a ladder while somebody above you is trying to knock you off is not a pleasant experience. Not only that but the ladder was heavy, requiring several men to carry it; and if too short it was useless, if too long easily thrown down. Assuming it was the correct length, the knack was to put the base of the ladder well away from the wall with its top resting just under the parapet. This meant a soldier trying to push it down had to lean over and risk being hit by an arrow. An escalade was seldom successful unless the defenders were taken by surprise or it was combined with other methods of attack.

Bombardment

If a quick surprise escalade failed the next stage was a siege, a principal component of which was the bombardment. However, the first step was to surround the castle to cut it off from supplies, particularly (if feasible) water. Casualties, hunger and thirst would eventually weaken the defenders, especially if large numbers of women and children had sought refuge inside.

The first siege engine was the mangonel or catapult, really a development of the Roman *onager* or 'wild ass'. It consisted of a wooden trestle mounted on a horizontal frame. At the bottom of the trestle was a thick skein of cords or sinew (the Romans used women's hair if available) through the middle of which was fixed one end of the throwing arm. The skein was twisted by means of capstans at each end, forcing the arm up tightly against the crossbar of the trestle. With the capstans locked, a windlass was used to pull back the arm, which was then held in position by a simple rope and hook trigger mechanism. A large rock was placed in the cup at the end of the arm. When the arm was released it sprang back to the vertical position, striking the crossbar (which was padded in the centre) and hurling the missile forward with great velocity. A range of 300 yards was achievable, and a continuous pounding by several machines over many days was likely to gradually break down a wall.

The second siege engine for bombardment was the trebuchet. This was a much larger machine, still based on a long throwing arm but with a sling at the end to hold the missile. The arm was wound back against the pull of a huge counterweight. When the arm was released it was swung forward by the counterweight falling. The range was similar to the mangonel, while its high-angle trajectory made it suitable for hurling sizeable rocks – up to two or three hundredweight – over walls as well as into them. Both these machines could also throw incendiary missiles over walls.

Battering rams

The ram could only be used when it could be brought up to the foot of a tower or wall. The crew had to be protected by a heavy beam shed roofed with wet cowhide against the heavy rocks, barrels of boiling oil or incendiary mixtures that might be dropped on them. The ram needed many hours of swinging against the wall to make a breach. Crews and damaged machines had to be replaced, while archers had to maintain covering fire to discourage the defenders on the ramparts. It was found that the corners of square towers were particularly vulnerable to attack by battering rams or, indeed, men equipped with picks.

Towers (also known as belfries)

The wheeled siege tower was designed to get infantry onto the top of a castle wall by means of a drawbridge lowered from the top of the tower. It was packed with soldiers to storm the ramparts as well as archers to keep up covering fire. Its sides, like the ram's, were covered with wet cowhides as protection against fire arrows. When a deep ditch, with or without water, protected a castle, it had first to be filled in so that the siege engines could be hauled across. Such in-filling was a long job so the attackers needed time on their side. Towers were heavy, cumbersome (requiring a lot of pushing), hard to manoeuvre and expensive to make. They were also vulnerable to shots from the castle's mangonels.

Tunnelling

This was resorted to against very thick walls or, more often, under the corners of a square tower. The idea was to dig a mine under the wall and prop it up with timber. When ready the tunnel would be filled with combustible material (e.g. timber) and set alight. As the props burnt through, that section of the wall would collapse.

FIXED DEFENCES
The ditch/moat

This formed a difficult barrier to cross and was intended to keep both the besiegers and their engines away from the base of the walls. It could be overcome with time by in-filling but a water-filled moat made tunnelling under the walls or towers virtually impossible.

Walls

'Curtain' walls, between towers, were anything from 8 to 20ft thick and up to 30ft high and could usually withstand a prolonged bombardment. By the 13th century castles were being built with both an inner and outer ring of curtain walls. If the outer defences fell then the garrison could retire to the inner walls (and towers), which were high enough to overlook the wall-walk on the outer walls.

Towers

Projecting out from the wall at intervals, these gave added height over the attackers but more importantly facilitated flanking fire down onto the enemy at the base of the curtain wall. They also broke up the wall-walk behind the ramparts. An enemy that secured a foothold on the wall would have to fight their way into the tower in order to reach the next stretch of wall-walk or to get to stairs leading down into the castle. Many castles had round towers, despite the space restrictions they created inside, as curved surfaces tended to deflect missiles and were more difficult for rams or tunnellers to damage. Inside the towers were various rooms for accommodation, stores or dungeons; access was by very narrow spiral staircases turning from the bottom to top in a clockwise direction, a severe handicap for a right-handed swordsman fighting against a man above him.

Gateways/gatehouses

At first gateways were often just simple doorways. However, they soon became the strongpoint of many castles, the place where an enemy was most likely to try to break through, so proper gatehouses were built, equipped with several defensive features. These included the familiar portcullis (the heavy iron grate that could be lowered to block the intruder's entrance) and thick wooden, iron-studded doors that could be barred shut behind the portcullis. If the castle had a moat or ditch then the drawbridge was another well-known feature. Where the defences included inner- and outer-wall systems then double gateways were necessary. In later castles the gatehouses replaced the keep as the 'last stand' strongpoint, where the captain had his residence, separated from the garrison.

These gatehouses were elaborate affairs. King Edward I's Beaumaris Castle in Anglesey is a great square of towering walls with massive round towers at each corner and towers of a D-shaped plan on two sides. In the centre of each of the other two sides are the gatehouses, a combination of a square tower with a gateway passing under it and flanked by two wall towers. They have both had an additional gateway added, consisting of two great drum towers bulging outwards, between which is a pit covered by a drawbridge. If an enemy broke through the drawbridge and the outer portcullis he had still to fight up the long passageway to the doors at the inner end, past other portcullises with more missiles raining down from both sides. If the lower part of a gatehouse was taken there was no internal stairway to reach the upper stories. These massive gatehouses became almost impregnable to direct assault.

Beaumaris Castle gatehouse

Arrow slits and parapet brackets

Arrow slits (and windows) were built into most towers, for crossbowmen (the longbow was too large to shoot through them). There was always a triangular space to the rear of the slit to allow the archer to move and adjust his aim. It is worth peering out of one of these slits to get a realistic idea of how much the firer could see – enough, but not a lot. With the development of gunpowder in the 14th century, many arrow slits were converted into upside-down 'keyhole' gun ports. The danger of exposing soldiers when shooting, or dropping things, at an enemy near the base of a tower was overcome in the late 13th century by constructing the parapet of the walkway on a series of stone brackets jutting out from the outer face of the wall. This left a gap down which rocks, sharpened logs, boiling oil and incendiaries could be dropped.

DEFENSIVE WEAPONS AND EQUIPMENT

Missiles

A considerable variety of missiles were available to the defenders on the walls or towers. Although crossbow bolts were fired from the arrow slits, the great bulk of the defenders were deployed on the wall-walk, on the top of towers and gatehouse. Archers and crossbowmen were both able to shoot from these positions, although they had to expose themselves to aim properly. Mangonels were sometimes sited on the tops of towers for counter-battery fire or to smash approaching siege towers. Rocks, sharpened logs and boiling water or oil (kept bubbling over a fire) were all stockpiled on the walls when an attack was threatened. Pitch could be poured down onto the roofs of rams and set alight with fire arrows.

Other devices

Large mattresses were sometimes lowered down a wall to soften the blows of a ram. Alternatively, a huge hook or grappling iron could be used to try to catch and drag away the ram. Long poles with hooked or forked ends were used to push down scaling ladders. Hand-to-hand fighting only occurred if the attackers gained a foothold through a breach or got onto a wall – then all the usual weapons came into play.

WELSH CASTLES OF EDWARD I

The castle building of Edward I represented an extension and completion of the scheme he inherited from his father, Henry III. All castles west of Chester, both royal and baronial, had suffered in some measure from attacks by the Welsh under the leadership of Llywellyn ap Gruffydd, notably in 1277 and 1282. The King's plan was to repair and rebuild where possible and, where not, to build new, more scientifically designed and more carefully located castles. Edward built all four great castles of North Wales (Conwy, Harlech, Caernarfon and Beaumaris), a fearsome ring of colossal fortresses that represents Europe's most ambitious and concentrated medieval building project.

The castles in North Wales were nearing completion when the third revolt of 1294–5 broke out. Several, including Cardigan and Caernarfon, were

besieged, their garrisons already depleted by the King's expedition to Gascony, but English control of the sea restricted the spread of the rebellion. Castles held out as long as provisions could be brought in by ship; Aberystwyth, Conwy, Criccieth and Harlech were supplied from Bristol and Ireland. Eventually Caernarfon was relieved and in the spring of 1295 work began on Edward's last castle – Beaumaris.

Edward experienced great difficulty in paying for his huge construction programme. Over twelve years he spent £60,000 (£35 million in modern money), over ten times his annual income, on building the castles and walled towns at Conwy, Caernarfon and Beaumaris and on refurbishing Criccieth. Edward's efforts have left Wales with a magnificent legacy of medieval military architecture of international importance.

Well worth a visit

The following is but a selection from scores of castles scattered all over the country. Others are recommended under Defence against Invasion (pp. 79–83).

Corfe, Dorset *p. 10*
Bodiam, Sussex *p. 34*
Carisbrooke, Isle of Wight *p. 35*
Pevensey, Sussex *p. 44*
Rochester, Kent *p. 46*
Tower of London *p. 51*
Warwick *p. 70*
Lincoln *p. 87*
Caerphilly, Wales *p. 123*
Conwy, Wales *p. 125*
Tantallon Castle, E. Lothian, Scotland *p. 136*
Edinburgh *p. 144*
Stirling, Scotland *p. 161*

Harlech Castle, one of Edward I's greatest achievements

SCOTLAND

BORDERS AND LOWLANDS

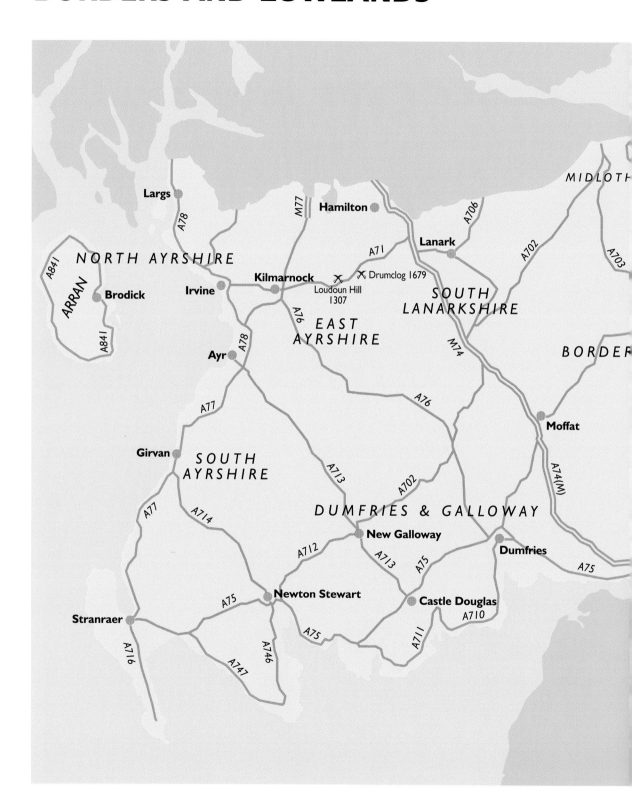

Largs

Hamilton

M77

Lanark

A706

MIDLOTH

A78

A702

A703

NORTH AYRSHIRE

A841

A71

Kilmarnock

Drumclog 1679

Loudoun Hill
1307

SOUTH
LANARKSHIRE

BORDER

ARRAN

Brodick

Irvine

A76

EAST
AYRSHIRE

A841

Ayr

A78

M74

A76

Moffat

A77

SOUTH
AYRSHIRE

A713

A702

DUMFRIES & GALLOWAY

A74(M)

Girvan

A77

A714

New Galloway

Dumfries

A712

A713

A75

A75

Stranraer

A75

Newton Stewart

Castle Douglas

A710

A716

A75

A711

A747

A746

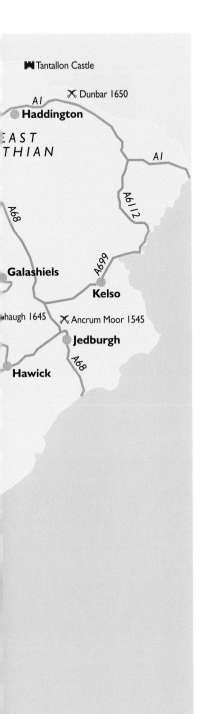

Ancrum Moor, Battle of, 1545 (Roxburgh)

Free. Easy access, open moorland. Parking possible on minor road. Five miles north of Jedburgh on the A68. A Waterloo monument on top of Peniel Heugh is visible from the road.

In 1544 Henry VIII sent an army into Scotland on a pillaging and destroying mission. In February 1545 this force of some 5000, most of whom were in fact German or Spanish mercenaries bolstered by 800 Borderers under Sir Ralph Evers, clashed with the Scottish force of Angus, Scott of Buccleuch and Leslie on Peniel Hill just off the Jedburgh road. Evers immediately ordered an attack uphill. The Scots made good use of their infamous Jedburgh axe with its billhook on one side and hook on the other to pull horsemen off their mounts and hack them to death. Then the Scottish spearmen advanced down the slope. At this critical moment the Borderers changed sides and joined Angus's line. This was more than enough to put the English to flight. Evers was killed and one hundred men were captured. It was a decisive victory that helped to unify Scotland.

Drumclog, Battle of, 1679 (Lanarkshire)

Free. Easy access, open country. Parking possible off-road. Drumclog is off the A71 midway between Hamilton and Kilmarnock.

In the late 1670s the struggle for control of the Church of Scotland became increasingly bitter, with the government punishing the low-church Presbyterians, known as Covenanters, with fines for not attending church and forced billeting of English troops. Soon western Scotland was on the point of rebellion, and the Archbishop of St Andrews, who led the government repression, was assassinated on 3 May 1679. John Graham of Claverhouse, with some 150 dragoons, was appointed to disperse unlawful gatherings of Covenanters. Warned of his approach, on 1 June the Covenanters deployed three squadrons of horse and four regiments of foot at Drumclog. Although something of a rabble with many poorly armed, they outnumbered Claverhouse by 10 to 1 and their position was strong, with marshy ground to their front. Claverhouse dismounted his dragoons and advanced boldly on the enemy only to be received by a massive counter-charge. The government troops, overwhelmed by sword, pike and pitchfork, turned to flee with the loss of a third of their number. The emboldened Covenanters unsuccessfully attacked Glasgow the next day.

Dunbar, Battle of, 1650 (East Lothian)

Free. Reasonable access, although a large cement work spoils a lot of the battlefield. Parking possible on minor roads. A mile south-east of Dunbar on the A1. Take the turning signed Cement Works and East Barns.

After the execution of Charles I the Scots proclaimed his eldest son Charles II. Parliament resolved to pre-empt any Royalist invasion of England by sending Cromwell into Scotland with an army of 20,000 men in July 1650. However the Scots were prepared and had strengthened and garrisoned Edinburgh, laid waste the country over which Cromwell would march and raised an army of 30,000 to oppose him under David Leslie, positioned behind fortifications outside Edinburgh. Cromwell, despite repeated efforts, was unable to force his way through and by 31 August was preparing to withdraw.

Leslie seized the opportunity to march his 23,000 men rapidly south to take a position of strength three miles south of Dunbar on Doon Hill. Cromwell would have to retreat between him and the sea with a hungry army half his size. Foolishly, on 3 September, Leslie moved his army down the hill and deployed with his left near Doon and his right near the pres-

Tantallon Castle, with its superb views out to sea

ent monument. Cromwell attacked the Scots right with six cavalry regiments while General Monk advanced against their centre. Some of Cromwell's horsemen got behind the Scots and Leslie's army began to falter. The Scots fought bravely but were cut down in large numbers. Some 5000 Scots surrendered, and many died of starvation en route to Durham where 2000 were locked up in the cathedral – only 200 survived to be transported to Virginia.

Loudoun Hill, Battle of, 1307 (Lanarkshire)

Free. Easy access, open country. Parking possible off-road. About seven miles west of Strathaven on the A71 to Kilmarnock. The battlefield lies to the north of the road, a mile south-west of Drumclog (above).

In April 1307 Robert the Bruce, using guerrilla tactics, ambushed the English at the Glen of Trool, causing heavy losses. Moving north, Bruce's troops met the English cavalry at Loudoun Hill on 10 May. Bruce chose his position carefully with boggy ground on each flank, and dug deep trenches to channel the English attack into the centre where he was strongest. The plan worked and the English were beaten back, withdrawing to Bothwell, near Glasgow.

Philiphaugh, Battle of, 1645 (Borders)

Free. Easy access, mostly open country. Parking off-road possible. Take the A707 south from Selkirk and turn left onto the A708. Philiphaugh Farm is on the right and the rest of the battlefield is ahead and to the right. Newark Castle is two miles further on.

As a reward for his services on behalf of Charles I at the Battle of Kilsyth (p. 144) Montrose was made Captain-General of Scotland but gradually his army began to melt away, and by September 1645 it had shrunk to little over 1000 men. Marching north over the border to confront him came Major-General Sir David Leslie with 6000 troops, of whom 5000 were cavalry. At dawn on 13 September, Leslie surprised Montrose in his encampment. The Scots were driven back to the area of Philiphaugh Farm and after a desperate brawling fight at close quarters they broke and ran while Montrose fled. Leslie marched all prisoners to Newark Castle and herded them into the courtyard where dragoons shot them down in cold blood; a thousand skeletons were discovered in 1810. The Covenanters also flung eighty women and children fugitives 50ft into the river at

Linlithgow Bridge. Montrose returned to fight for Charles II in 1650 but was captured and executed in Edinburgh.

Tantallon Castle (East Lothian) (HS)

£. Usual hours but closed Thursday afternoons and Fridays in winter. Shop. Parking. Tel. 01620 892727. Two miles east of North Berwick on the A198, and signposted off the A1 west of Dunbar.

Built in 1350, Tantallon is a classic example of a wall cutting off the approach to a headland. Behind the curtain wall and towers is a flat grassy courtyard, around the perimeter of which the cliffs are so sheer that no further walls were necessary. A path led down the cliff face to the rocky shore below. The castle had a stormy history with the walls being strengthened in the 16th century to resist artillery, though that didn't stop Cromwell taking it by force in 1650. It is possible to climb up the stairs of the massive wall to the wall-walk at the top for magnificent views of the sea and the tiny island of Bass Rock as well as inland. There are good interpretive displays including a replica gun.

MILITARY MUSEUMS

There are well over 300 military museums in Britain but as they form only part of our military heritage, only some 75 can be covered in a Guide of this length. Those wanting a comprehensive list are recommended to consult Terence and Shirley Wise's *Guide to Military Museums and Other Places of Military Interest*, the 10th edition of which was published in 2001. The Internet is another valuable source of information.

'Military museums' means all types of 'Service' museums, including Royal Navy, Royal Marines, Army and Royal Air Force establishments together with those focused on arms, armour, artillery, military vehicles, aircraft and ships. All those included are well worth a visit (as are many that have had to be left out); they give the visitor a fascinating look at Britain's Services and what they have achieved. Opinion polls continue to show that of all the country's institutions the Armed Services remain at the top of the list in terms of public respect, esteem and trust.

To help the visitor understand the significance of the more common exhibits in Service museums, some background information is given below on the history of our regular Services, the wars and campaigns in which they fought, and the honours awarded to commemorate exceptional service.

THE ROYAL NAVY (RN) AND ROYAL MARINES (RM)

The RN is the senior Service. This is because Britain has had a permanent, or regular, Navy since Henry VIII established it in the 16th century whereas the regular Army dates its foundation to the middle of the 17th century, and the RAF was not formed until the end of the First World War. The Royal Marines started off as soldiers who fought on ships – soldiers of the sea – so were, and remain, a part of the RN.

HMS *Warrior*, the world's first steam-powered battleship, now on show at Portsmouth

As an island nation Britain has always primarily depended for defence of its shores and trade on the warships of the RN.

Warships were, and still are, floating gun platforms. Initially their purpose was to destroy enemy ships and later came shore bombardment, first with guns and now with missiles. Even submarines and aircraft carriers are 'gun platforms', the former firing torpedoes, the latter aircraft. Warships today are vulnerable to attack from the air from aircraft and missiles, from torpedoes and mines, as well as enemy surface ships. For this reason RN ships have highly sophisticated defences, and naval gunfire as such is now often the weapon of last resort.

The big naval actions between battle fleets slugging it out with their guns (and aircraft) ended with the huge American and Japanese engagements in the Pacific in the Second World War. Britain's most famous fleet victory remains Trafalgar. Her last fleet action, an indecisive one, was at Jutland in the First World War. Perhaps her most deadly struggle was the Battle of the Atlantic in the Second World War, a campaign lasting many months, victory in which saved Britain from economic strangulation, even starvation. It is highly unlikely the RN will ever fight a fleet battle again. The nearest it has come to doing so in recent years was in the Falklands in 1982 when she suffered several sinkings, not from Argentinian naval guns but from missiles fired from aircraft. The Gulf War of 1991 and the Iraq War of 2003 saw the RN playing an important, but subordinate, role launching missiles and aircraft at land targets often hundreds of miles away, projecting military power overseas today requires the RN to base her much-reduced fleet on two or three aircraft carriers and their escorts (frigates). Such a fleet gives Britain enormous flexibility in the choice of when and where to operate.

For those interested in seeing the RN from its birth to modern times the Royal Naval Dockyard at Portsmouth (p. 45) is a must. Portsmouth has always been, and remains, the home of the RN. The highlights of any visit are HMS *Victory*, Nelson's flagship at Trafalgar, and HMS *Warrior*. Not to be missed are Henry VIII's warship the *Mary Rose* and the Royal Naval Museum itself. Next door, at Southsea, is the magnificent Royal Marines' Museum (p. 47).

THE BRITISH ARMY

While there are large, comprehensive Army museums such as the National Army Museum and the Imperial War Museum (p. 52), and there are Corps museums such as that of today's Royal Logistics Corps, most military museums are Regimental ones. Over the last 350 years the British Army has founded its structure, its success, its life in peace and war, on the Regiment. The honour of the Regiment, loyalty to the Regiment and service in the Regiment have formed the foundation of hundreds of victories as well as maintaining unit cohesion during disastrous defeats and retreats. Britain's regular standing Army has been composed of Regiments since the middle of the 17th century when the monarchy was restored after the Civil War. The Regiment has provided the home and the family, sometimes the only home or family, of countless soldiers down the centuries.

It is Regiments that make up the fighting element of the Army. There are Guards Regiments (elite infantry and cavalry) and there are infantry and cavalry Regiments of 'the line' – armies always used to fight in lines. Then there is the Royal Regiment of Artillery. Most other Corps are there to support, supply or in other ways assist the so-called 'teeth' arms. Discounting the Royal Artillery the oldest Regiment is the Life Guards, formed in 1661 to guard the person of King Charles II after the Restoration. Today the Household Cavalry (the Life Guards and Blues and Royals), along with the Foot Guards Regiments, still perform royal duties as well as fielding combat units. At one stage at the height of the Napoleonic Wars there were 104 British infantry Regiments, many with more than one battalion. In the First World War many Regiments put over thirty battalions into service at some stage.

Colours and drums of the Queen's Own Highlanders

Through the years cutbacks by penny-pinching politicians seeking an elusive 'peace dividend' have forced virtually all Regiments to undergo numerous disbandments, amalgamations and title changes. Despite all this the 'Regiment', immensely proud of its traditions and the battle honours of its forebears, still inspires many soldiers. Just one example of how amalgamations have not destroyed the Regimental spirit is today's King's Royal Hussars, a cavalry Regiment mounted in heavy tanks rather than horses that was formed in 1992 from its predecessor Regiments (the 10th, 11th, 14th and 20th Hussars). At the time of writing (early 2005) its four tank (called 'sabre') squadrons are A (10th Hussar) Squadron, B (11th Hussar) Squadron, C (14th Hussar) Squadron and D (20th Hussar) Squadron. Its most celebrated battle honour is 'Balaklava' and the 'Charge of the Light Brigade' in which the 11th Hussars participated. Every year it is recalled by special celebrations. In October 2004 a large party from the Regiment walked down 'the valley of death' in the Crimea in which the charge was made exactly 150 years before. Officers and soldiers on ceremonial parades still wear the unique crimson trousers of Lord Cardigan's 11th Hussars.

In the 350 years since the beginnings of the British Army, its soldiers have done an immense amount of fighting and dying – far more than any other regular army in the world, and almost all of it overseas.

In regimental museums you will see an amazing display of military history. There will be weapons, uniforms, drums, silver, medals, equipment, pictures, photographs, maps, displays, panoramas and personal mementos covering every war, campaign or battle that the Regiment has participated in from Blenheim to Baghdad. In many there will also be some of the old Colours (or Guidons for cavalry) of the Regiment. Each infantry Regiment has two, the Queen's (or King's) Colour and the Regimental Colour, both of which are replaced on amalgamation or when worn out. They are rich silk tasselled flags on which are embroidered in gold the Regiment's badge and selected battle honours (names of the famous battles in which it fought). These Colours were originally carried into battle by the Regiment's two most junior officers, as the Regiment's rallying point in action. To lose a Colour was a disgrace – it rarely happened, although many a young officer died defending them. One wounded officer in the Essex Regiment saved a Colour when the enemy surrounded him by ripping it from the staff and wrapping it round his body.

The major wars or campaigns in which the British Army has fought with distinction since its founding up to the end of the Second World War are listed below, with one or two of the major battles in brackets afterwards.

War of the Spanish Succession, 1701–14 (Blenheim)
Jacobite Risings, 1715 (Sheriffmuir) and 1745 (Culloden)
War of the Austrian Succession, 1740–8 (Fontenoy)
Seven Years' War, 1756–63 (Minden)
American War of Independence, 1775–83 (Yorktown)
French Revolutionary/Napoleonic Wars, 1792–1815 (Waterloo)
Wars of conquest in India, 1803–5 (Assaye)
Peninsular War, 1808–14 (Salamanca)
War of 1812 with America, 1812–15 (Lundy's Lane)
Wars of conquest in India, 1843–9 (Chilianwala)
Crimean War, 1853–6 (Balaklava)
Indian Mutiny, 1857–8 (Storming of Delhi)
Afghan War, 1878–80 (Maiwand)
Zulu War, 1879 (Rorke's Drift)
Sudan Wars, 1882–5 (Tel el-Kabir) and 1896–8 (Omdurman)
First Boer War, 1880–1 (Majuba Hill)
Second Boer War, 1899–1902 (Colenso)
First World War, 1914–18 (The Somme)
Second World War, 1939–45 (El Alamein)

Since 1946 barely a year has passed without a British soldier being under hostile fire somewhere. Again the list of areas of operations is impressive – Palestine, Malaya, Korea, Cyprus, Kenya, Egypt (Suez), Borneo, South Arabia, Northern Ireland, the Falklands, Kuwait (Gulf War), Bosnia, Kosovo, Afghanistan, Sierra Leone and Iraq. No modern army in the world can match the British for operational experience.

THE ROYAL AIR FORCE

The RAF is the junior of the three Services, formed at the end of the First World War from the Royal Flying Corps established in May 1912 as part of the Army. The RFC played a critical role during all the major battles of the First World War and by 1916 was losing two pilots a day. By the time of the Somme offensive it had 421 operational aircraft in 27 squadrons, together with 4 kite balloon squadrons with 14 balloons. By the end of the war RFC personnel had won 11 Victoria Crosses and at the time of its disbandment and the formation of the RAF there were 4000 aircraft in service and 114,000 men in uniform.

During the Second World War the RAF played a vital role in every theatre of war, but particularly in the skies above North Africa, Italy, north-west Europe and England. Fighter Command saved Britain from invasion in 1940 in what turned out to be the longest, most sustained and deadly air battle ever fought. As Prime Minister Churchill said, 'Never in the field of human conflict has so much been owed by so many to so few.'

The post-Second World War RAF, like the other two Services, has suffered numerous and drastic cutbacks, reducing its manpower to about 45,000 personnel operating strike aircraft such as the Tornado, Harrier 'jump jets', helicopters like the Sea King, the Hercules transport and the Nimrod command and surveillance aircraft. The RAF has played a critical role in recent hostilities in the Gulf, Afghanistan and Iraq.

MEDALS AND DECORATIONS

Virtually all military museums display a dazzling collection of gallantry awards, decorations and campaign medals, often going back as far as the Napoleonic Wars. It is worth having some basic knowledge of medals, as this enhances the interest of the impressive collections on show. They will usually be in sets awarded to individuals, varying in number from a single medal to a huge chestful that necessitated special supports under the wearer's uniform to take the weight. The late Field Marshal Montgomery of Second World War fame had ten rows of ribbons made up of nearly forty decorations and medals.

It is important to distinguish between awards for gallantry, decorations and medals. Gallantry awards are for courageous action in the face of the enemy, examples being the Victoria Cross (VC), Conspicuous Gallantry Cross (CGC), Distinguished Service Cross (DSC), Air Force Cross (AFC) and Military Cross (MC). Decorations are normally given for distinguished service by senior commanders not personally involved in fighting. Examples include Officer and Member of the Order of the British Empire (OBE and MBE). Medals are divided into two categories; campaign medals are bestowed for active service in a theatre of operations for a given period, such as the North Africa Star, Atlantic Star, Air Crew Europe Star and Defence Medal from the Second World War, and more recently the Korea Medal and General Service Medal. Other medals are awarded for service other than in an operational situation, examples being the Long Service and Good Conduct, Jubilee and Coronation Medals.

Often a campaign medal will have a number of clasps (bars), each with the name of a different battle or engagement in which the holder took part. The 1962 General Service Medal for example has several clasps including 'South Arabia' and 'Northern Ireland' while the Crimean War Medal has clasps for 'Alma', 'Inkerman', 'Sevastopol' and 'Balaklava', all battles in that war.

Medals won by the soldiers of the Queen's Lancashire Regiment

the Military Medal and Bar. Miraculously, he survived the war, was commissioned into the Burton Army Cadet Force during the Second World War and died aged eighty-three in 1974.

It is well worth looking out for VCs on display. They will always be given pride of place, as befits the highest award for gallantry. The VC was instituted in 1856 after the Crimean War as, prior to this, Britain had no way of rewarding bravery in battle. It can only be awarded for action in combat during which the recipient's life was in grave danger from enemy fire. As recently as the Iraq War in 2003 Trooper Christopher Finney, an eighteen-year-old soldier in the Blues and Royals, was awarded the George Cross (GC) for great gallantry under heavy fire from attacking aircraft. He did not qualify for the VC as the fire was coming from American aircraft – 'friendly fire'! The GC is the second-highest award for bravery and can be won by civilians as well as soldiers. All gallantry awards can be made

It is possible to win a gallantry award twice or even three times, in which case a small rosette in the centre of the ribbon shows the second and subsequent awards. The holder of two MCs would be described as having an 'MC and Bar'. The Mentioned in Dispatches (MiD) award is the lowest level of a bravery award and is indicated by a small bronze oak leaf in the centre of a campaign medal ribbon. The most decorated NCO of the First World War was Lance-Corporal William Coltman of the North Staffordshire Regiment, who was awarded the Victoria Cross, the Distinguished Conduct Medal and Bar and

posthumously; indeed today the chances of living to wear the Victoria Cross are slim. At the time of writing (early 2005) there are only fourteen living holders of the VC. Twelve VCs have been won since the end of the Second World War – four in Korea, one in Borneo (a Gurkha), four in Vietnam (Australians), two in the Falklands and one in Iraq. This most recent award for two acts of exceptional bravery was to Private Johnson Beharry of the Princess of Wales's Royal Regiment, who is currently the only holder of the VC still serving in the Forces. In all 1355 have been awarded, 634 of them in the

First World War. The VC is a Commonwealth award and it is interesting to note that after Britain with 988, the country with the most winners is India with 137. A set of medals with a VC can now fetch huge sums if they come up for sale. The present record is £178,000 for the set belonging to Major-General Daniel Beak VC, DSO, MC and Bar.

To finish this feature I cannot resist recounting what must be one of the most rare and amazing stories of the winning of a VC. Sergeant Norman Jackson, RAF, was a crewmember of a Lancaster bomber on a raid over Germany in 1944. At 22,000ft the aircraft was attacked by a German fighter whose cannon shells hit an engine, which caught fire. Jackson grabbed a fire extinguisher and, holding on with one hand, crawled out onto the wing. He subdued the fire but, just as success seemed possible, the fighter reappeared and Jackson was wounded in the legs and lost the extinguisher. The engine caught fire again and the slipstream lifted him off the wing and flung him backwards. He was now being dragged along on his parachute behind the twisting, falling bomber like a fish on a line. His comrades desperately paid out the

cords to try to get him clear before they baled out of the doomed aircraft.

Jackson suddenly broke free but immediately realized the canopy had caught fire. The cords were also smouldering so he gripped the rigging lines with his bare hands to extinguish them. Because the canopy was torn and had holes burnt in it Jackson was plunging to earth much too quickly. Miraculously he landed in some thick bushes, which broke his fall. His ankles were broken, his hands and face were badly burned and he had shrapnel wounds in his legs and back. He was captured and survived. His VC and other medals are to be auctioned shortly and are expected to fetch well over £120,000. Likely bidders include the RAF Museum at Hendon and Lord Ashcroft, who has Britain's largest private collection of VCs.

Well worth a visit

Royal Naval Museum, Portsmouth *p. 45*
Royal Marines Museum, Southsea *p. 47*
Imperial War Museum, London *p. 52*
National Army Museum, London *p. 52*
RAF Museum, Hendon *p. 53*

Reconstructed Battle of Britain operations room, at the Battle of Britain Museum

CENTRAL SCOTLAND

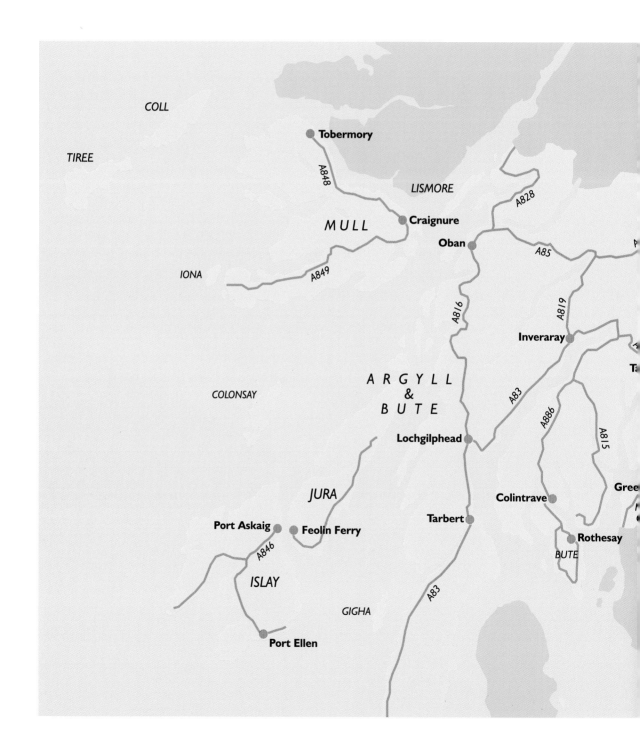

The Antonine Roman Wall Walkway Trust (Stirling)

Free. Easy access, well-signposted paths and walks. Cycling possible. Refreshments in Croy village. Picnic areas. Parking. Tel. 01236 827242. Ten miles north-east of central Glasgow off the A80. At Condorrat take the B8048 then the B802 to Croy.

The section of the Antonine Wall on Croy Hill has one of the best-preserved parts of the ditch and has been developed by the Walkway Trust so that visitors can explore the area along well-maintained and signposted paths. There is a fine view from the top of Croy Hill and the site of a Roman fort nearby with a gap in the ditch where the underlying rock proved too hard for the Roman engineers. Along the walk from Croy Hill towards Dullatur there is a well-preserved stretch of the ditch and rampart. For a description of the Wall itself see p. 119. It requires a little more imagination from visitors than Hadrian's Wall, but a visit is still very much worthwhile.

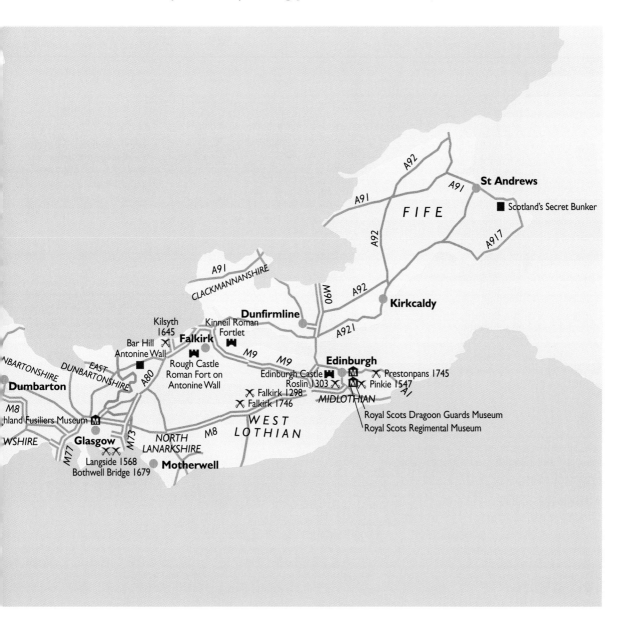

Bar Hill Roman Fort (Dunbartonshire) (HS)

Free. Open access. Parking possible nearby. Some walking required to reach fort. Eight miles north-east of Glasgow off the A803. Take the B8023 from Kirkintilloch and the fort is signposted from Twechar village.

The highest fort on the line of the Antonine wall, containing the foundations of the headquarters building and bathhouse. It was a small fort ($3^1/_2$ acres) that housed an infantry cohort but was built, as indicated by inscriptions, by detachments of the II Augusta and XX Valeria Legions. This is the best site to appreciate the strategic significance of the Wall and enjoy the magnificent views over the Kelvin Valley.

Bothwell Bridge, Battle of, 1679 (Lanark)

Free. Reasonable access to bridge, but parking difficult. Largely urban area. Seven miles south-east of Glasgow on the A724. The modern bridge has a monument on the Bothwell side.

An engagement in the religious wars in Scotland fought between the Scottish loyalists under the Duke of Monmouth and the Covenanters commanded by their preachers. Monmouth's march on 22 June from Bothwell to Hamilton was blocked by the rebels defending the bridge over the River Clyde. The bridge was 120ft long and had a central gateway. Monmouth's leading troops charged the bridge and as the defenders' ammunition ran out eventually succeeded in pushing the Covenanters back. This allowed more Highlanders over the bridge together with some cavalry, and these reinforcements soon scattered the Covenanters. The pursuit was vigorous; some 600 men were cut down and around 1300 captured.

Edinburgh Castle (Edinburgh) (HS)

££££. Usual hours. Shop. Refreshments. Guided tours. Free audio-visual tour. School visits. Parking. Tel. 0131 2259846. www.edinburghcastle.biz The Castle, Edinburgh. You can see it from most locations in the city!

The castle's story is the story of Scotland. Visitors should be prepared for a three-hour tour as there is much to see. Of particular interest are the Laich Hall, the vaults, the 'Honours of the Kingdom' exhibition telling the story of Scotland's crown jewels, the giant siege gun (Mons Meg), dog cemetery, the half-moon battery, gatehouse, Great Hall towers and battlements. There are also three excellent military museums within the castle to which entrance is free: the National War Museum of Scotland (p. 146), the Royal Scots (p. 147) and the Royal Scots Dragoon Guards (p. 147).

Falkirk, Battle of, 1298 (Stirling)

Free. Access easy but the battle took place in the town on land now built over. Wallace Street and Thornhill Road are thought to mark the centre of the field.

Fought on 22 July 1298 between the forces of Edward I of England and the Scots commanded by Sir William Wallace. Wallace, who was deserted by two English barons on the eve of battle, drew up his army behind some boggy ground in three schiltrons. His total army was some 15,000 strong, mostly infantry but with 1000 archers and a mounted reserve. The English cavalry foolishly charged into the boggy ground where they were shot down by the Scottish bowmen. A second cavalry attack could make little headway against the long spears of the schiltrons. Just when their intervention could have sealed a victory for Wallace his cavalry reserve turned and rode off. Wallace fought on but the English brought forward their archers and slingers. This proved too much for the Scots and the schiltrons broke up as the men abandoned the fight. Wallace escaped but seven years later he was caught and hanged, drawn and quartered.

Falkirk, Battle of, 1746 (Stirling)

Free. Easy access, much of the battlefield unspoilt. Parking possible nearby. Take the B803 out of Falkirk up the hill past the railway station then turn right opposite the hospital, then right again into a housing estate. A monument can be found at the entrance to Bantaskin Park.

Fought on 17 January 1746 between the Jacobites of Prince Charlie under General Hawley and the English army under Lord George Murray. The Jacobites with some 8000 men had formed up on Falkirk Moor and at 4 p.m., as light was fading, Hawley ordered an attack, which began with a charge by three cavalry regiments against the Highlanders' right. However, a close-range musket volley emptied many saddles and the surviving horsemen retreated. The Highlanders then rushed forward, sword in hand. The English, blinded by driving sleet and rain, offered little resistance. Several English regiments turned to run but the Scottish advance was temporarily checked by Murray's second line. However, more Jacobite reinforcements finally forced the English to retreat.

Kilsyth, Battle of, 1645 (Stirling)

Free. Easy access, although much of the battlefield is now under a reservoir. Parking possible. Take the A803 from Kilsyth. Turn left into the grounds of Colzium House and you will see the Montrose memorial. The battlefield lies to the east.

A Civil War battle between the Royalists under the Marquis of Montrose and the Scottish Parliamentary force under General Baillie. On 14 August 1645, Montrose, with 5000 men including some Irish infantry and Highlanders, was encamped just east of Kilsyth. His main weakness was in the small number of his cavalry. The next day Baillie approached determined to sweep the Royalists out of his path.

When Baillie saw the Royalists' position he determined to outflank them to the north and turned to his left to do so. It was hot, the ground was boggy and the Parliamentarians soon began to struggle and straggle. Montrose saw his chance and sent his clansmen forward in a furious charge. However, the steady firing of musketeers and the levelled pikes of the Parliamentarians checked the rush. Montrose sent the seventy-year-old Earl of Airlie in to support his Highlanders and turned his attention to an attempt by Baillie to attack his left flank. Using his small cavalry force Montrose crashed into the Parliamentarian right and at the same time ordered a general advance. After some desperate fighting at close quarters the Parliamentarians broke. There was little mercy for those who could not escape.

Kinneil Roman Fortlet (West Lothian) (HS)

Free. Open access. In grounds of Kinneil House (public park). Parking available. In Bo'ness. Follow signs for Kinneil House off the A993.

An Antonine Wall fortlet that has been partially restored along with a section of the wall. There is a small museum of finds.

Langside, Battle of, 1568 (Glasgow)

Free. Reasonable access, although the site is in central Glasgow with parking problems. Queen's Park, central Glasgow, close to the Victoria Infirmary. A 58ft battlefield memorial facing Clincart Hill marks the site of Glasgow's most important military encounter.

Fought on 13 May 1568 between the forces of Mary Queen of Scots and those of her half-brother James Earl of Moray, who had been appointed Regent of Scotland after Mary's forced abdication. Moray had positioned his troops on Langside Hill, while Mary's forces were on the lesser Clincart Hill (now the site of Langside College) about half a mile to the east. After an unsuccessful mounted charge, Mary's infantry approached Langside Hill up what is now Battlefield Road. They were met by gunfire and other forces coming down from the site of Pathhead Farm. Between these two wings of Moray's forces, archers and then cavalry attacked the oncoming army. It was more than Mary's men could take and they disappeared leaving a hundred dead and more wounded behind. It was all over in less than an hour , and Mary headed for sanctuary in England.

Edinburgh Castle, beautifully preserved and with lots to do and see

Rough Castle; the pits for hiding sharpened stakes are still very evident

National War Museum of Scotland (Edinburgh Castle)

££££, included in entry to the castle. Usual hours. Shop. Refreshments. Sound guide. School visits. Research facilities. Parking. Tel. 0131 2257534. www.nms.ac.uk/war/home/index.asp Edinburgh Castle.

This museum explores over 400 years of Scotland's military experience. There are some 35,000 objects, covering all three Services, in six major exhibitions covering the history of Scottish warfare including weapons and the civilian experience.

Pinkie, Battle of, 1547 (East Lothian)

Free. Access possible, but much of the ground covered by the town of Musselburgh. Parking possible. Musselburgh, seven miles east of Edinburgh on the A1. The best viewpoint is from the summit of Falside Hill, climbed from the roundabout just off the A1. The castle at the top is a private residence.

In 1543 Henry VIII arranged a marriage between his six-year-old son Edward and the infant Mary Queen of Scots. He was enraged when the Scots decided against it, and following Henry's death in early 1547 the Lord Protector, the Duke of Somerset, with 80 cannons, 8000 foot and 4000 cavalry marched across the border to enforce the betrothal. The Earl of Arran, Mary's Regent, assembled an army of 25,000 men at Edinburgh and confronted the English behind the line of the River Esk south of Musselburgh.

The battle was fought on 10 September. As the English advanced the Scots foolishly abandoned their defensive position and advanced over the river to meet their enemy. Somerset deployed on Falside Hill with cavalry on each flank and a fleet of warships at sea guarding his extreme right. The fire of the fleet dispersed Arran's left wing, and his dense mass of pikemen in the centre were charged by the English horse, although the long spears were able to

keep the cavalry attackers at bay. Then, at last, the English cannons were brought into action against the dense and vulnerable target of the schiltron. The effect was devastating. The cannonballs cut swaths through the Scottish ranks. English archers and arquebusiers added their fire and their cavalry rallied for another charge. The Scots' attempted orderly withdrawal quickly dissolved into panicked flight.

Prestonpans, Battle of, 1745 (East Lothian)

Free. Mostly accessible. Parking possible. The eastern outskirts of Prestonpans. Best approached by leaving the A1 at the Tranent roundabout.

A battle fought on 21 September 1745 in the Jacobite Rebellion between the English/Hanoverian army under Sir John Cope and the insurgent Highlanders under Lord George Murray, each side mustering around 3000 men. They clashed east of Prestonpans. Initially Cope drew up his force facing south between Bankton House and Meadowmill. Murray, however, made a concealed night march across his front and deployed facing west towards Edinburgh. This forced Cope to change his front and before they were organized the Highlanders charged. Cope's men only fired once before the clansmen hit them. After a brief mêlée the English fled leaving 300 dead and 1600 prisoners.

Roslin, Battle of, 1303 (Edinburgh)

Free. Easy access. Parking possible. Four miles south of Edinburgh. Turn off the A701 onto the B7006 to Roslin.

Probably the bloodiest battle fought on Scottish soil, but not well documented, this was really a series of three clashes between some 8000 Scots led by John Comyn and 30,000 English under Sir John Segrave, fought around Roslin village or the Glen of Roslin on 24 February 1303. The English were divided into three separate forces, which brought about their undoing. First the Scots surrounded and surprised one division, comprehensively defeating it. The second English division then attacked, but their charge was broken by Scottish arrows, with many English being driven over a precipice. After fighting all day the Scots were still able, by skilful use of bowmen, to defeat the last English force. It was an outstanding victory, and as late as the 19th century farmers were ploughing up cartloads of bones in the area.

Rough Castle Roman Fort (Stirling) (HS)

Free. Open access any reasonable time. Parking. Signposted from the A803 near Bonnybridge west of Falkirk.

The best site on the Antonine Wall for viewing a well-preserved rampart and ditch, with the earthworks of a fort. There is also a section of the military way (road) and a system of defensive pits for concealing sharpened stakes.

Royal Scots Dragoon Guards Museum (Edinburgh Castle)

Free, included in Castle entry charge. Usual hours. Shop. Refreshments. School visits. Castle parking, restricted in July and August. Tel. 0131 3105101. Edinburgh Castle.

A fascinating collection of exhibits telling the story of this cavalry regiment from the formation of its forebears up to the Gulf War and Iraq with uniforms, weapons, paintings, medals and silver. The highlight is the illuminated Eagle and Standard of the French 45th Regiment captured in the famous charge of the Scots Greys at Waterloo. Recent exhibits illustrate service in the 1991 Gulf War , Bosnia, Kosovo and Iraq in 2003.

The Royal Scots Regimental Museum (Edinburgh Castle)

Free, included in Castle entry charge. Usual hours. Shop. Refreshments. School visits. Castle parking, restricted in July and August. Tel. 0131 3105016. Edinburgh Castle.

This regiment was raised in 1633 by King Charles I, making it the oldest in the British Army. The museum tells its story from its formation through to the Gulf War of 1991 with displays of uniforms, weapons, equipment, medals, paintings, silver and other artefacts.

Scotland's Secret Bunker (Fife)

£. Usual hours April–October. Parking. Tel. 01333 310301. www.secretbunker.co.uk Six miles south-east of St Andrews. Turn left at junction of B9131 and B940 and follow brown tourist signs.

Scotland's secret underground nuclear command centre was designed to house up to 300 Scottish government officials and military commanders in the event of nuclear war. It comprises a labyrinth of tunnels and operations rooms 100ft below ground, all encased in 15ft of reinforced concrete. The accommodation, dining rooms, power plant, communications centre, cinemas, broadcasting studios and computer room are all preserved with authentic artefacts.

Scotland's secret bunker; fortunately it was never used

HIGHLANDS AND ISLANDS

WESTERN
ISLES

LEWIS

A857

A857

A858

A859

Stornoway

HARRIS

Tarbert

An T-ob

NORTH
UIST

Lochmaddy

Uig

A87

RAASAY

Dunvegan Dun Beag Portree

A863

BENBECULA

SOUTH
UIST

A865

SKYE

Lochboisdale

Elgol

A851

Dun Telve

Ardvasar

BARRA

RUM

Mallaig

EIGG

A830

ARGYLL

A861

A884

A828

A82

John o'

Thurso

A836

A838

Tongue

A9

Kylestrome

A838 A836

A897

A894

A9

Brora

Ullapool

Dornoch

HIGHLAND

A832

A835

A9

Dingwall

Auldearn
1645 A96 Elgin

Fort George
The Highlanders' Nairn
Regimental Museum

A890

Inverness Culloden 1746

Kyle of Lochalsh

A82

A939

Glenshiel 1719
A87

A9

Aviemore

Fort Augustus

Kingussie

A82

A86

Fort William

A9

Killiecrankie
1689

A93

Glencoe Massacre 1692

PERTH & KINR

A827

Inchtu
of Roma

Dunkeld 1689

A85

A85

A9

Perth

The Black Watch Regimental Museum

D
Mo

06W

STIRLING

The Argyll and Southern Highlanders Museum Sheriffmuir 1715

Stirling Castle Stirling Bridge 1297

Bannockburn 1314 Stirling

A811

M9

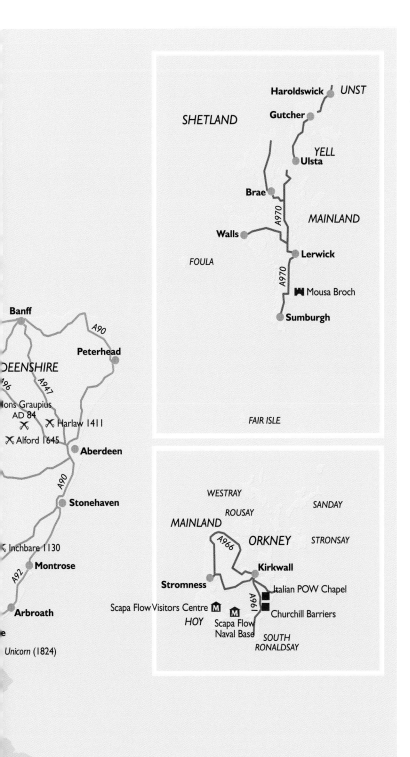

Alford, Battle of, 1645 (Aberdeen)

Free. East access, open country. Parking in Alford or off the A944. About twenty-five miles west of Aberdeen on the A944. The battlefield is a mile west of Alford village to the south of the road. The bridge carrying the A944 over the River Don is the site of the ford used by Baillie's force.

An English Civil War clash between the Royalists under the Marquis of Montrose and Covenanters commanded by General Baillie – both sides numbering around 2000 men. On 2 July 1645 Baillie discovered Montrose's force deployed to the south of the River Don on Gallowhill, half a mile west of Alford village. Believing he only faced a rearguard, Baillie advanced across the Mountgarrie Ford, the only crossing point. However, on crossing the Covenanters were charged by cavalry and Irish infantry on both flanks. Montrose then launched his centre down the hill. Most of the Covenanters were cut down and it became more a bloodbath than a battle. Baillie escaped but some 1600 of his men perished.

The Argyll and Sutherland Highlanders Museum (Stirling)

Free, but donations welcome, entry charge to Stirling Castle. Usual hours, October–Easter 10 a.m.–4.15 p.m. Shop. Refreshments. Parking. Tel. 01786 475165. Stirling Castle.

The Regiment has been based at Stirling Castle for over a hundred years and its museum is one of the highlights of any visit to the castle. The museum is divided into two sections with displays of Colours, pipe banners, uniforms, weapons, equipment, medals, paintings, photographs and memorabilia spanning all the wars in which the Regiment fought including the Crimea, the Indian Mutiny, both World Wars, Korea, Malaya, Aden, the Gulf and Iraq.

Bannockburn, Battle of, 1314 (Stirling) (NTS)

££ (for Heritage Centre charge). Centre open usual hours except January. Easy access to the parts of the battlefield not urbanized. Shop. Café. Audio-visual display of Robert the Bruce and the battle. Parking. Tel. 01786 812664. One mile south-west of Stirling. It is well signposted from the M9. The Heritage Centre lies alongside the rotunda and Robert the Bruce monument.

A battle in the Scottish Wars of Independence fought on 23 and 24 June 1314 between the English King Edward II and the Scots under Robert the Bruce. In the summer of 1314 the Scots had Stirling Castle under siege and the battle of Bannockburn took place when Edward marched north with a large army to its relief.

On the morning of 23 June, Edward's army of some 16,000 men, including 1000 mounted knights, marched north out of Falkirk along the old Roman road, now the A9. He had two days to reach the castle as the governor had agreed to surrender if not relieved by then. Bruce, having only around 8000 men, was heavily outnumbered and decided to take up a defensive, blocking position

Robert the Bruce's statue above the battle site (Battlefields Trust)

on the plateau of woodland known as 'The Park', which stretched south of the castle for some two miles. Just before the road crossed the stream known as Bannock Burn was an open piece of ground suitable for cavalry, called 'The Entry'. Here Bruce dug and camouflaged and scattered pointed caltrops to maim horses. His main line behind the burn and the obstacles ran from dense woods beyond the Borestone on his right to the burn on the left, and along the high ground overlooking the low ground called the Carse. The Scottish position was a strong one although its front stretched for well over a mile.

Edward advanced in ten 'battles' (divisions) and on approaching the burn his vanguard of 1500 horse and foot under the Earl of Gloucester advanced over it to attack frontally, while some 800 horse under the Earl of Clifford were sent to outflank the Scottish left. Leading the vanguard was an English knight called Sir Henry de Bohun who, on recognizing Bruce, immediately spurred forward, levelled his lance and rode straight for his adversary, who was mounted on a pony rather than his warhorse. Bruce managed to dodge the lance point and, rising in his stirrups, swung his battleaxe with such force and accuracy that it split open de Bohun's helmet and skull. The Scots rushed forward and drove the English vanguard back over the burn. Bruce called off any pursuit.

Meanwhile Clifford's force had clashed with some 500 of Randolph Moray's foot near St Ninian's Church. The English horse found the hedgehog-like long spears of the Scottish schiltron were invulnerable to mounted attack as the horses shied away from the bristling steel. The knights hurled their axes and maces but the infantry could not be broken. A Scottish advance drove the English into retreat, leaving Clifford dead on the field.

Edward had had enough. He regrouped his battered and somewhat demoralized army before moving late that evening to camp about a mile east of the castle with their backs to the Bannock Burn. The sun was shining on 24 June when Bruce advanced down to the Carse to attack the English who awaited them on the narrow ground of their encampment. The archers on both sides opened the fight. The English bowmen appeared to be getting the upper hand when some of their cavalry charged the schiltron of Edward Bruce, thereby screening it from the archers. Moray's schiltron then attacked the English right and Sir James Douglas stormed

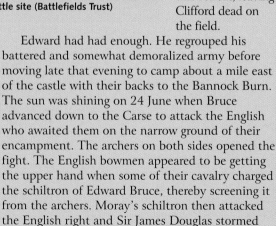

forward into their centre. Edward's horsemen, deployed in front of their infantry, could make no headway against the long spears, and the bowmen were trapped behind the horses and unable to fire. Edward's infantry were penned in the rear by the mass of men to their front. The English were slowly pushed back by the solid wall of spears and shields. The arrival of Scottish reinforcements in the form of some 3000 armed civilians finally tipped the

balance, and the English turned to flee. Edward rode for refuge in the castle while his army disintegrated.

Pursuit was relentless and English casualties heavy. Bannockburn was a decisive victory but it did not end the war, which dragged on until 1328 when the Treaty of Northampton recognized Robert Bruce as King of Scotland.

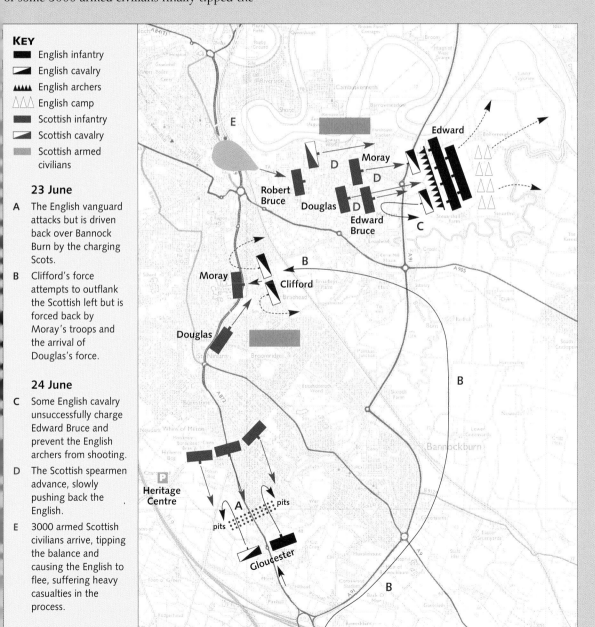

KEY

- English infantry
- English cavalry
- English archers
- English camp
- Scottish infantry
- Scottish cavalry
- Scottish armed civilians

23 June

A   The English vanguard attacks but is driven back over Bannock Burn by the charging Scots.

B   Clifford's force attempts to outflank the Scottish left but is forced back by Moray's troops and the arrival of Douglas's force.

24 June

C   Some English cavalry unsuccessfully charge Edward Bruce and prevent the English archers from shooting.

D   The Scottish spearmen advance, slowly pushing back the English.

E   3000 armed Scottish civilians arrive, tipping the balance and causing the English to flee, suffering heavy casualties in the process.

Auldearn, Battle of, 1645 (Nairn)

Free. Easy access, open country. Parking in Auldearn village. Two miles east of Nairn on the A96. The Scottish National Trust preserves the Boath Doocot and has erected a viewpoint with a plan and description of the battle.

An English Civil War battle fought on 9 May 1645 between the Scottish Royalists under the Marquis of Montrose with less than 1500 foot and 250 horse and the Covenanters under Sir John Urry with 4000 foot and 600 horse. Montrose had encamped near Aldearn, and deployed a small part of his force on Castle Hill, where the present Boath Doocot stands, with King Charles's great golden banner prominently displayed. The muske-teers on the left wing were stationed in the scattered houses of the village with orders to fire fast and give the impression of much larger numbers. Montrose kept the majority of his force concealed in two bodies behind Castle Hill with the aim of launching them in a surprise double flanking attack as the enemy advanced.

Because of boggy ground the Covenanters' attack, when it came, was piecemeal, frontal and directed towards the standard. Unfortunately for Montrose, the MacDonalds in the centre of his line, who were supposed to stay on the defensive, spotted their bitter enemies the Campbells leading the Covenanter advance and charged forward despite being heavily out-numbered. However, Montrose and the left wing were able to crash into Urry's right flank and after a stiff fight the Covenanters withdrew to Inverness. It was a remarkable victory for Montrose.

The Black Watch Regimental Museum (Perth)

Free, donations appreciated. Usual hours May–September Monday–Saturday. October–April Monday–Friday 10 a.m.– 3.30 p.m. Shop. Refreshments available in adjacent Sports Centre. Picnic area. Audio tours available. School visits. Parking. Tel. 0131 3108530. www.theblackwatch.co.uk/museum Balhousie Castle, Hay Street, Perth.

This museum tells the story of the oldest Highland Regiment, raised in 1725. There are seven rooms of dis-plays, each depicting a different period of the Regiment's history including the North American Wars, Napoleonic campaigns, the Crimea, two World Wars and more recent conflicts such as the Gulf and Iraq. There are numerous artefacts, medals, uniforms, Colours and a magnificent collection of paintings. An unusual exhibit is the key to Spandau prison

A piper of the Black Watch, the oldest Highland Regiment

which was destroyed when its only surviving prisoner, Hitler's deputy Rudolph Hess, died. Of particular interest is the display of Field Marshal Earl Wavell's swords and medals, and those of the three genera-tions of his family that served in the Regiment – a family tradition com-mon in the Highlands.

Dun Beag ('Little Fort') (Isle of Skye) (HS)

Free. Open access at any reasonable time. Parking available. Signposted just north of Bracadale on the A863.

A comparatively well-preserved broch with two chambers and a stairway that leads up. Although set on a com-manding position it is only a short walk from the road.

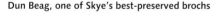
Dun Beag, one of Skye's best-preserved brochs

Dunkeld, Battle of, 1689 (Perth)

Free. Easy access to the village of Dunkeld. Parking possible. Twelve miles south of Killicrankie on the A9.

A battle fought on 19 August 1689 between a rebel Jacobite army of 4000 under Colonel Cannon and a government force of 1200 of the newly raised 26th Foot (Cameronian Regiment), who were defending the village of Dunkeld, commanded by Lieutenant-Colonel Cleland. The Highlanders, led by their colonel, attacked by launching a wild, traditional clansmen's charge, waving swords and yelling battle cries against the fortified church, houses and Dunkeld House. The Cameronians drove them back with pikes and halberds, which proved excellent weapons at close quarters. After four hours of bitter fighting and with many houses ablaze, the Jacobites fell back dispirited and exhausted. They marched away leaving some 300 casualties to the defenders' 45.

Dun Telve (Highland) (HS)

Free. Open access at any reasonable time. Parking possible in a layby. Signposted on a minor road south of Glenelg.

Viewed from the roadside this broch looks almost complete with walls up to 35ft high, though at the rear much of the wall has collapsed. It is well worth exploring inside to see the galleries and stairway.

Dupplin Moor (Muir), Battle of, 1332 (Perth)

Free. The site of this battle is uncertain but is likely to be close to Bridge of Earn village, probably rising ground immediately south of the Bridge of Earn on the A912 three miles south of Perth. The stone cross in St Serf's church at Dunning once marked the site.

This battle was not only the turning point in the Scottish Wars but also the birthplace of the archery tactics that the English used so successfully in the Hundred Years War. Under Edward Balliol, a mixed group of aristocratic Scottish exiles ('the disinherited') and English adventurers invaded Scotland. On 9 August 1332 they were met south of Perth at the River Earn by the Scottish army of 20,000 under the Earl of Mar. Although heavily outnumbered, the rebels made a successful night attack across the river. The Scots rallied and at dawn counter-attacked. However, Balliol's men-at-arms fell back up the slopes of Dupplin Muir and formed a tight phalanx of spearmen flanked by archers. Mar's men charged up the slope and locked spears but on the flanks the enemy archers turned inwards and poured a devastating hail of arrows into their flanks and rear. Those that could broke away and fled.

Fort George (Inverness) (HS)

£££. Usual hours. Shop. Refreshments. Parking. Tel. 01667 462777. Ardesier village, some six miles west of Nairn on the B9006. It is well signposted off the A96.

Built between 1748 and 1769, this magnificent fort covers over forty-two acres and remains virtually unaltered. It is perhaps the most remarkable piece of military architecture in Britain, incorporating the very latest defensive ideas of the time. The main defence is a massive circuit of ramparts one mile in circumference, fronted by stone walls so constructed that no attacker would be safe from defensive fire. Under the ramparts are huge 'bomb proof' casements of brick-built barracks that could house the entire garrison of around 2500 men. Visitors can see barrack blocks with reconstructions of army life of different periods, the magazine that contains the splendid Seafield Collection of arms and military equipment, the Highlanders' Regimental Museum (p. 156) and the chapel. The Fort is still used by the Army and thus retains a strong military atmosphere.

Glencoe, Massacre of, 1692 (Argyll)

Free. Easy access. Remote glens and highland area. Parking possible. The A82 passes through the glen on the way to Oban or Fort William.

Although this is not a battlefield site, it is included because the massacre that took place in this dark glen on a bitter night in February 1692 has become so well known.

In 1691 King William III decided the best way of bringing some semblance of law and order to the Highlands after the Jacobite rebellion was to grant an amnesty to all clan chieftains who swore allegiance by 1 January 1692. MacIan, chief of the Macdonalds of Glencoe, delayed until the last moment and when he arrived to take the oath at Fort William there was no magistrate available. The Secretary of State for Scotland, Sir John Dalrymple, prevailed upon the

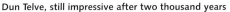

Dun Telve, still impressive after two thousand years

Culloden Moor, over which the Highlanders made their charge. Part of the English position is marked by the flag left of centre (Battlefields Trust)

Culloden, Battle of, 1746 (Inverness) (NTS)

£££ (visitor centre). Usual hours daily all year. Shop. Restaurant. Guided tours. Living history presentations (summer only). Video cinema. Audio-visual programme. Special facilities for disabled and visually impaired visitors. School visits. Parking. Tel. 01463 790607.
Three miles east of Inverness. Signposted off the A96.

The decisive battle of the Jacobite Rebellion led by Charles Stuart (Bonnie Prince Charlie). It was fought on 16 April 1746, a blustery, sleet-filled morning, when the English Hanoverian Army of some 9000 under the Duke of Cumberland crushed Charles Stuart's 5000 Jacobites.

On 15 April Charles had drawn up his army on Drummossie Moor south-east of Culloden House to await the arrival of the English. As time wore on with no enemy in sight, hunger got the better of many Scots who broke ranks to scavenge for cabbage leaves. It became apparent that the open rough ground chosen was hardly suitable for meeting a more numerous, disciplined force well supplied with cannons and cavalry. By late afternoon with no English to fight it was decided to take the offensive with a night march and launch a surprise attack on Cumberland, who was encamped near Nairn. At 7 p.m. at least 1000 men were missing, out searching for food. As many refused to return until they had found it, Charles was forced to start without them. Night marches are notoriously difficult and this one was worse than most. As the sullen, half-starved men struggled through the pitch-black night large gaps appeared in the column and much cursing and stumbling ensured that the English sentries raised the alarm as the leading units approached. With all chance of surprise gone, Charles's adviser, Lord George Murray, recommended retreat, so the Jacobites turned round and spent the rest of the night trailing back to Culloden. Morale was desperately low and the men were exhausted, famished and bitterly critical of the order, counter-order and disorder of the previous ten hours.

Little rest was possible as dawn brought news of the English approach. With great difficulty and considerable delay Charles drew up his 5000 men in two lines. On the right of the first line was the Athol Brigade under Murray, in the centre Lord John Drummond, and the Macdonalds on the left. The second line had some cavalry although most dismounted to fight as infantry. Some 600 yards away Cumberland began to draw up his army, also in two lines, with seven regiments in the first flanked by cavalry on the right. Another seven infantry regiments formed the second. Ten 3-pounder cannons were positioned at intervals along the front.

The opening cannon shots came from the Jacobites at 1 p.m. This brought an accurate and effective response from the English guns, which forced the Jacobite gunners to abandon their pieces. Cumberland's artillery continued firing and began to knock holes in the rebels' ranks. The Jacobites had been forced to stand for hours in the rain without food or sleep and now they were unable to respond properly. At last Charles ordered the attack. With the exception of the Macdonalds on the left, who held back at first, the rebel line rushed forward in a wild charge, straight at the guns and muskets 600 yards away. The speed with which they covered the ground was astonishing. But as the distance closed the cannon fire and the long lines of levelled muskets firing volley after volley took a terrible toll. By the time the survivors reached the English line and hand-to-hand fighting started the English advantage in numbers was too great to overcome. In less than an hour it was all over. Some 1200 Jacobites died on Culloden Moor. Prince Charlie escaped to France and never returned to Britain. Cumberland earned the nickname 'The Butcher' for the atrocities he unleashed on the Highlands. When he returned to London in triumph he had the flower 'Sweet William' named after him. In Scotland a particularly unpleasant weed was later re-named 'Stinking Willie'.

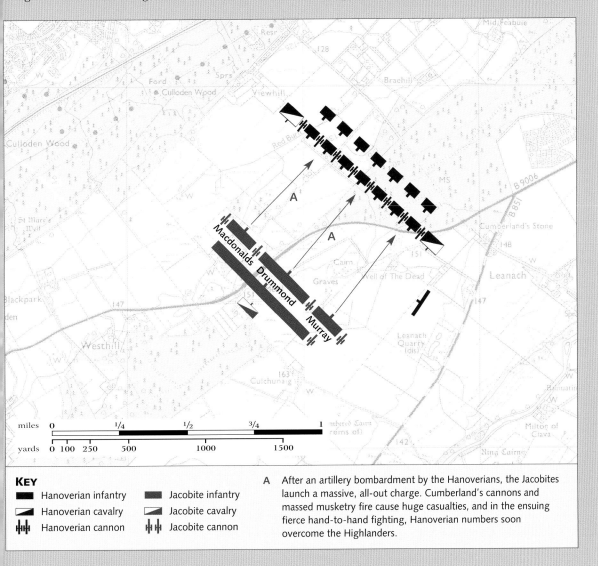

KEY

■	Hanoverian infantry	■	Jacobite infantry
◤	Hanoverian cavalry	◤	Jacobite cavalry
╫	Hanoverian cannon	╫╫	Jacobite cannon

A After an artillery bombardment by the Hanoverians, the Jacobites launch a massive, all-out charge. Cumberland's cannons and massed musketry fire cause huge casualties, and in the ensuing fierce hand-to-hand fighting, Hanoverian numbers soon overcome the Highlanders.

king to punish the Macdonalds as an example to the other Scottish clans.

So Dalrymple dispatched a regiment commanded by Campbell of Glenlyon, which accepted MacIan's hospitality for two weeks before Campbell ordered it to strike. At midnight on 12 February the massacre began. MacIan was shot and thirty-seven others – men, women and children – were butchered, the remainder scattered into the snow-covered hills to survive if they could. The murderous treachery of the Campbells is still remembered today.

Glenshiel, Battle of, 1719 (Ross-shire)

Free. Easy access. Some parking off main road. The A87 from Invergarry to the Kyle of Lochalsh runs through Glen Shiel. The fighting took place just east of the road bridge over the River Shiel. There is a green boggy area with a cairn marking the spot where the leaders of the Monro regiment fell.

Britain and Spain went to war in 1718, and the Spaniards agreed to support a Jacobite rising. The main Spanish force sailed from Cadiz in early 1719 but was scattered by storms. A smaller force under George Keith, unaware of this disaster, landed on the west coast of Scotland in April 1719. He had around 300 Spanish troops and was joined by around 1000 Highlanders under the Marquis of Tullibardine. General Wightman, with 1100 men, including a Dutch contingent, and four mortars was sent to put down the rebellion.

The Jacobites had set up a blocking position covering the bridge in the glen at Shiel. It was protected on the right by the river, on the left by a ravine and to the front by barricades. On 10 June Wightman attacked. The mortars opened fire, followed up with a flank attack against the Jacobite left that succeeded in getting in their rear and routing them. The Spaniards retired to another defensive position but surrendered the next day.

Harlaw, Battle of, 1411 (Aberdeenshire)

Free. Reasonable access. Some parking. The eastern outskirts of Inverurie.

A clash between marauding Highlanders under Donald, chief of the Camerons with a force numbered at 10,000, against defending lowlanders with a numerically inferior, though well-armed, force under the Earl of Mar. Arriving at Harlaw, which was a flat moor edging up to the rise of a hill, the Highlanders launched their usual wild, uncontrolled charge, which was met by a compact body of spearmen who held their own. Wave after wave of attackers threw themselves at the spearmen with significant losses to both sides. The result was inconclusive as the casualties were so heavy that both armies drew off when they could fight no more.

The Highlanders' Regimental Museum (Inverness-shire)

Free (donations welcome). Usual hours. Fort George has refreshments (summer only). Parking. Tel. 01463 224380. In Fort George, Ardesier village six miles west of Nairn off B9006. Follow Fort George signs off the A96.

The museum is housed in the old Lieutenant Governor's and Fort Major's quarters and tells the story of the Seaforth, Cameron Highlanders, Lovat Scouts and Queen's Own Highlanders from their raising to the present day. The first floor contains exhibits from the 18th and 19th centuries, including a splendid Gallantry Awards Room. The second floor is devoted to colonial wars and the First and Second World Wars, and includes the Lovat Scouts. The third floor displays exhibits from the campaigns in which the regiments served since 1945 including Malaya, Aden, Brunei, Northern Ireland, the Gulf and Iraq.

HM Frigate *Unicorn* (Dundee)

£. Usual hours April–October daily; November–March closed Monday and Tuesday. Shop. Refreshments. School visits. Parking on quayside. Tel. 01382 200900. www.frigateunicorn.org Victoria Dock, Dundee next to the Tay road bridge and a few minutes' walk from city centre.

HM Frigate *Unicorn* is the world's last unreconstructed wooden sailing ship. She was launched in 1824 and was only decommissioned in 1968, having been used as a training ship as recently as the Second World War. It is well worth exploring the gundeck, lower and orlop decks, hold, captain's cabin, forecastle and quarterdeck.

Inchbare, Battle of, 1130 (Angus)

Free. Easy access. Parking possible off-road. Turn off the A92 onto the B966 north of Brechin. The site is about 300 yards south of the Westwater bridge over the North Esk.

A battle fought in the Scottish Wars between King David I's army under Edward De Morville and rebels under the Earl of Moray. De Morville commanded a large army of some 3500 knights and horse with 5000 foot but no archers. Moray had mustered over 15,000 lightly armed clansmen.

De Morville planned to set an ambush on the plain south of the ford over the River North Esk at Inchbare. He placed his foot on high ground and his horse hidden behind nearby hills. However, as Moray approached over the ford from the north and was deploying, a party of Norman knights ruined the plan by charging out prematurely, forcing De Morville to commit the rest of his mounted men. Moray had time to form his men into a tight defensive half-circle with their backs to the ford. The day was spent in repeated charges by De Morville's men, each of which was beaten off by archery and a wall of spears. Moray rashly accepted a personal challenge and was struck down. When De Morville received some 2400 mounted reinforcements, Moray's younger brother, who had taken command, wisely opted to withdraw across the ford in the failing light. Some 2000 fell on either side.

Inchtuthill Roman Legionary Fortress (Perthshire)

Free. Access easy. Parking possible on minor road but short walk required to site. On the north bank of the River Tay, two miles west of Meikleour village on the Coupar Angus to Dunkeld road (A984).

A fortress built in AD 83 as the advance headquarters of Agricola for his campaigns against the Caledonian tribes. It held a legion of 5000 men. The legion was withdrawn in 87 to calm trouble in the East, but before leaving was ordered to demolish the fortress. Excavations have revealed thousands of iron nails bent by being pulled from the timber, as well as about a million in a pit beneath a workshop. Sections of the rampart and ditch can still be seen.

The Scapa Flow visitors' centre is housed in the oil pumping station at Lyness, which supplied fuel to the British Fleet

Mons Graupius, Battle of, AD 84 (Aberdeenshire)

Still very uncertain, but possibly in the Grampian Hills west of Inverurie. Here the discovery of the camp of Durno, the largest marching camp in northern Scotland, near the mount at Bennachie makes this a possible site.

Between AD 80 and 81 Agricola, the Roman governor of Britain, had brought the whole of southern Scotland under Roman domination. In 82 he began his final push into the north with three legions and auxiliaries; his line of advance can still be traced by the remains of his marching camps. In 84 Agricola got the pitched battle he had long sought at what the Romans knew as Mons Graupius (Graupian Hill). While the legions remained in reserve, the 8000 Roman infantry auxiliaries and 3000 cavalry fought and defeated between 20,000 and 30,000 Caledonian warriors, killing many thousands

Mortlach, Battle of, 1010 (Banff)

Free. Easy access, open country and golf course. Parking possible off-road. Immediately west of Dufftown on the B9009 on and around the golf course. Balvenie Castle is open in the summer.

A battle fought by King Malcolm II against Viking raiders. The Danes approached from Carron House on Speyside four miles west of Dufftown and camped at a place called Little Conval. Malcolm's army came from the east and camped on the other side of the river at Auchindoun. The fighting took place near the 'Giant's Chair' (a distinctively shaped nearby rock) and the monastery of Mortlach. The Scots launched an attack with the usual wild rush but quickly lost three of their leaders in the mêlée, and they fell back in some disorder. King Malcolm is then said to have prayed for divine help before leading another assault. This time the Vikings retreated. Malcolm reputedly threw the Danish leader off his horse and strangled him. There was considerable slaughter of the fleeing Vikings and grave pits have been discovered in the grounds of Balvenie Castle.

Mousa Broch (Shetland) (HS)

Free. £££ for the daily boat trip from Sandwick. Summer, limited hours, only in fair weather. On the island of Mousa, reached by ferry from Sand Lodge Pier near Sandwick. There is a convenient bus service from Lerwick.

The world's only near-complete broch, a primitive Iron Age castle dating from Roman times. It stands over 40ft high, making it very dark inside. A stairway runs between the outer and inner walls, leading to a wall-walk at the top.

Ruthven Barracks (Inverness) (HS)

Free. Easy access. Parking possible. Signposted off the A86 at Kingussie.

After the 1715 Jacobite uprising, the government decided to tighten its grip on the Highlands by building four fortified barracks at strategic locations. Ruthven Barracks is one of them, and all remains of the earlier castle were removed to make way for the structure you see today. In 1745 some 200 Jacobites attacked the barracks but were beaten off by a mere 12 soldiers commanded by a Sergeant Molloy. After the Battle of Culloden (p. 154), the Jacobites set fire to the barracks and dispersed, their rebellion defeated. Today all that remains are the exterior walls of two barrack blocks and the stables. Worth a visit for the stillness and atmosphere of history.

Scapa Flow (Orkney)

Donations accepted. Usual hours for visitors' centre Monday–Friday; mid-May–September also open Saturday and Sunday. Shop. Tel. 01856 791300. www.scapaflow.co.uk Lyness, Hoy, Orkney. The centre is reached by a short ferry trip across Scapa Flow from Orkney mainland.

Scapa Flow, the Royal Navy's most northern base, played a crucial role in the two World Wars. The visitors'

Killiecrankie, Battle of, 1689 (Perthshire) (NTS)

Free. Easy access. Visitors' centre open usual hours 31 March–31 October with exhibition of the battle, shop and snack bar. Site open all year. Picnic area. Guided walks. Parking in Centre car park only. The A9 west from Pitlochry runs through the Pass of Killiecrankie. The battlefield lies to the north of the road close to the village of Aldclune. The whole area is an excellent place for walks, which are best started from the Visitors' Centre where guides are available if required.

A battle after the deposition of James II between the forces of the Jacobite commander Viscount Dundee and the Scottish government army under General Mackay. On 27 July 1689 Mackay, at the head of some 5000 men, was marching through the pass of Killiecrankie. As he waited at Urrard House for his army to close up it was reported that the rebels were only a short distance away at Aldclune and were prepared to fight despite numbering only 3500 clansmen.

As the government army marched out of the pass, Mackay realized he would need to secure the higher ground to his right. Accordingly he executed a right wheel and pushed his way up the slope, which was covered with trees and scrub. As he deployed he found that the clansmen had already formed up opposite and on a higher ridge only 'short musket shot' away. Mackay resolved to remain on the defensive. In order to fully occupy the position he decided to spread out his seven infantry regiments in a three-rank line instead of six, leaving a substantial gap in his centre. Dundee extended his own line for fear of being outflanked. All this shuffling around took up to two hours.

Mackay opened fire with his three light cannons but it did not last long as the carriages disintegrated. As the sun set Dundee gave the order the clansmen had been waiting for – a Highland charge. The clansmen swept down the slope, many naked from the waist up and wielding huge broadswords. The speed and fury of the yelling Highlanders took the waiting red-coated infantry by surprise and only one volley of musket fire was possible for most of the regiments under attack. Before they could reload or even plug in their bayonets the charge hit them. As they had rushed

Soldier's Leap, famously jumped across by Donald MacBean (Battlefields Trust)

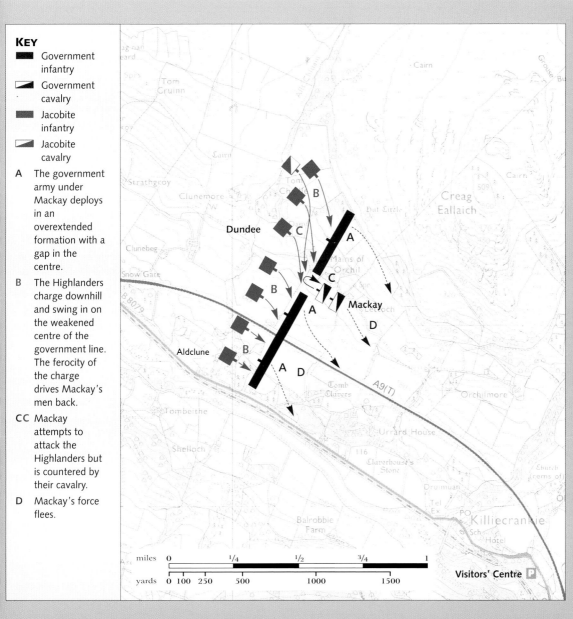

KEY

▬ Government infantry

◣ Government cavalry

▬ Jacobite infantry

◣ Jacobite cavalry

A The government army under Mackay deploys in an overextended formation with a gap in the centre.

B The Highlanders charge downhill and swing in on the weakened centre of the government line. The ferocity of the charge drives Mackay's men back.

CC Mackay attempts to attack the Highlanders but is countered by their cavalry.

D Mackay's force flees.

miles 0   ¼   ½   ¾   1

yards 0   100   250   500   1000   1500

down the hill the slope fell away gradually to the Highlanders' right and thus the charge swung in that direction and became more concentrated against the thinly held centre and right. In a close-quarter fight the English soldiers, many of them new recruits, barely stood a chance. Although they outnumbered their attackers the regiments on Mackay's right gave way. In a desperate attempt to salvage the battle Mackay launched his cavalry that had been held in reserve onto the Highlanders' flank. However, this was countered by a charge by the Highlanders' troop of horse. This final assault sealed Dundee's victory, although at the moment of triumph he was mortally wounded by a musket ball.

The clansmen harried their enemy until they reached the baggage train whereupon the scramble for loot stopped the killing. One soldier, Donald MacBean, was pursued by a Highlander who fired his pistol at him. On coming to a stream some 18ft across MacBean took a mighty leap and just cleared the water. He survived to write his memoirs. 'Soldier's Leap' can be visited today.

Sheriffmuir, Battle of, 1715 (Perthshire)

Free. Easy access, a wild, largely untouched area. Parking possible. Six miles north of Stirling, on the open ground immediately north-east of Dunblane off the A9.

None of Queen Anne's children survived her death and so Parliament secured the throne for James I's great-grandson, the German-speaking Protestant George I. However, within a year the 'Restoration Standard' was raised in Scotland in support of Prince James Stuart, son of the deposed James II. The Jacobites, under the Earl of Mar, had some 7000 men, and were opposed by the British government forces under the Duke of Argyll with some 3500.

On the bitterly cold morning of 13 November the two armies were drawn up opposite each other a mile apart, on the moor immediately north-east of Dunblane. Argyll deployed his infantry in two lines, six regiments in the first and two in the second with cavalry on each flank. Mar with 6000 infantry and 1000 cavalry similarly adopted a two-line deployment flanked by cavalry. At 11 a.m. Mar advanced to the attack with his right wing of both infantry and cavalry. As he approached, the line of

advance inclined slightly left. Argyll moved some infantry to his right and on this flank found that he outflanked Mar's left. Thus the right flanks of both armies advanced successfully.

The wild Highland charge with clansmen abandoning their muskets and surging forward screaming and waving their swords, supported by cavalry, was too much for the Hanoverian left. It was cut to pieces and within ten minutes the survivors had fled the field. On the Jacobite left an advance by a mob of Highlanders was forced back by sustained musketry and a flank charge by Argyll's dragoons. This success was followed up by the whole of the Hanoverian right and a lengthy and bitter struggle at close quarters took place. The Highlanders were driven back for almost two miles, over the River Allen. Both the armies had triumphed on their right and were now divided by some considerable distance with the original battlefield almost deserted. Both commanders marched their victorious troops back to the battlefield but it was then almost dusk so the armies finally withdrew, Argyll to Dunblane and Mar to Ardoch.

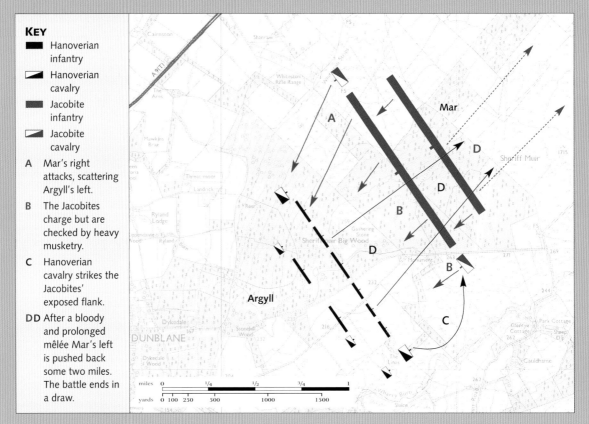

KEY

■ Hanoverian infantry

◤ Hanoverian cavalry

■ Jacobite infantry

◤ Jacobite cavalry

A Mar's right attacks, scattering Argyll's left.

B The Jacobites charge but are checked by heavy musketry.

C Hanoverian cavalry strikes the Jacobites' exposed flank.

DD After a bloody and prolonged mêlée Mar's left is pushed back some two miles. The battle ends in a draw.

Stirling Castle, impressively situated on an outcrop of volcanic rock

centre is housed in the oil pumping station at Lyness, which supplied fuel to the British Fleet. Artefacts include guns salvaged from the German High Seas Fleet scuttled in Scapa Flow in 1919. There is a large photographic display and an audio-visual display of wartime life in Orkney with sound and light effects. On Orkney mainland the Churchill barriers and the Italian prisoner-of-war chapel are worth seeing.

Stirling Bridge, Battle of, 1297 (Stirling)

Free. Easy access to site of bridge although it has been covered over by subsequent building. Parking in Stirling. The old bridge has gone but the later footbridge (not the road bridge) gives a good impression of its predecessor. The best view of the site is from the walls of Stirling Castle.

While Edward I remained in England to crush a baronial rebellion, he sent an army into Scotland under the Earl of Surrey to put down the rebels under William Wallace, who awaited the English on the slopes of Abbey Craig in Stirling. Wallace's position behind the River Forth was a strong one as the river was 250ft wide and fast-flowing with only one bridge available to an attacker, although there was a ford downstream at which he placed a detachment. Wallace had some 10,000 men and was confident that he could see off the English although they outnumbered him by 4 to 1.

On 11 September Surrey, with astonishing stupidity, advanced two-abreast over the bridge. Once the vanguard was across Wallace launched his army in a furious downhill charge. They were met by English knights spurring uphill. Outnumbered, on the far side of the bridge, the English were soon in difficulties. Seeing this, Surrey sent yet more knights thundering over the bridge, which promptly collapsed under the crush – it may have been weakened beforehand by partially sawing through the timbers. Powerless to intervene, the English east of the river were slaughtered. Surrey fled to Berwick Castle while Wallace was proclaimed 'Guardian of Scotland'.

Stirling Castle (Stirling) (HS)

£££. Usual hours. Shop. Refreshments. Exhibitions. Parking. Tel. 01786 450000. In Stirling, a steep walk from the town centre.

One of the grandest of all Scottish castles, both in its situation on commanding rock outcrops – the views from the walls are worth the visit alone – and in its architecture. Unfortunately, traces of the castle's early life have been obscured by structures dating from 1500 onwards. Nevertheless, there are some magnificent buildings within the outer defences including the Great Hall, the Gatehouse, the Palace of James V, the Chapel Royal of James VI and the artillery fortifications of the 16th–18th centuries. There are displays on the castle's history including a medieval kitchen.

PICTURE CREDITS

The author and publishers would like to thank all those who have given their permission to reproduce copyright material.

Photographs by Damien Noonan have been credited DN.
Photographs from the Battlefields Trust have been credited BT.

p. ii Apsley House, The Wellington Museum; p. iii Board of Trustees of the Royal Armouries; p. Cabinet War Rooms; p. 3 Corbis; p. 4 Board of Trustees of the Royal Armouries; p. 5 Heritage Image Partnership; p. 9 Lincoln Castle; p. 11 Bovington Tank Museum; p. 12 DN; p. 13 Fleet Air Arm Museum; p. 16 DN; p. 18 Battlefields Trust; p. 22 Soldiers of Gloucestershire Museum (J. Matthews); p. 23 DN; p. 29 Airborne Forces Museum; p. 30 BT; p. 32 (top) Battle of Britain Museum, Kent, (bottom) Battle Abbey; p. 33 Bletchley Park Trust Ltd; p. 34 DN; p. 35 DN; p. 36 Explosion: The Museum of Naval Firepower; p. 38 English Heritage; p. 40 BT; p. 43 Museum of Technology; p. 44 DN; p. 45 Crown Copyright; p. 46 DN; p. 47 Royal Green Jackets' Museum; p. 49 DN; p. 51 *HMS* Belfast; p. 52 Corel Corporation; p. 53 RAF Museum Hendon; p. 54 Getty; p. 55 English Heritage; p. 60 DN; p. 61 DN; p. 63 BT; p. 64 BT; p. 68 BT; p. 70 RAF Museum Cosford; p. 71 Warwick Castle; p. 73 BT; p. 74 BT; p. 76 BT; p. 78 BT; p. 80 DN; p. 81 DN; p. 82 DN; p. 85 DN; p. 86 (top) Cholmondeley Collection of Model Soldiers, (bottom) The Harwich Society; p. 87 Lincoln Castle; p. 88 BT; p. 90 RAF Air Defence Radar Museum; p. 91 Royal Anglian Regiment Museum; p. 92 Crown Copyright; p. 95 Deva Roman Experience; p. 96 Imperial War Museum North; p. 97 Stockport Air Raid Shelters; p. 101 Eden Camp; p. 102 BT; p. 104 Green Howards Regimental Museum; p. 105 Harperley Prisoner of War Camp; p. 106 HMS *Trincomalee*; p. 108 BT; p. 111 Board of Trustees of the Royal Armouries; p. 112 BT; p. 115 DN; p. 116 DN; p. 118 DN; p. 119 DN; p. 123 (top) Caerleon Roman Legionary Museum, (bottom) Caenarfon Air World; p. 124 (top) Corel Corporation, (bottom) Castell Henllys Fort; p. 125 Corel Corporation; p. 126 DN; p. 127 Royal Regiment of Wales Museum; p. 128 DN; p. 130 Corel Corporation; p. 131 Corel Corporation; p. 136 DN; p. 137 Crown Copyright; p. 138 Queen's Own Highlanders; p. 140 Queen's Lancashire Regiment; p. 141 Battle of Britain Museum, Kent; p. 145 Corel Corporation; p. 146 DN; p. 147 Scotland's Secret Bunker; p. 150 BT; p. 152 (top) Black Watch Regimental Museum, (bottom) DN; p. 153 DN; p. 154 BT; p. 157 Scapa Flow; p. 158 BT; p. 161 DN.

INDEX OF BATTLES

Principal entries are in **bold**. Maps and illustrations are in *italics*. All dates are AD unless stated BC.

A

Adwalton Moor (1643), *98*, **99**
Agincourt (1415), 4, 44
Alford (1645), **149**, *149*
Aliwal (1846), 78
Alma (1854), 53, *104*, 140
Ancrum Moor (1545), *134*, **135**
Ashdown (871), *28*, **30–1**, *30*, *31*
Ashingdon (1016), *84*, **85**
Assaye (1803), 139
Atlantic (1939–45), 95, 137
Auldearn (1645), *148*, **152**

B

Balaklava (1854), 78, 139, 140
Bannockburn (1314), 4, *148*, **150–1**, *150*, *151*
Barnet (1471), *28*, **50**
Bigbury Heights (54 BC), *29*, **32–3**, 57
Blenheim (1706), 139
Blore Heath (1459), *62*, **63**
Boroughbridge (1322), *98*, **99**, 107
Bosworth (1485), 5, *72*, **74–5**, *74*, *75*
Bothwell Bridge (1679), *143*, **144**
Bradock Down (1643), **10**, *11*
Britain (1940), 2, **92–3**, *92*
  Chapel, 56
  home defences, 83
  Memorial Flight, 83, *84*, 85
  Museum, 32, *32*, 83
  Operations Room, 52
  RAF Museum Hendon, 53
  Spitfire and Hurricane Memorial Building, 48
  Tangmere, 49
Brunanburgh (937), *98*, **100**
Byland (1322), *98*, **100**

C

Caractacus's Last Stand (51), *62*, **63**
Chalgrove Field (1643), *28*, **35**
Cheriton (1644), 7, *28*, **37**, *37*
Chilianwala (1849), 139
Colenso (1899), 139
Crécy (1346), 4
Cropredy Bridge (1644), *28*, **35–6**
Culloden (1746), *148*, **154–5**, *154*, *155*
  Highlanders and Jacobites, 7, 139
  last land battle in Britain, 2, 7
  Ruthven Barracks, 157

D

Delhi, Storming of (1857), 139
Drumclog (1679), *134*, **135**
Dunbar (1650), 7, *134*, **135–6**
Dunkeld (1689), *148*, **153**
Dupplin Moor (1332), *148*, **153**
Dyrham (577), *11*, **14–15**, *15*, 79

E

Edgcote (1649), *28*, *72*, **73**, *73*
Edgehill (1642), 6, 7, *62*, **64**, *64*, *65*
El Alamein (1942), 139
Ethandun (878), 2, *11*, **13**, 79
Evesham (1265), *62*, **63**, *63*, **66**

F

Falkirk (1298), *143*, **144**
Falkirk (1746), *143*, **144**
Flodden (1513), 5, *98*, **102–3**, *102*, *103*
Fontenoy (1745), 139
Fulford Gate (1066), *98*, **101**

G

Glenshiel (1719), *148*, **156**

H

Halidon Hill (1331), 4, *98*, **104**
Harfleur (1415), 4
Harlaw (1411), *149*, **156**
Hastings (1066), *28*, **40–1**, *40*, *41*
  Battle Abbey, 29, 32
  Bayeux tapestry, *3*
  composition of Saxon army, 2, 3
  Fulford Gate and, 101,
  Stamford Bridge and, 114
Hedgeley Moor (1464), *98*, **105**
Hexham (1464), *98*, **105**
Homildon Hill (1402), *98*, **106**
Hopton Heath (1643), *62*, **66**

H

Inchbare (1130), *149*, **156**
Inkerman (1854), 140

I

Jutland (1916), 137

K

Killiecrankie (1689), 7, *148*, **158–9**, *158*, *159*
Kilsyth (1645), *143*, **144–5**

L

Langport (1645), *11*, **17**
Langside (1568), *143*, **145**
Lansdown Hill (1643), 7, *11*, **18–19**, *18*, *19*

Lewes (1264), 4, *28*, **42**, *42*, 63
Lincoln (1141), *84*, **87**
Lostwithiel (1644), *11*, **17**
Loudoun Hill (1307), *134*, **136**
Lundy's Lane (1812), 139

M

Maiwand (1880), 139
Majuba Hill (1881), 139
Maldon (991), 2, *84*, **88–9**, *88*, *89*
Mancetter (60), *58*, 61, *62*, **66**
Marston Moor (1644), 7, *98*, **108–9**, *108*, *109*
Minden (1759), 139
Mons (1914), 53
Mons Graupius (84) 57, 58, *149*, **157**
Monte Cassino, 32, 53
Mortimer's Cross (1461), 5, **67**, *67*, 112
Mortlach (1010), *148*, **157**
Mount Badon (c500), 10, *11*, **17**, 79
Myton (1319), *98*, 99, 107

N

Nantwich (1644), *94*, **96**
Naseby (1645), 6, 7, *72*, **76–7**, *76*, *77*, 97
Neville's Cross (1346), *98*, **107**
Newark (1644), *72*, **73**
Newburn Ford (1640), *98*, **107**
Newbury (1643), *28*, **43**
Newbury (1644), *28*, **43–4**
Northallerton (1138), 4, *98*, **110**, *110*
Northampton (1460), 5, *72*, **78**, *78*

O

Omdurman (1898), 78, 139
Otterburn (1388), *98*, **107**, **111**

P

Philiphaugh (1645), *134*, **136**
Pilleth (1402), *122*, **126**
Pinkie (1547), *143*, **146**
Powick Bridge (1642), 62, **66**, **70**
Preston (1648), 6, *94*, **96**
Preston (1715), *94*, **97**
Prestonpans (1745), 7, *143*, **146–7**

R

Rorke's Drift (1879), 127, *127*, 139
Roslin (1303), *143*, **147**
Roundway Down (1643), *11*, **20–1**
Rowton Heath (1645), *94*, **97**

S

Salamanca (1812), 139
Sedgemoor (1685), 7, *11*, **21–2**
Sevastopol (1854), 140
Sheriffmuir (1715), 7, *148*, **160**, *160*
Shrewsbury (1403), 4, *62*, **68–9**, *68*, *69*
Somme (1916), 139
St Albans (1455), 2, *28*, **48**
St Albans (1461), 2, *28*, **48**, 112
Stamford Bridge (1066), 3, 40, *98*, **114**
Stirling Bridge (1297), *148*, **161**
Stoke Field (1487), *72*, **78**
Stow-on-the-Wold (1646), 6, *11*, **22–3**
Stratton (1643), *11*, **23**

T

Tel el-Kabir (1872), 139
Tewkesbury (1471), *11*, 23, *62*
Tobruk (1941), 32
Towton (1461), 5, 23, *98*, **112**, *112*, *113*
Trafalgar (1805), 38, 45, 82, 137

U

Ulundi (1879), 78

W

Wakefield (1460), *98*, 112, **115**
Walmer Beach (55 BC), *29*, **49**, *58*, 61
Waterloo (1815)
    Apsley House, 50
    Diorama, 47, *47*
    Fort Nelson, 38
    National Army Museum, 53
    Wellington's map, 46
Winceby (1643), *84*
Worcester (1651), 7, *62*, **71**

Y

Yorktown (1781), 139

INDEX OF SITES

Principal entries are in **bold**. Maps and illustrations are in *italics*.

A

Aberystwyth Castle, 131
Ackling Dyke Roman Road, **10**, *11*, 61
Adjutant General's Corps Museum, *28*, **29**
Airborne Forces Museum, *28*, **29**, *29*
Alauna Roman Fort and Senhouse Roman Museum, *94*, **95**
Aldershot Military Museum, *28*, **29**
Animals in War Memorial, *50*, **54**, *54*
Antonine Roman Wall Walkway Trust, **143**, *143*
Antonine Wall, **119**, *119*, 147
Apsley House: Wellington Museum, **50**, *50*
Arbeia Roman Fort and Museum, *98*, **99**, 118
Argyll and Sutherland Highlanders Museum, *148*, **149**
Army Medical Services Museum, *28*, **29**
Army Transport Museum, *98*, **99**
Artists Rifles, Royal Academy, 56

B

Badbury Rings, **10**, *11*, 26
Bar Hill Roman Fort, 119, *143*, **144**
Battle Abbey, *28*, **29**, *32*, *40*
Battle of Britain Chapel, 56
Battle of Britain Memorial Flight, 83, *84*, **85**, *93*
Battle of Britain Monument, *50*, **54**
Battle of Britain Museum, *29*, **32**, *32*, 83, *141*
Beaumaris Castle, 130, *130*, 131
Bedfordshire and Hertfordshire Regiment Museum, *28*, **32**

Belgium National Monument, *50*, **54**
Berwick-on-Tweed Barracks and Town Ramparts, 81, *98*, **99**
Birdoswald Roman Fort, *94*, **95**, 118
Black Watch Regimental Museum, *148*, **152**, *152*
Bletchley Park, *28*, **33–4**, *33*
Bodiam Castle, *28*, **34**, *34*, 131
Border Regiment and King's Own Royal Border Regiment Museums, *94*, **95**
Bovington Tank Museum, **10**, *11*
Britain at War Experience, **50**, *50*
Burgh Castle, 78, *84*, **85**, *85*

C

Cabinet War Rooms, **50**, *50*
Caerleon (Isca) Roman Fortress and Legionary Museum, 117, *122*, **123**, *123*
Caernarvon Air World, *122*, **123**, *123*
Caernarvon Castle, 127, 131
Caerphilly Castle, *122*, **123–4**, *124*, 131
Calshot Castle, *28*, **34**
Canadian Memorial, *50*, **54**
Cardigan Castle, 131
Carisbrooke Castle, 6, *28*, **35**, *35*, 81, 131
Castell Henllys Iron Age Fort, 26, *122*, **124**, *124*
Cavalry Memorial, *50*, **54–5**
Cenotaph, *50*, **55**, *55*
Chatham Historic Dockyard, *28*, **35**
Chesters Fort and Museum, *98*, **100**, 118
Chindit Forces Memorial, *50*, **55**
Cholmondeley Collection of Model Soldiers, *84*, **86**, *86*

Cobbaton Combat Vehicle Collection, **10**, *11*
Conwy Castle, *122*, **125**, *125*, 131
Corbridge Roman Fort and Museum, *98*, **100**, 118
Corfe Castle, **10**, *11*, 12, *12*, 131
Crownhill Fort, *11*, **12**, 82

D

D-Day Museum, *28*, **36**
Deal Castle, *29*, **36**, 81
Deva Roman Experience, *94*, **95**, *95*
Devil's Dyke, 80, *84*, **86**
Devon and Dorset Regimental Museum (Keep Military Museum), *11*, **12**
Doncaster Aero Venture, *98*, **100**
Dover Castle, *29*, **36**, 46, 79, 83, 128
Duke of Cornwall's Light Infantry Museum, *11*, **12**
Dun Beag, 27, *148*, **152**, *152*
Dun Telve, 26, 27, *148*, **153**, *153*

E

Eden Camp, *98*, **100**, *101*
Edinburgh Castle, 131, *143*, **144**, *145*
Explosion: The Museum of Naval Firepower, *29*, **36**, *36*

F

Firepower: The Royal Artillery Museum, *50*, **51**
First World War Artillery Memorial, 54
Fleam Dyke Path, 80, *84*, **86**
Fleet Air Arm Memorial, *50*, **55**

Fleet Air Arm Museum, *11*, **13**, *13*
Fort Amherst, *28*, **38**, 82
Fort Brockhurst, *28*, **38**, *38*, 82
Fort George, *148*, **153**
Fort Nelson, *28*, **38**, 82
Fort Paull, *98*, 100–1
Fusiliers Museum of Northumberland, *98*, **101**

G

Glencoe, Massacre of, *148*, **153**, 156
Greenhead Roman Army Museum, *98*, **104**, 118
Green Howards Regimental Museum, *98*, **104**, *104*
Guards Division Memorial, *50*, **55**
Gunpowder Mills, *29*, **38**
Gurkha Museum, *28*, 29, **38**
Gurkha Regiment's Memorial, *50*, **55**

H

Hadrian's Wall, 59, 80, 114, **116–18**, *116–18*, 119, 143
Half Moon Battery, Pendennis Castle, *10*, 13, 20, 83
Hambledon Hill, *11*, **13**, 26
Ham Hill, *11*, **13**, 26
Harlech Castle, 6, *122*, **125**, 131, *131*
Harperly Prisoner of War Camp, *98*, **105**, *105*
Harwich Redoubt, 82, *84*, **86**, *86*
Highlanders' Regimental Museum, *148*, **156**
Historic Warships Visitors' Centre, *94*, **95**
HM Frigate *Unicorn*, *149*, **156**
HMS *Belfast*, *50*, **51**, *51*
HMS *Trincomalee*, *98*, **106**, *106*
Hod Hill, *11*, **16**, *16*, 25, 26
Household Cavalry Museum, *28*, **39**
Housesteads Roman Fort and Museum, *98*, **106**, 118
HQ No 11 (Fighter) Group Battle of Britain Operations Room, *50*, **52**
Hurst Castle, *28*, **39**

I

Imperial Camel Corps Memorial, *50*, **55**
Imperial War Museum, *50*, **52**, 138, 141
Imperial War Museum Duxford, 83, *84*, **87**, 93
Imperial War Museum North, *94*, **96**, *96*
Inchtuthill Roman Legionary Fortress, 59, 61, *148*, **156**
Infantry and Small Arms School Corps Weapons Collection, *11*, **16**

K

Kelvedon Heath Nuclear Bunker, 83, *84*, **87**
King's Own Scottish Borderers Museum, *98*, **106**
King's Royal Hussars Museum, *28*, 29, **39**
Kinneil Roman Fortlet, 119, *143*, **145**
Knap Hill, *11*, **16**, 26

L

Liddington Castle, *11*, **17**
Light Infantry Museum, *28*, 29, **39**
Lincoln Castle, *84*, **87**, *87*, 131
Lindisfarne Castle, 81, *98*, **107**
Lunt Roman Fort, 61, *62*, **66**

M

Machine Gun Corps Memorial, *50*, **55–6**
Maiden Castle, *11*, 16, **17**, 25, 26, *26–7*
Malta GC Monument, *50*, **56**
Martello Towers, *29*, **39**, 79, **82**, *82*
Military Museum of Sussex, *28*, **39**
Military Vehicle Museum, *98*, **107**
Monument to the Women of World War II, *50*, **56**
Mousa Broch, 26, *27*, *149*, **157**
Museum of Army Flying, *28*, **43**
Museum of D-Day Aviation, *28*, **43**
Museum of Technology, *28*, **43**, *43*

N

National Army Museum, *50*, **52–3**, 138, 141
National Maritime Museum, *50*, **53**
National War Museum of Scotland, *143*, 144, **146**
Nelson Museum, *122*, **125**
Newhaven Fort, *28*, **44**, 83
Norfolk Nelson Museum, *84*, **90**
Nothe Fort and Military Museum, *11*, **20**, 82

O

Offa's Dyke (Gloucestershire), *11*, **20**
Offa's Dyke (Shropshire), *62*, 66, **80**
Offa's Dyke (Wales), *122*, **125–6**, *126*
Old Contemptibles Chapel, 56
Old Sarum and Castle, *11*, **20**

P

Pendennis Castle, *10*, 13, **20**, 81, 128
Pevensey Castle and Roman Saxon Shore Fort, *28*, **44**, 79, 83, *128*, 131
Portchester Castle and Roman Saxon Shore Fort, *28*, **44**, *44*, 79
Portland Castle, *11*, **20**, 81
Portsmouth Historic Dockyard, *28*, **45**, *45*, 81, 137, *137*
Prince of Wales's Own Regiment of Yorkshire Museum, *98*, **111**
Princess of Wales's Royal Regiment, *29*, **46**

Q

Queen's Dragoon Guards Museum, *122*, **126–7**
Queen's Lancashire Regiment Museum, *94*, **97**, *140*
Queen's Royal Lancers' Regimental Museum, *72*, **78**

R

RAF Air Defence Radar Museum, *84*, **90**, *90*
RAF Manston History Museum, *29*, **46**, 83

RAF Museum Cosford, *62*, **70**, *70*, 93

RAF Museum Hendon, *50*, **53**, *53*, 83, 93, 141

RAF Regiment Museum, *84*, **90**

Rame Peninsula Forts, *11*, **20**

Richborough Castle and Saxon Shore Fort, *29*, **46**, 61, *61*, 79

Rochester Castle, *28*, **46**, *46*, 131

Roman Road, Blackstone Edge, *98*, **111**

Rough Castle Roman Fort, 119, *143*, *146*, **147**

Royal Air Force Memorial, *50*, **56**

Royal Anglian Regiment Museum, *84*, 87, **90**, *91*

Royal Armouries Museum, *98*, **111**, *111*

Royal Artillery Memorial 1910, *50*, **56**

Royal Artillery Memorial 1925, *50*, **56**

Royal Dragoon Guards Museum, *98*, **111**

Royal Engineers' Museum, *28*, **46**

Royal Fusiliers Memorial, 56

Royal Gloucestershire, Berkshire and Wiltshire Regiment Museum, *11*, **21**

Royal Green Jackets' Museum, *28*, **47**, *47*

Royal Gunpowder Mills, *84*, **90–1**

Royal Logistics Corps Museum, *28*, **47**

Royal Marines' Memorial, *50*, **56**

Royal Marines Museum, *28*, **47–8**, 137, 141

Royal Military Canal, *29*, **48**, 82

Royal Naval Museum, **45**, 141

Royal Navy and Merchant Marine Memorial, 56

Royal Navy Submarine Museum, *28*, **48**

Royal Norfolk Regiment Museum, *84*, **91**

Royal Regiment of Fusiliers' Museum, *50*, **53**

Royal Regiment of Wales Museum, *122*, **127**, *127*

Royal Scots Dragoons Guards Museum, *143*, 144, **147**

Royal Scots Regimental Museum, *143*, 144, **147**

Royal Signals Museum, *11*, **21**

Royal Welch Fusiliers Museum, *122*, **127**

Rumps Hill-forts, *10*, **21**, 26

Ruthven Barracks, *148*, **157**

S

Saxon Burh (Dorset), *11*, **21**

Scapa Flow, *149*, **157**, *157*, **161**

Scotland's Secret Bunker, 83, *143*, **147**, *147*

Segedunum Roman Fort and Museum, *98*, **114**, 118

Soldiers of Gloucestershire Museum, *11*, **22**, *22*

Somerset Military Museum, *11*, **22**

South Cadbury Castle, *11*, **22**, *23*, 26, 79

Spitfire and Hurricane Memorial Building, *29*, **48**, 83

St Mawes Castle, *10*, **21**, 81

Staffordshire Regiment Museum, *62*, **70**

Stanwick Iron Age Fort, 26, *98*, **114**, *115*

Stirling Castle, 131, *148*, **161**, *161*

Stockport Air Raid Shelters, *94*, **97**, *97*

T

Tangmere Military Aviation Museum, *28*, **49**, 83

Tantallon Castle, 131, *135*, **136**, *136*

Temple of Mithras, *98*, **114**, 118

13th/18th Royal Hussars and Light Dragoons Museum, *98*, **114**

Tilbury Fort, 83, *84*, **91**

Tomb of the Unknown Warrior, *50*, **56**

Tower of London, *50*, **51–2**, *52*, 53, 81, 128, 131

U

Upnor Castle, *28*, **49**, 81

V

Victoria Cross and George Cross Memorial, *50*, **56**

Vindolanda Roman Fort and Chesterholm Museum, *98*, **115**, 118

W

Walmer Castle, *29*, **49**, *49*

Warwick Castle, *62*, **70**, *71*, 131

West Wansdyke, *11*, **23**, 80